The Road to Somewhere

The Road to Somewhere

A FATHER AND SON IN SEARCH OF THE OLD WORLD

JAMES DODSON

WILLIAM HEINEMANN : LONDON

Published in the United Kingdom in 2004 by William Heinemann

1 3 5 7 9 10 8 6 4 2

Copyright © James Dodson 2004

The right of James Dodson to be identified as the author of this work has been asserted
by him in accordance with the Copyright, Designs and Patents Act, 1988

William Heinemann
The Random House Group Limited
20 Vauxhall Bridge Road, London, SW1V 2SA

Random House Australia (Pty) Limited
20 Alfred Street, Milsons Point, Sydney
New South Wales 2061, Australia

Random House New Zealand Limited
18 Poland Road, Glenfield
Auckland 10, New Zealand

Random House (Pty) Limited
Endulini, 5a Jubilee Road, Parktown 2193, South Africa

The Random House Group Limited Reg. No. 954009

www.randomhouse.co.uk

A CIP catalogue record for this book
is available from the British Library

Papers used by Random House are natural, recyclable products made from
wood grown in sustainable forests. The manufacturing processes conform to the
environmental regulations of the country of origin

Printed and bound in Great Britain by
Mackays of Chatham Plc, Chatham, Kent

ISBN 0 434 01205 X

For Jack and the Queen Mum

CONTENTS

ACKNOWLEDGMENTS

Every journey has a midwife, goes an old Moorish proverb, and ours certainly had many of those, but none more helpful than Pat Robinson, a legendary bookseller who cleaned out her shelves on Africa and beyond to inspire Nibs and his father to take off for parts unknown. She's a classy lady and a treasured friend and we owe her much for years of friendship and wisdom.

A special thank you to Alison Bennie for allowing her dearly beloved boy to take off into the wild blue, and to Kathleen Bennie for having the good Glaswegian sense to go part of the way with us. Thank you Dame Wendy for unerring instincts and leading us the rest of the way home.

Charles Churchill, the boys of Summer Fields, Martin and Brigge Skan of Chewton Glen Hotel—thank you all and see you again soon, I hope.

Thanks to Hugh and Susan Klutz, Dr. Rick and Susie Berta, Bob and Claire Tracy, Jerry and Lenoir Lancaster—beloved redneck kin who came far just to crack open a lobster and share a few laughs. Thank you, old travel pals Caroline and Edie Hazard—we won't miss dinner in London next time. Ditto Lee Walburn, Col. Bob and Mary Day, Doug and Lindy Bragg.

Much gratitude to Professor Benedetta Fantugini for making Florence unforgettable, and to Daphne Mazzanti for understanding our need for a swim. Thank you, Rafiki Tour for refunding our Africa money, Chief Stewart Corscadden for sorting out my airline screwups, and Chet from the embassy who clearly meant well, wherever you are. I hope you enjoyed your Swiss vacation.

Finally, once again, Brian Tart and Ginger Barber. Editor and agent extraordinare. Friends for life.

Ask where the good road is, the Godly paths you used to walk in, in the days of long ago. Travel there, and you will find rest for your soul.

—Jeremiah 6:16

And bound on that journey you find your attorney (who started that morning from Devon);
He's a bit undersized, and you don't feel surprised when he tells you he's only eleven.

—W. S. Gilbert

There are two types of travel—first class and traveling with children.

—Robert Benchley

Time to Mourn,
Time to Dance

My truck was the first one in the nursery parking lot that fine September morning. I was buying flowers for the wedding reception, thinking how nice it was that the summer tourists had vanished and thoughtfully left the best weather for us locals, when I heard a gasp and turned to see an elderly woman sitting in her Cadillac, ashen faced, holding a tray of African violets on her lap, apparently unable to move.

"Ma'am?" I said to her. "Are you okay?"

"Come here," she replied quietly.

I put down my mums and walked over, placing a hand on the roof of her car, leaning in. She turned up her radio and stared at it, gripping the wheel. An announcer was going on excitedly about a swirling cloud of black smoke that was now clearly visible the length and breadth of Manhattan Island.

After a few moments I said, "Is that in New York?"

She nodded gravely.

"What happened?"

"An airplane just flew into the World Trade Center," she replied. She pronounced the word aero-plane, the old-fashioned way, like an English blueblood who'd never flown in one.

"I'll be damned."

She said nothing. And then explained quietly, "My grandson Tommy works there."

Of course, I didn't know what to say. I could see she was almost rigid with shock and fear. I moved my hand gently to her shoulder, thinking of my own mother, who had been dead almost exactly a year—thinking of my son,

Jack, too, quite suddenly and unexpectedly. We'd just arrived home from a summer of trying to wander around the world like a couple real-life Huck Finns, a freewheeling caprice of discovery during which nothing basically went as I expected it to. The spiritual pilgrimage I'd quietly hoped for turned out to be more of a Hope and Crosby road show. But curiously, for all of our bungled hopes, wrong turns, and failed objectives, I wouldn't swap the places we'd seen, the characters we'd met, and the laughs we'd had together for anything.

"Don't worry," I assured her. "The World Trade Center is an awfully big place. I'm sure he's fine."

She glanced up at me with disbelief.

"I don't think you understand, young man," she said, her voice wavering with emotion, as if I'd simply not been listening. "That was the second plane to hit the Trade Center. Both towers are on fire." She paused to let the meaning of that sink in, touching one of her African violet blooms. "Nothing is ever going to be the same again, I'm afraid, dear."

The party tents were already up, the bonfires laid and waiting. But in the procession of numbing days following the terrorist attacks on New York's twin Trade Towers and Washington's Pentagon, we decided to postpone the lobster bake and wedding reception.

Eight thousand people were still missing in the rubble of the collapsed towers alone. Five hundred were estimated to be dead in Washington, another hundred in a quiet Pennsylvania pasture. The horrifying estimates were incomprehensible, almost biblical in scope. How could we possibly bless rings, celebrate a second-chance union, tell tales of our boys' adventure abroad, eat lobster, and kick up our heels to an Irish fiddle band when so many we knew, or simply knew of, were devastated. Besides, with the airlines in such turmoil, flights were being canceled right and left. A dozen people phoned to say they simply couldn't get here from there—a dark twist on the old Maine tourist joke.

But then someone else called, plucky friends from Georgia, who said they hoped we hadn't canceled the party because they were coming anyway. Soon others were phoning up to say they'd simply decided to drive instead of fly—to take an unexpected road trip and see America the old-fashioned way, maybe even try and make a second honeymoon out of the weekend.

"There's a time to weep, pal, and a time to laugh; a time to mourn and a time to dance," drawled my old college roommate Hugh, more or less appropriating Ecclesiastes. "Damn it, boy, we need a reason to laugh and dance. So start cookin' that lobster!"

So the bonfires were lit, the Guinness keg tapped.

More people actually showed up than we invited—friends brought friends who'd been holed up staring at the TV for days. The overflow crowd held hands in a vast circle of friends and neighbors, of grief and celebration. A prayer was said for the dead, the missing, the families torn asunder. Then the rings were blessed, the lobster and grilled salmon served, the dancing commenced.

Toward the end of the evening, someone touched my arm. I was pleased to see it was Jack, my sidekick from the road that summer.

"Hi, Dad," he said pleasantly, slugging down a Coke. "How's it going?"

He was barefoot, his nice white dress shirt hopelessly soiled with grass, hair mussed, sweating in the cool evening air. He'd been playing tag on the darkened lawn and dancing with a group of other children, spinning wildly to an Irish reel.

I said it was going pretty well, considering what an unbelievable week we'd all just been through. But I was pleased we'd decided to have the party after all and others, to judge by the rates lobster and wedding cake were vanishing, seemed to appreciate the decision as well. I asked how he was doing because we really hadn't had a chance to talk about our big trip yet. Just days after we came home, Jack had ventured into the brave new world of Mount Ararat Middle School, a hectic resumption of our ordinary lives.

"Great," he said but then fell silent. "Hey, Dad," he added in a more thoughtful voice, "I was wondering about something. Do you think if this thing had happened last year we would have tried to go around the world?"

He meant, of course, the terrorist attacks that we were weighing incalcuably on all our minds and spirits. Ironically, Jack and I had been forced to cut short our summer odyssey because of trouble in some of the more exotic places we'd hoped to visit—including canceling a long-talked-about swing through Africa. We'd only gotten about halfway around the world—to the backyard of Western civilization, as I said, trying to put an optimistic face on things—before calling it quits and coming home. A certain innocence or hubris was clearly gone as a result of 9/11 and I'd pretty much been wondering the same thing he had ever since meeting the woman in the nursery parking lot, wondering if anybody for a very long time would travel the way we had done.

"Probably not," I admitted, draping an arm around his shoulders. For a moment we stood together knocking back Coke and Guinness respectively, watching our friends and neighbors make complete fools of themselves on a dance floor beneath a waning harvest moon. What a nice sight it was. I was touched that they'd cared to come so far, and really pleased to see my old college roomie was an even worse dancer than me.

"So it's good, I guess, that we did it when we did."

"I think so, Boss. Remember that crazy night in Parga?"

"Yeah," he said with a slow rising grin. "That was awesome."

Then he went off to rejoin the dance.

I walked over to the food tent where my new wife was serving the last piece of wedding cake to an attractive older lady. She looked familiar but I couldn't place a name. Then it came to me who she was. She was the woman from the nursery parking lot. She'd come with friends from town. Good for her, I thought. Grief at least can make proper neighbors of strangers.

"How is your grandson?" I finally worked up the nerve to ask her.

"Oh, he's fine. He had a head cold that morning and decided to stay home from work. Can you believe it?"

I shook my head and thanked her for coming and went to get a scoop of the Maine blueberry cobbler before it disappeared, too, thinking how strange it was that a head cold could save your life. There were thousands of stories like this being told and retold across America tonight, each one sadder or more unbelievable than the last.

Sorrow, as someone said, is sacred ground. But perhaps as Jack and I had discovered on the road that summer, as the ancients themselves advised, eating and laughing and dancing with friends really does help push back the fear and darkness for a little while. The cobbler was all gone so I went and found my bride and led her to the dance floor at a risk to her lovely feet.

"This reminds me of that night in Chianti," Wendy said with a sly smile, picking up where Jack left off, as the fiddles slowed to an old-fashioned waltz. "The night Sister Patrice locked us out of the convent."

I smiled back at her with maybe the first true and uncomplicated happiness I'd felt for many days, a much needed lift to the spirit, forgetting for the moment to worry where I placed my clumsy feet or wonder how we'd all get through the uncertain days and weeks ahead, remembering instead a funny evening among the olive trees of an older world that already felt like something that happened to a boy.

ONE

Nibs the Lost Boy

Early that afternoon, as the skies cleared and the summer sun returned to England, Jack and I set off up Greenwich Hill with our ball gloves in hand.

"Dad," he said a bit anxiously as we neared the top of the ancient hill where King Henry VIII brought the first of his many virgin brides home to the palace bed nearly six centuries ago, "do you think anybody will mind if we throw the baseball up here? I mean, it looks kind of busy."

"The world is a busy place, Nibs," I assured him, placing a supportive hand on his shoulder—partly to ease his worry, partly to ease my aching knees. "But that's no reason to stay home in the hutch. Besides, we're only going to pitch a quick inning or two. My guess is, nobody will have a clue what we're really up to."

The hike up the famous long hill, as my huffing and puffing proved, was either harder than it looked or I was simply in worse shape than I feared. In either case, the enclosed stone terrace of the Royal Observatory was indeed crowded with packs of giggly, jostling French and Japanese students who'd already occupied most of the space around the Prime Meridian, our trip's first objective, zero degrees longitude, the place where measured time begins.

Starting here and now, the plan was for Jack and me to do something we'd talked about doing since he was a small boy perched on a large bed in a quiet dormer room demanding I read him one more adventure book of far-off places or, better yet, make up one of my ridiculously embroidered stories in which he and I wander about the ancient world slaying dragons, saving beautiful damsels, meeting friendly wizards, fighting black knights, and feasting on M&Ms and popcorn, generally having a legendary high old time.

"Dad," he said to me one night after I'd made up a particularly rollicking adventure which included storming a dark castle, becoming invisible in the nick of time, being personally thanked by the good Queen Gertrude, and riding a loyal camel named Sam all the way across the Sahara to enjoy a swell Kool-Aid party at the foot of the great pyramids, "do you think we could we really *do* that stuff sometime?"

"What's that, Boss?" I was hoping he meant fall asleep.

"See dragons and wizards and visit real castles and things like that."

I hated to have to tell the cute little cuss that even though there might be a few Medieval castles left standing around Europe, there really weren't wizards and dragons and such roaming the world anymore. Pity. So I said what any self-respecting parent says when faced with the reality that the only person in danger of falling asleep is them.

"Sure," I promised. "Someday. When you're a bit older."

Well, a promise is a promise and Jack was a good bit older and someday, as they say, was finally here. Only the stated objective of our long-promised odyssey had changed and matured a bit over the intervening years. Thus, instead of going in search of dragons and wizards, per se, we embraced the more ambitious and perhaps more implausible aim to try and travel entirely around the world during the first full summer of the new millennium, to wander like a pair of Mark Twain's proverbial innocents abroad and see whatever we could see for the two months of summer freedom allotted to us before Jack (a big fan of mythology, a good student of history) moved on to the mysteries of Mount Ararat Middle School.

The emphasis was on *try* because forty thousand miles, the approximate distance I calculated we needed to cover in order to see the exotic places we hoped to see, is a lot of ground to place beneath your feet in less than eight weeks. The experienced traveler in me was realistic enough to think we'd probably only be able to knock off all of Continental Europe, several Mediterranean countries, and possibly a bit of Africa at the tail end of the enterprise. Jack, on the other hand, fueled by those distant dormer room dreams and unburdened by too much travel experience abroad, was thinking big and appeared to have no doubt that we could somehow manage to squeeze in the Pyramids of Giza, the River Jordan, and maybe a friendly hike along the Great Wall of China on his birthday at the end of August. As unlikely as I knew it was that we could reach these exotic compass points in the course of just fifty or so days of dedicated vagabonding, I also didn't want to dampen my son's appetite and enthusiasm for exploring a complex world he was on the threshold of inheriting by insisting those places were out of the question.

By design ours was a largely unstructured and open-ended odyssey and the simple truth was, we—well, I—had no firm idea how far we might get and no clue where exactly we might wind up, because the point of embarking on a journey of discovery is to let the road unfold and lead where it will, show you what it needs or wants to show you. Thus, aside from a couple advance hotel bookings (one made in London and another in Paris on Bastille Day) plus a refundable reservation deposit plunked down on a ten-day safari I dearly hoped we would be able to take in East Africa toward the end of August (my own childhood fantasy trip), we had no accommodations reserved in advance, nor any firm travel schedule etched in stone.

I realize no one in their right mind really travels this way anymore, of course, certainly not abroad—going where personal whimsy and the winds of chance blow them, with little more than a good road map and an atlas of curiosities in their own heads to guide them. But it struck me that if ever there was maybe an opportune moment in time to undertake such a boyishly unstructured tromp through the Old World, to see what was beyond the horizon of our safe and conventional lives on a seaside hill in Maine, that moment was this summer.

Western Civilization, after all, was celebrating its second millennium of survival and Jack was about to turn eleven, the age boys in Medieval times were apprenticed to knights in order to learn the ways of the world; the age boys in Periclean Athens were dispatched to the country to learn the art of civility at the elbows of rural scholars; the age scientists say a boy first begins to notice the musk of life and almost every religion insists he's finally a young man.

As for me, the expedition's de facto field commander, chief financial patron, and head bottle washer, well, I was rapidly approaching the end of my forties, fast nearing that celebrated plateau of midlife when the intelligent man, as a valued older friend of mine likes to point out, honestly appraises his various strengths and weaknesses and begins to accept the remote possibility that he won't ever pitch for the Boston Red Sox, not even in short relief.

Between the idea and the action, as some celebrated poet or possibly bitter ex–Red Sox manager once advised, *there* lies the shadow of the matter. Though the world, for the moment at least, seemed no more acutely perilous at the start of summer 2001 than it had at any given point in my memory, I was old enough to realistically understand there were enough natural and man-made dangers on this planet to keep me on my toes and Jack's mom—my friend, coparent, and former wife—gently worried out of her mind back home in Maine, reminders that there were plenty of people who do unspeakable things to each other and perfect strangers every minute of the day and maybe twice on Sunday. History, with its impressive ledger of Holy Roman Crusades, conquests, civil wars, Inquisitions, jihads, plagues, mass murders, revolutions, and Reformations, as someone who was clearly on the losing end of things was supposed to have said, is simply a laundry list of man's staggering inhumanity to his neighbor, and if you think about it too long and hard it's a wonder anybody has the nerve to leave the yard for a quart of milk.

But having said this, civilization makes up pretty nicely where history sometimes makes a real sow's breakfast of things, and you don't have to be related to either Kenneth Clark or Ariel and Will Durant to realize that the origins of such wonders as the Italian Renaissance, English poetry, French food, Greek mythology, and the black rhino of Kenya were pretty nifty things to consider leaving home to investigate, even at the risk of making the evening news in the most unpleasant way possible.

There were other less glamorous obstacles to our trip, to be sure. Jack would have to miss theater camp and playing Cal Ripkin baseball and I'd have to forfeit most of the decent all-too-brief gardening and golf weather in Maine. Both of us would miss the heart of Red Sox season (no great loss to me—I'm a seasoned Fenway sufferer—but Jack is a *true* believer in the boys from Beantown) and Jack would miss trips to Moosehead Lake and vital general goofing off time with his best pal Andrew Tufts. To be blunt about it, I also wasn't even certain my wallet could deliver the grandiose boys' adventure my mouth had promised so many years ago up in that dormer bedroom. I mean, honestly now, all security concerns aside, how much did it *cost* to wander around the world like a couple New Age Medieval spiritual pilgrims? Frankly speaking, based on my own work-related travels, I didn't have much more than a few unsettling rough cost estimates tapped out late at night on the office calculator to go by, and those totals were almost enough to quell the budding world explorer in any responsible American middle-class taxpaying grown-up. Not to put too fine a point on the naysaying, that sum didn't even take into consideration the nearly two *months* I would have to take off work in order to try and do the trip.

No, as several of my fellow parental contemporaries at various youth baseball and basketball games in the days and weeks preceding the start of our unplanned global caprice took pains to point out, there was no shortage of perfectly good and practical reasons why it was one thing to talk about doing this sort of thing with your kid and *another* to actually try and do it.

At the end of the day, I decided, there was really only one reason that mattered to Jack and me—we simply wanted to go.

On a deeper level, I had a few private best hopes for believing a trip of this nature would be good for the Jack of the New Millennium. Recently, he'd played Nibs the Lost Boy in his school production of *Peter Pan*—perfectly cast, in my view, as a boy who's having so much fun in Neverland he can't see the point of going back to the real world, where he has to remember to pick up his towels and make up his bed and make certain his book report is properly signed and turned in on Thursday.

If my Nibs the Lost Boy was polite to a fault, sweet to the core, an excellent student, and almost equally smitten with Pedro Martinez's fastball and the flattering attentions of a certain pretty girl called Bethany Bellnap, he was also one of the dreamiest boys you're ever likely to encounter, prone to forget where he left his geography project, ball glove, or even good old Jack Pillow, the somewhat tattered, frequently mended icon of those distant storytelling days up in his dormer bedroom, a small Peter Rabbit–themed pillow he'd had since his mom and I brought him home from the hospital.

The fact that he still *had* good old Jack Pillow in tow spoke eloquently about his innocent view of the world beyond our hill in Maine. He was, as they say in guidance counseling circles, a "young" ten-year-old—*unspotted from the world,* as the Book of Common Prayer so aptly sums up the profile. A bit of a worrier, a deep and sensitive thinker, clearly a lad who took folks directly at their word, he didn't appear to have a cynical bone in his rapidly growing body. And as much as I wanted to nurture and preserve these admirable qualities in him, it was illogical and perhaps even dangerous to think I could keep him safely swaddled up this way—and hidden from the perils and seductions of the world at large—forever.

Travel broadens the mind, I suppose it's true, while TV simply broadens the butt. Thanks to his passion for playing until he dropped at any game involving a ball, Jack's rear end was probably in pretty good shape for the start of a New Millennium, but a summer away from the influence of Game Boy and the Disney Channel and maybe even Red Sox baseball, I calculated, wouldn't do either one of us on the home team any particular harm.

On the contrary, apart from the sheer boyish fun we might kick up on a freewheeling road trip to parts unknown, the *real* benefit of a summer jaunt around the Western civilized world on its two thousandth birthday, in search of the origins of some of our species' higher achievements in art and science and history and faith—my unapologetic paternal hidden agenda, as it were—was that such a roving chautauqua might go a long way toward broadening a young man's thinking and responsibly prepare him—not to mention *me*—for that sad but inevitable day when Nibs the Lost Boy finally grew up for good and said a fond goodbye to a dirt road in Maine and ventured out to find his own way through life, a tale as old as Telemachus and his worrying dad, Odysseus.

I think Mark Twain, patron saint of lost boys everywhere, stated the case pretty nicely when he set off on an almost identical journey of discovery two years after the end of the American Civil War. *The man who is a pessimist before forty-eight knows too much*, he declared. *If he is an optimist after that, he knows too damn little*.

As the ancient gods of sweet irony would have it, the father of this unlettered enterprise was exactly forty-eight years old this first summer of the brand-new age. And to be blunt, I still wasn't certain whether my collected years of wandering about had made me a natural optimist, who stubbornly refused to accept the verdict that the world is crowded with too many perils to consider leaving home, or a learned pessimist afflicted with terminal wanderlust, who simply chose to hope for the best and was willing to risk whatever it took to get back in touch with his inner eighth grader in a place most folks only read about in picture books.

On the title page of my own favorite childhood book, an *Illustrated Treasury of the World's Greatest Legends, Myths and Poems*, which still reposed somewhere on a shelf in my office, my late father, an adman with a poet's heart whom I affectionately called Opti the Mystic, quoting some long forgotten Eastern sage, inscribed these words: *A great man is he who does not lose his child's heart. Wherever this world takes you, Bo, please keep yours . . .*

The truth was, I hadn't been *Bo* in many long years. But maybe it was time, for the span of a few summer weeks at least, to be Bo again. More importantly, as a father fast approaching midlife with a son who recalled his own father's grace in so many visible and intangible ways, the double meaning of my father's wish wasn't entirely lost on me.

Thus, wherever we wound up on the road to *somewhere*—east of the moon or west of the sun or maybe just some interesting place in between—I finally decided, maybe Nibs the Lost Boy and I could teach each other something valuable, about finding and preserving a boy's heart in each other.

So there we were, Once Upon a Time, as they say in fairy tales, at the top of an ancient hill, having taken a tempestuous king's summit with ball gloves in hand and paid our five quid admission and filtered through the gates of the Royal Observatory museum to the spot where longitudinal time on this planet as we know it, officially called Greenwich Mean Time, is marked, measured, and commences.

Without much ado we found an open spot among the jostling French teenagers and took positions on each side of the famous glass-encased meridian line that splits east from west and transects the courtyard floor below a large red illuminated chronometer where milliseconds perpetually whirl in a mad fugue of passing moments, proving *tempus* really does *fugit*. I gently flipped the baseball to Jack across the time line. He caught it and blushed and glanced around to see if anyone took offense at us playing catch like a couple runaway Little Leaguers.

"Hey, Dad," he asked casually, "can I throw overhand?"

In an effort to make up for missing baseball, I'd larkishly suggested to Jack that we cart along our gloves and a couple baseballs and get in a spot of throwing practice at least once a day, wherever we happened to be. That way, I reasoned, we could see the wonders of the world *and* work on his pitching technique. I envisioned Jack developing into a fine shortstop or a third baseman, to be honest, though he clearly saw himself as the future Pedro Martinez.

"Better wait till we find an open field somewhere, Nibs," I replied, catching another gentle pitch. "We might bean somebody and tick off the Queen Mum."

The Queen Mum, I should explain, was Jack's maternal grandmother, Kathleen Bennie, my former wife's disgustingly responsible mother (trust me, it's kind of complicated), a retired school principal and superintendent who had thoughtfully agreed to accompany us for the first ten days or so of the trip through England before she headed off to her native Scottish homeland for her semiannual inspection tour of the premises.

In addition to being Jack's grandmother, Kate was one of my closest friends on earth—a good-hearted if somewhat moralistic agnostic dame of wartime Glasgow and daughter of the "Red Tide" Clyde, who'd grown up to marry a brilliant Paisley scientist and immigrate to America, reading (at least twice, probably three times) virtually every book published since Pliny the Younger along the way, and becoming, in due course, our own family's New World version of Britain's beloved Queen Mum.

We—well, *I*—called her this with all due irreverence because she harbored an unlikely if deeply felt affection for the oldest member of the otherwise dopey Royal family of Britain, another Scotswoman who uncomplainingly accepted her "intolerable burden" of serving as a reluctant king's wife during Britain's darkest days, a one-woman Royal and Ancient who steadfastly refused to budge from London when the Germans were attempting to bomb the city by the Thames back to the Stone Age.

Except for Kate's quiet agnosticism and the fact that she was a card-carrying, George Bernard Shaw–loving socialist school superintendent who detested frilly hats and the idea of anybody making the slightest fuss over her person, *our* QM otherwise struck me as an awful lot like *their* QM—even down to the somewhat goofy and embarrassed smile and the way she waddled along with an oversized handbag that held everything from Shakespeare's complete folios to an endless supply of Kleenex and an extra pair of sensible flat shoes.

Their Queen Mum, I'd read in that morning's *Times*, was off visiting a garden show at Battersea, while *our* Queen Mum was presently taking the slow shuttle bus up long Greenwich Hill.

As I pointed out to Jack, neither of these royal and ancient dames would be terribly pleased to see us throwing a hard baseball over tender heads in a crowded public venue, but our Queen Mum at least would certainly be pleased to see that Nibs the Lost Boy was safely smiling again.

"I gather you're feeling better," I said as nonchalantly as possible, underhanding another pitch. Unfortunately, it fell short of his glove and landed on the glass of the Prime Meridian with an unsettling crack, causing several fellow Meridian visitors to turn and glare uncomprehendingly at us. To his credit, Jack expertly fielded the errant toss with a cool flip of his glove, proving he had the makings of a future Cal Ripkin after all.

"Fine. *Why?*" He seemed truly baffled why I'd ask such a silly thing.

"Just wondering. Glad to see England's sun shining and you smiling again. That's all."

This was so Jack, sweetly oblivious to the fact that the three of us—him, the QM, and me—had just been through one of the most intense experiences of our lives, an unexpected ordeal that began when our half-empty American Airlines Airbus 300 lifted off the runway at Boston's Logan Airport and tilted in the beautiful summer sky toward London.

We weren't ten feet off the ground when Nibs, a seasoned flier who'd never shown the first inkling of fear in the air in many years of long distance travel, suddenly began hyperventilating and wondering with quiet urgency, between gasps for air, clutching my arm, if we could "maybe get off the airplane."

Of course, that had been quite impossible. We were already one thousand feet in the air and climbing at sixty feet per second, so I hastily summoned an attendant and together we escorted Jack to the rear galley of the plane, where Kate, two more attendants, and finally a senior pilot deadheading to London joined us, a small congregation of worried grown-ups quietly doing their best to assure a suddenly mysteriously terrified little boy that the airplane he was riding on wasn't going to crash in the ocean.

In a nutshell, nothing we said made a dint in his inexplicable panic and only the introduction of an oxygen mask and tank and the presence of Jack Pillow seemed to calm him down for the balance of the Atlantic crossing. And so, for the next six hours Jack huddled beneath a blanket in the seat beside me, the plastic mask clamped weirdly to his suddenly small and slightly ashen face, breathing easier but by no means easy. He watched an old Chevy Chase movie and appeared to drift in and out of an uneasy sleep while I attempted to read my biography of Dante Alighieri, wondering if I'd made an awful misjudgment about our fitness to wander around the world together.

At one point about four hours into the flight, I glanced over from my book and discovered him staring out the window of the airplane at cloud tops, lost in the upper atmosphere of his own thoughts.

"Jack," I attempted to reassure him, massaging his blanketed arm, "everything will be all right. The plane is fine. Trust me. Have I ever lied to you?"

He glanced at me, looking far younger than his actual calendar age.

"How do you know that?" he said from under his oxygen mask.

I smiled. "Because my father used to tell me I didn't have a good enough memory to be a successful liar. He was right. I can't remember what I ate for breakfast this morning. And that's no lie."

For what it's worth, making my son laugh seems to be one of my few talents on this earth. When life becomes a little overwhelming, I invariably resort to a lame joke—my own little defense mechanism, I guess, against unraveling panic. The truth was, Jack was an experienced flier who'd flown with me many times to places like Scotland and Hawaii, never once evincing the slightest trace of worry for his fate or the airplane's safety. I'd never seen him like this and, frankly, it frightened me as much as it obviously did him. For her part, the Queen Mum was busy being the Rock of Gibraltar over some obscure arty unreadable novel in the seat directly in front of us, but I knew she was worried to pieces about Nibs, as well.

"No, I mean how do you know something won't *happen?*"

"Something will happen, Boss," I said as calmly as possible, "but I have faith that it will be good."

He nodded fractionally and glanced back out the window at the clouds. "What exactly *is* faith?" he asked after a quiet bit.

I gazed at him for a moment. Jack was a founding member of the chapel choir at the small Episcopal church we regularly attended, and we'd had scores of conversations over the years, in some form or another, about the subject of faith. But maybe he just needed to hear my latest take on the subject, especially as it related to the suspension of disbelief that we wouldn't at any given moment plummet into the sea five miles below us.

I smiled at Nibs and, neglecting to properly credit Luther, proposed that faith was something beneath your left nipple, a reason to keep on smiling no matter what. Keep heart and you kept faith. It sounded trite, perhaps, but that was pretty much the essence of what I'd learned thus far in life that really mattered through good times and bad. I had faith the airplane would get us to England and the rest would basically be up to us.

He glanced at me and actually smiled a bit beneath the foggy Plexiglas of his oxygen mask, though in truth the smile looked decidedly forced. That was Jack's way, I think, of trying to reassure me.

It wasn't until the plane's wheels finally touched down at Heathrow, in any case, that the mystery of what unaccountably spooked him to the marrow began to reveal itself. The night before our departure, he explained as we taxied up and made our way through the airport's endless maze of arrival corridors toward customs, he and his stepbrother Charlie watched a few minutes of a television program on plane crashes, specifically the preview of a forthcoming documentary on people who had "miraculously" survived plane crashes and lived to tell about the experience.

"It's not that I really thought our plane *would* crash or anything," he attempted his best to assure me, almost his old Lost Boy self again but clearly relieved to be earthbound. "It's just that I realized it *could.*"

I'd nodded understandingly, suddenly remembering that this was the same cute tyke who once caused a minor disruption by refusing to return to the school building after his first fire drill in kindergarten because, as he later explained it in a calm logic that was difficult to deny, wherever there was a fire drill proved there might be a fire. Maybe his airplane terrors had simply been an extension of that logic—a kind of prefiguring of the worst that could happen. Or maybe, as fire-lit mythology and a thousand years of church doctrine seem to agree, eleven years really is about the time a boy begins to notice the wider world and its myriad joys and random terrors. The trick, of course, at the heart of growing up, is somehow learning to safely distinguish which path to take to the former and which to avoid to the latter.

I draped a reassuring arm around his slim shoulders and politely shoved him toward the customs officer, who asked, with perfect BBC diction, what the nature and purpose of our travels to Britain were.

"We're going around the world." Jack spoke up for us both, still a little pale at the gills, holding tight to Jack Pillow.

"Very good," the officer said with surprise, smiling and glancing at me for clarification. Under the circumstances, after what we'd just been through, I felt the sudden urge to repress my responsible adult side and try and leaven the mood just a bit, a theme I would pretty much adopt for the rest of the summer. When in doubt, make Jack laugh or at least smile—this became my silent travel motto. My role in this expedition to ancient wonders, I decided, would probably be at least as much court jester as it was knight errant.

"Just your usual garden variety summer holiday," I explained. "Warwick Castle. The Tower of London. Shakespeare at Avon. Warm beer and cold showers." I leaned forward and nodded discreetly at the old biddy waiting politely behind us in line for her personal interview with British immigration.

"See that elderly lady there, the one who is trying her best to look like somebody's innocent Scottish granny?" He nodded solemnly. "If I were you, I would have her taken off and strip searched. For one thing, she's carrying the unabridged Oxford Dictionary and some awfully dangerous looking knitting needles."

He glanced again at the Queen Mum and smiled; she smiled back at him, the very picture of Glaswegan granniness.

"I trust, madam," he said to her pleasantly, "that you are traveling with these gentlemen?"

"That's right," she replied crisply and marched dutifully forward, depositing her massive bag directly on my foot.

"And what, pray thee, have we *here?*" declared a plumy voice all the way from the Age of Reason. "A pair of whimsical Colonials performing what appears to be . . . some *crude* form of American recreation?"

There was a great deal of chuckling from the other tourists still loitering around to see if somebody was going to make me pay for cracking the Prime Meridian.

Jack's pitching arm froze in midair, his blue eyes widening. Our little game of catch had been detected by a powder-wigged gentleman who'd come out of the observatory museum to investigate our activities beneath a violently arched eyebrow.

"It's called baseball," I explained to him, hoping our inquisitor had at least a sense of humor to go with his lacy waistcoat. "It won't be invented for another hundred years or so. By then, I'm sorry to say, you'll be dead."

He smiled graciously. "Very witty, sir. You should be encouraged to take the stage. Or possibly flogged."

We carried on like this for a bit, until it suddenly came to me who he was—Nevil Maskelyne, the king's infamous royal astronomer who did everything he could to prevent humble Yorkshire clockmaker John

Harrison from proving the existence of global longitude and claiming the scientific adulation of his age for his brilliant discovery.

"You know," mused the young actor playing Maskelyne, leaning over to speak confidentially with Jack, "there was a time, lad, when men such as ourselves controlled the very passage of time itself. By that I mean to say that emperors and popes established calendars, kings named months and days of the week." He pointed a tapered finger at the museum proper, where three or four of Harrison's famous sea clocks were housed and kept on display. "But the clocks inside that building and the creation of this very Prime Meridian changed circumstances forever. Instead of men ruling time, time ruled the lives of men! And henceforth, science ruled the clockwork heavens and controlled *all* our lives!"

It was a nice little speech, probably rendered dozens of times a day during the long summer tourist season. Jack nodded, smiled appreciatively, and murmured, "Oh cool . . . ," all the while thumping his glove gently and impatiently with his balled fist the way all baseball-addicted boys do when they're anxious to keep throwing the ball.

I wasn't sure he fully grasped the scientific significance of what our man from the eighteenth century was getting at, but a clever idea suddenly came to me how to illustrate the point.

"In that case," I injected, casually tossing the ball back across the Meridian to Jack, who caught it, rather cheekily, Willie Mays style, like an apple dropping into a basket, "by sending this baseball back exactly the way it came, have I, in effect, sir, *reversed* time or at least momentarily suspended its forward passage?"

"Intriguing question!" Maskelyne appeared delighted with my little impromptu inquiry to reason, no doubt because all the world is a stage and the crowd of curious onlookers had begun to grow.

"What a positively beguiling theoretical *notion*!" he declared, cocking a bluestocking hip, narrowing an eye, and lifting a theatrical finger to his temple. "By moving that crudely stitched object that appears to be covered by the skin of some albino bovine creature backward through space and time, you have enacted, or so you claim, a process whereby time's ineluctable passage is, per force, somehow reversed? Is that the crux of your fanciful theoretical premise, sir?"

"Yep," I admitted, trying my best not to blush.

"You *should* be commended for your Newtonian cleverness," he insisted, bowing elegantly from the waist. Then he smirked and glanced at his audience. "Or else placed in stocks and severely *thrashed* for being such a pathetic heathen and heretic!"

Just then, wouldn't you know it, our Queen Mum hove into view, carrying her vast canvas bag and looking deeply worried—as if she gravely feared that whatever trouble I'd gotten her grandson into was going to wind up splashed all over the front page of the London *Sun*—YANK RUNS AMOK AT GREENWICH! BEANS INNOCENTS WITH STRANGE LEATHER ORB! ADVOCATES REVERSING TIME THROUGH MINDLESS GAME!

Good lad that he is, Jack immediately sashayed over and gave his flushed agnostic granny a welcoming hug, as if he hadn't seen her in weeks rather than minutes.

"And how long shall we have the pleasure of your company in England?" Maskelyne wondered to me, smiling after Jack, sounding more like the young actor playing him than the snotty astronomer who made such a royal nuisance of himself.

"As long as it takes to go as far as we can," I said, and explained the rough theory behind of our little field expedition to Who Knows Where.

He complimented me on such a novel idea, artfully noting that during the Age of Reason promising young men who displayed any intellectual or social potential were invariably sent on similar "grand tours" of enlightenment to the capitals of the Continent and beyond, including the Middle East and China.

"Look at Byron, look at Shelley," he trilled plummily, naming two of my favorite Romantic poets. "From Cambridge to Chillon, the Ponte Vecchio to the ancient Peloponnesus!"

"Right! Look at John, Paul, George, and Ringo," I chipped in helpfully. "Liverpool to New York, Ed Sullivan to an ashram!"

He summed up with a familiar quotation from Shakespeare. "A noble enterprise, sir. As a famous English bard might say, 'Then comes the time, who lives t'see it/that going shall be us'd with feet!' "

"*Exactly*, Lord Hamlet."

With this, though, the actor gave a sudden powerful shudder of revulsion, reverting quickly to the loathsome Nevil Maskelyne. "That's *Lear*, you unwashed soppit!"

"Are you behaving?" the Queen Mum demanded to know, sounding remarkably like the retired school superintendent she was, when I finally sidled over, gently punching my own mitt, an old Little Leaguer's catcher's mitt that was fraying at the seams and actually too small for my adult hand, a relic scrounged from a barrel at the back of our garage back home.

"Not entirely," I reassured her, pointing out that she'd probably just saved me from a royal flogging for momentarily confusing a mad Danish prince with a mad English king.

"Good thing you'll be having a refresher course soon, James," she said primly, digging into her vast canvas thing for a tissue to blow her nose or a knitting needle to smack me with.

Both of us knew that the primary reason she'd agreed to accompany us on the British leg of our journey was Jack—a chance to spend nearly a fortnight with her first male and (in some ways) favorite grandchild on foreign holiday. Another reason she agreed to tag along and good-naturedly suffer my constant abuse of her royal and ancient person was that I'd shamelessly dangled the carrot of promising to take her to a Royal Shakespearean Company's performance of *Hamlet, Prince of Denmark* at Stratford-upon-Avon. *Hamlet* was Mum's favorite play, for reasons known only to her, a play I find about as much fun as watching someone mop a floor in a shopping mall. I know what an uncultured Philistine boob that makes me out to be because Mum, who isn't nearly as innocent as she looks to people in British Immigration, reminds me of this cultural reality all the time.

"That guy in the wig said Dad was a heretic." Jack appeared to take great pleasure in revealing my public shame to his private grandmother.

"Actually, if you can believe it," I elaborated a little woundedly, "he called me an unwashed soppit! By the way," I asked the human Unabridged Oxford Dictionary, "what exactly *is* an unwashed soppit?"

"I'm not entirely certain," she was forced to admit, "but it pretty well describes you, I think." She turned to Jack and smiled with a forbearance she rarely extends to any of her former sons-in-law, of which

I happen to be the only one. "A heretic, Lamb, is someone who challenges the existing order of things. They're often ahead of their time in thinking and philosophy."

"Right," I agreed. "Like your socialist granny who claims to be a naturalized American citizen but steadfastly refuses to eat a charcoal-grilled steak, vote for a Republican, or watch the Super Bowl. I expect her to be deported any day now, Jack. Better get your goodbyes in now."

"Daughter of the Red Tide Clyde," the QM reminded me with a blithe little shrug, as we shuttled toward the observatory museum's front door.

"Don't be such a boring old agnostic," I sharply rebuked her, paraphrasing Robert Frost. "Actually be something."

She smiled tolerantly and Jack loped ahead inside to find Harrison's clocks. Kate used the opportunity to whisper, "So how's our worried lad really doing?"

I explained that he finally seemed to be settling down, though the side trip the three of us had made through the hokey, overpriced London Dungeons on the way to Greenwich Hill had clearly been another sensational miscalculation on my part.

For reasons that now eluded me, I'd thought Jack might find the place as much of a hoot as his fearless older sister, Maggie, had when I brought her with me to London two years previously. She'd adored the gaudy spectacle of blood and gore and the simulated horror of everything awful that had ever happened to the citizens of old London Town: the Plague, the Great Fire, Jack the Ripper, trial by a Dark Ages judge, beheadings and hangings and various ingenious forms of Medieval torture—all rendered with ghoulish enthusiasm by painted-up wraiths who leapt out from dark corners amid swirling electronic fogs to jolt squealing teenagers and make Midwestern tourists soil their walking shorts.

Jack, on the other hand, who has a powerful aversion to any loud noise, as I normally do, had endured the Medieval fun house with fingers plugged protectively into both his ears, a grimace of pure disgust on his face, and a visible pallor at the end of the ordeal that dangerously resembled his whacked-out countenance over the Atlantic

Ocean. Lunch at Covent Garden and a soothing rooftop tour of the city on the Big Red Bus served to ease his anxiety a bit, but I made a firm mental note not to try anything like the London Dungeons again wherever we went from here.

Up ahead in the gallery of Flamsteed House, where clockmaker Harrison once sought the advice and counsel of Sir Edmond Halley, a tale handsomely told in Dava Sobel's lovely book *Longitude*, which Jack and Kate had given me one Christmas, Jack had reached the first of John Harrison's famous sea clocks, so-called "H-1," a huge, ornate brass and steel timekeeper with various unseen wheels and mechanisms that, thanks to Nevil Maskelyne, sat forgotten and decaying in a damp storage place until it was meticulously restored and began running in 1933, after an interval of 167 years.

H-2 and H-3 were also working, minutely advancing the summer underfoot while a white-haired museum guide named Nick thoughtfully materialized on whispering crepe soles to explain the complicated functions of the world famous clocks to Jack and his grandmother, a wealth of scientific detail and operational minutiae that flew, let me be honest, straight over my head.

"Those suckers remind me," I heard myself mumble to no one in particular, "of Mr. Peabody's incredible Way Back Machine."

"Of . . . *what?*" Nick the time guide abruptly paused in his enthusiastic narration, fixing me with a woolly eye. He didn't seem at all pleased to have been interrupted, or maybe he was slightly annoyed by the fact that I was mindlessly thumping my own ball glove. The truth was, the observatory loo was closed for repairs and I really had to go.

I explained to him that Mr. Peabody was a beagle-like dog who invented a special Way Back Machine that enabled both him and Sherman, a brainy kid about Jack's age, to climb aboard and travel back through time to personally experience Arthur's round table or Madam Curie's laboratory and other pivotal moments in human history like that. My favorite episode was the one where Sherman and Mr. Peabody wound up at Custer's Last Stand and narrowly escaped with only a bunch of arrows dangling from their hindquarters. That episode never failed to crack me up, I explained. But I guess you had to actually see it or something.

Nick nodded and sniffed.

"American telly-vision, eh? Sounds more like a story basically *stolen* from H. G. Wells."

He turned his full attention warmly back to the Queen Mum, who seemed to be hanging on his every scientific word. I was half-tempted to pull him aside and warn him that the QM was a natural menace to the fun and personal freedom of eighth-grade boys everywhere until I heard him going on about his fast-approaching retirement from the National Trust and the Royal Observatory staff, in a fortnight's time, his needy dahlia garden in Luton, nine grandchildren who irregularly phoned, and a pension he hoped would take him for a lengthy "ramble" through the ruins of Italy and Greece.

"Always meant to do that but time simply flitted away," he explained to her a bit wistfully by the exit door of the museum.

"As Ben Jonson was supposed to have said, time really is the old bald deceiver and you'd best do today what you dare not put off till tomorrow!" And with this bit of woolly parting wisdom, he smiled tenderly at Mum and patted Jack thoughtfully on the head.

"Carry on, my good chap," he declared to me as if I were just some dumb jerk hired to carry the steamer trunks on our Old World expedition.

"Lovely man," the Queen Mum remarked as we filtered out the Royal Observatory gate and passed through the nicely landscaped grounds toward the waiting shuttle bus. Our first full day of trying to go around the world had been so tense and draining we were all going to ride back down the famous hill where time begins.

"At least he didn't call me an unwashed soppit," I agreed, thumping my glove.

TWO

An Unscheduled Odyssey

Back at the Hotel Edward Lear, the frazzled Russian woman running the place nearly tackled me in the lobby when I ventured downstairs a couple hours later to ask if she might know if there happened to be a local clinic or hospital emergency room anywhere around Marble Arch. On the boat ride back from Greenwich, Jack had announced he felt "funny" and suddenly began hyperventilating all over again. Kate suspected acute travel fatigue while I suspected an international plot to scuttle our summer abroad.

The mistress of Lear thrust a scrap of paper into my face.

"Your friend Iris phone to say you should call her back as soon as possible. Here is number. Please call *now*."

I looked at the illegible scrawl on the paper and admitted to her that I didn't know a living soul named Iris, in London or anywhere else on the planet. But I would be most grateful if she could reveal the location of the nearest walk-in medical clinic or hospital emergency room.

"You are *sick*?" Somehow she made it sound more like an accusation than a simple geographical question.

I explained to her that my son was having a bit of trouble breathing. He'd had this problem before we arrived, I pointed out, and it might be an allergic reaction to something or maybe simple exhaustion. "We just want to have him looked over to be on the safe side."

"You will phone Iris?" As she glared at me, I realized who she reminded me of. She was a dead ringer for the late Leonid Brezhnev. Except Brezhnev was prettier.

"Sure. What about that clinic, though?" I persisted.

"Good." The woman nodded and shuffled back to her stool behind the cluttered counter and began flipping through a scholarly periodical that showed a depressing amount of boiled white flesh and appeared to be called *Bare Bums of the Baltic* or something poetic like that.

Apparently she wasn't planning to give me a clinic until I gave Iris a jingle. Since there was no telephone up in our room, I picked up the house phone and dialed the number on the scrap of paper.

The phone on the counter rang and Madame Brezhnev promptly lifted the receiver.

"Hotel Edward Lear," she said.

"Excuse me," I replied, setting down my own reciever. "I think I somehow mistakenly dialed the hotel instead of Iris."

"No problem." She hung up and went back to her boiled bare bums.

I dialed once more. Her phone rang again.

"Hotel Edward Lear," she repeated in my ear.

"Look," I said to the receiver, "I think you gave me the *hotel's* telephone number instead of this Iris person's."

"Is not possible," she snapped, and hung up on me.

I stared across the lobby, a bit dumbfounded, debating whether it made more sense to give up and go back upstairs and check on Jack or make a lunge for her throat.

"Could it be possible that the person who phoned was named *Edie?*" We were scheduled to meet friends from back home for an early dinner in Soho, and it suddenly occurred to me that Madame Brezhnev might have mistaken Edie for Iris.

"Who is *Edie?* I don't know this Edie person," she grunted, visibly irritated that I was horning in on her valuable private reading time.

"I think Edie might be *Iris,*" I put to her gently. "Or at least I hope so."

"I do not know who . . . *Edie* is."

"Look," I said, "could you at least tell me where there is a local clinic or hospital?"

"I have no idea," she admitted with a shrug.

"In that case," I said, "would you please phone us a taxi?"

"Okay." She released a heavy politburo sigh as I fled for both of our protections, leaning forward to call after me: "But what if *Iris* phones again?"

I wandered distractedly back up the Lear's poorly lit, insanely vertical stairway, more or less in the general direction of our grim fourth-floor "guest room," where Jack was supposed to be resting on his prison-sized bunk and watching Englishman Tim Henman attempt to advance to the quarter finals of Wimbledon on our minuscule black-and-white television set (the kind of high-quality video appliance American gas stations give you free if you fill up your car twice).

I made a mental note, as I climbed, to strangle to death with my bare hands the friend who whimsically proposed that we try her favorite London digs, "save money and have fun" by spending the night at the Hotel Edward Lear. "Charming, *very* reasonable, and perfect for traveling families" she evangelized, citing the establishment's handy location at Marble Arch and proximity to Hyde Park and Speaker's Corner.

For reasons that also now escaped me, I'd foolishly ditched the modest but comfortable Knightsbridge hotel across Hyde Park where I customarily stayed in London in favor of this run-down guest house that had once been the home of Britain's most celebrated nonsense poet, the guy who wrote "The Owl and the Pussycat" and other ditties for small children and the mentally defective.

Poets, I suppose, are a pretty fair barometer of the times they inhabit (or at least the houses they choose to dwell in) so it probably shouldn't have come as a big surprise for me to learn (from a yellowing framed magazine story nailed to the peeling wallpaper of a hallway where I paused to rest from my brutal ascent up the stairs) that Edward Lear, author of some of the world's most beloved childhood poems was, in fact, the twentieth child born to a bankrupt suburban stockbroker and a mentally ill woman who hardly noticed his existence. An epileptic, asthmatic, shortsighted, and sexually abused boy brought up in wrenching poverty by a domineering older sister, Lear grew up to become an agile social climber and celibate homosexual who chose to make his living giving drawing lessons to Queen Victoria and selling his possibly drug-induced nonsense verse and pencil sketches of faraway places to court wannabes and minor pillars of the empire.

What on earth had I been thinking? And who the *hell* was Iris?

Back at the room, I discovered Jack sitting rigidly on his bed, pallid as the faded Edwardian wallpaper, staring wide-eyed at the TV set, breathing like a dying man on an iron lung.

"Dad," he said, between gasps, "what does she mean that her son is going to die and go to paradise but he'll have seventy-two virgins waiting for him?"

I glanced bewilderedly at the TV set and saw that Tim Henman and the summer idyll of Wimbledon had been replaced by a bleak BBC documentary on the Palestinian Intifada and the rapid growth of "suicide camps" along the West Bank. A proud Palestinian mother was boasting to her interviewer that her son Ahmad—a kid about Jack's size, wearing over his young face the famous checkered scarf of a Palestinian freedom fighter—would soon kill many Jews and possibly Americans and be rewarded, as a result, by many virgin wives in heaven.

"It means he's going to be so busy taking out the trash for his arguing wives he'll wish he was back on earth playing war games with his buddies," I said and immediately helped Nibs to his feet and handed him Jack Pillow and snapped off the damned documentary.

Our taxi driver was a man of Middle Eastern descent. *Oh perfect*, I thought. His named was Muhammad. He had a photograph of a pretty little girl taped to his dashboard.

"We need to go to the closest hospital," I said urgently to him.

He nodded understandingly. "The Great Ormond Street Hospital for Children is not far. No more than five minutes."

Muhammad's tires squealed and I gripped the seat and glanced behind me at Jack and the Queen Mum in the backseat. Jack was leaning heavily into his grandmother's amply padded side, still gasping shallowly for air but now also appearing to fight off the urge to fall asleep, as well. He looked frighteningly pale and limp. I must have looked a fright to him, too.

"It's okay, Lamb," Kate said soothingly to him, staring at me with those round no-nonsense superintendent eyes of her. "You can go to sleep if you like. Rest now . . ."

His eyes fluttered open.

"I don't want to fall asleep," he murmured, then fell silent, then added almost dreamily, "Dad . . . why do the Arabs want to kill Americans?"

I turned and stared a little embarrassedly at Muhammad's unshaven profile. *Kids say the darndest things on vacation.* But before I could say this he glanced at me calmly and turned the wheel sharply and we sped up a narrow alley between several tall brick buildings.

"Is that your daughter?" I asked him, pointing to the photograph of the pretty little girl.

"Yes. She has been to Ormond Street many times lately. That's why I know how to get there quickly."

"Is she okay?"

He smiled thinly and gave the faintest shrug of a man who has been to hell and back in his own way.

"We do not know. She is tiny and refuses to grow. They do not know why exactly." He accelerated, and a blur of parked cars flew by the Toyota's windows. "But we have good doctors there, so we have hope," he added.

I glanced back at Jack again. He appeared to be asleep now. Kate's eyes met mine. She looked more worried than ever.

I asked Muhammad where he came from. It was either that or scream.

"Iran," he answered simply.

"Some of my favorite poets are ancient Persians," I said, apropos of absolutely nothing whatsoever except my frantically scrambling state of mind.

"It is very sad about Iran," he commented, turning the wheel and making the tires beneath us squeal again.

"Very beautiful, I hear."

"Very sad and very beautiful," He spoke English as skillfully as he hurled a private taxi through southwest London's crowded back streets. We took a final corner on two wheels and skidded to a halt in front of the children's hospital made famous by an endowment by Scotsman James Barrie, author of *Peter Pan*. If I hadn't been in such a mad dash and careening state of personal semi-panic I might have realized what a sweet irony this was—to be bringing a real-life Lost Boy to a house of healing built by the magic of a boy who simply refused to grow up.

Curiously, Muhammad was out the door before I was, opening the Queen Mum's door and gently helping my son shakily to his feet.

For a crazy second or two, while Mum gathered her things and got out, the three of us stood there in the pretty five o'clock sunlight of a nice English summer afternoon.

"Muhammad," I used the opportunity to say. "Do you think people from the Middle East really hate Americans?"

He looked slightly taken aback but quickly realized what I was attempting to do.

"Not at all," he answered calmly, placing a gentle hand on Jack's shoulder. He looked my son directly in the eyes, though I'm not sure Jack was really capable of looking back at him by this point in time. "Most Iranians I know like Americans very much. My daughter would love to see America."

"What's her name?" I asked him.

"Her name is Simi."

When Jack and his grandmother were safely inside, being led by a nurse to an examination room, I went back to pay Muhammad and thank him for his kindness and his driving skills. I handed him a twenty-pound note and told him to keep the change, but he refused to accept my money.

"Your son is probably just weary from traveling," he said, lighting a cigarette. He offered me one but I declined. I was dying to get back inside to Jack and Kate but hesitated a moment, feeling as if I really ought to say something more to him, though I didn't have a clue what that might be. We were worried fathers from different worlds.

"Well, in any case, thanks," I said insufficiently, wondering if I should add that I sincerely hoped his little Simi would begin to grow very soon.

"What Persian poets do you like so much?" he asked pleasantly out of the blue, looking at me with large, calm, deeply shadowed eyes.

I said I really liked the love poems of Rumi and the meditations of Muhammad Hafiz, the famous Sufi mystic who had such great influence over Ralph Waldo Emerson. Emerson, I needlessly explained, attended college in the same small New England town where we resided. He'd been called the father of transcendentalism, which simply meant he saw traces of God or the divine everywhere he looked. The older I got, the more I seemed to relate to this simple view of life, which made me something of a latter-day dirt road transcendentalist even though, technically speaking, I was Episcopalian.

Muhammad smiled, took a patient drag of his cigarette, and said he had heard of Emerson. He fell silent as if trying to think of something more to say to me.

"God wants to see more playfulness and laughter in your eyes," he added, squinting at me as the smoke leaked from both nostrils. "For that is your greatest witness to him. Your heart and my heart are very old friends. We knew each other's souls, perhaps we played footsie together in the Beloved's womb."

He gave me the faintest of smiles. "I think that is Hafiz, but you can tell your son that is a friendly message from his taxi driver, if you like."

"I will," I assured him and started to walk away, a little amazed and perhaps even shaken by what had just happened.

At the hospital door, I paused and waved my hand. Leaning on his taxi, Muhammad waved back. He seemed to be in no hurry at all. Then he took another long drag on his cigarette. The sky rumbled somewhere off to the west. It was going to rain.

A few minutes after midnight, the Queen Mum stepped out of the tiny curtained cubicle to stretch her legs and hunt down a decent cup of tea while I replaced her vigil on the hard plastic chair by the bed where Jack was now soundly sleeping. I'd briefly slipped out to try and find a cup of coffee and something useful to read while we waited to be released from the hospital. I'd come back with a sensationally bad cup of Nescafé and an early edition of the *Daily Telegraph* which was reporting that Prince Charles had hinted publicly for the first time that he might make an honest woman of Camilla Parker Bowles and that Englishman Tim Henman's quest to become the first Brit in almost fifty years to reach the finals of Wimbledon had been cruelly suspended due to rain, leaving Britain's best hopes dangling two-sets-to-one over Goran Ivanisevic.

What an unplanned odyssey we'd had through the plumbing of the British medical system.

The Great Ormond Street Hospital had examined Jack to determine if he was in any immediate medical danger and then sent us via ambulance to London City University Hospital for more extensive pediatric tests. There, we'd waited for almost three hours to see a kind but thorough Pakistani physican who'd run an impressive battery of tests on Jack's lungs and blood composition and finally given him a mild sedative to help him rest.

The doctor's initial diagnosis ruled out infectious ailments and unknown allergies. Rather, he believed Nibs the Lost Boy was suffering from extreme anxiety brought on by a number of possible factors—the lingering effects of the plane crash documentary playing on his fervid imagination, a random episode of flight panic triggered by physical exhaustion due to our late arrival and sudden foreign surroundings, possibly even the jolt of discovering there were boys his age who believed they would go straight to heaven for blowing themselves up and taking a few innocent bystanders with them.

Sirens whooped mutely in the distance. Someone wheeled a gurney past our closed curtain and I heard a young person moaning in pain. "Knife wound," a clipped English voice called out as the gurney squeaked off down the corridor, the moaning fading away.

Suddenly Jack opened his eyes and stared at me. His eyes looked clearer than they had since our hike up Greenwich Hill.

"Hey, Boss," I said quietly. "Welcome back. The Queen of England was just here. Sorry you missed her. She said you should come by Buckingham Palace for tea and a biscuit, though. Nice lady."

"Hi, Dad." He yawned a bit. "Have I been sleeping long?"

"Five or six hours. You needed it. Frankly, so did we."

"Did we miss supper with Caroline and Edie?"

"Yeah. No big deal. We'll catch 'em back in Maine. Maybe we'll take Iris to dinner instead."

His smooth brow wrinkled up. "Who's *Iris?*"

"Long story. Best told with a stout shot of vodka. You rest. The doctor will release us shortly."

"Can I ask you something?"

"Sure."

He thought for a moment, rubbing an eye.

"How can women, like, wear lipstick or something and not get it on their food when they eat?"

I loved how Jack's brain worked. The fact that you had no idea what goofy question or peculiar observation was going to come out of his mouth next made life with Jack an ongoing adventure. It also meant he was feeling much better.

"You know," I was forced to admit. "I haven't a clue. That's one of the great unanswered questions of mankind. Another one is how they can possibly reach a bare hand into a working garbage disposal to retrieve the smallest object."

Now he smiled, which meant I was at least doing my job.

Back home we had an original oil painting of a Medieval court jester hanging in the foyer of our house; the jester was crouched, holding a small ball in one hand, ready to leap or fall like a buffoon, looking a little worried but clearly determined to make someone—the king himself, perhaps, or simply a child on a summer lawn—laugh and smile with much needed mirth. The painting was by a gifted Maine artist I'd never met, but I sometimes had the feeling, crazy as it sounds, that she'd modeled the jester after me.

I told Jack what Muhammad the taxi driver said about God wanting to see laughter in his eyes. The jester in me did, too. He liked that.

"Do you think the Red Sox will get to the World Series this year?" he wondered out of the blue.

"Maybe," I said. "You can never tell. It's only June."

Actually, with the Red Sox you can *always* tell. They were one of life's rare *non*-mysteries. They would win like world beaters until mid-September and then collapse like a two-dollar beach chair in the playoffs. Some things are uncertain in this life, but the Red Sox can always be counted on to break the hearts of their faithful followers. Someday I would have to break this sobering news to Jack. But for now, touchingly, he was a true believer in the warriors of Fenway Park.

"Dad, do we have to go home now?"

"Nope. We're just going back to our luxury hotel," I said. "Personally, I'd rather find a nice comfy wooden bench in Hyde Park."

"No," he said, a little worriedly, "I mean *home* home."

"Do you want to go home?"

"No, sir. I'd like to keep going. This was our trip. We were supposed to go to Paris and Africa and stuff."

"You're right. Then we'll keep going. Look out, world."

"Great," he said, almost sounding like good old Nibsy again. Amazing what a little bed rest and a slug of grape-flavored sedative will do. "So where are we going tomorrow?"

"I don't know exactly," I admitted. "Maybe England's greatest Medieval castle or some dumb play in Stratford-upon-Avon by a guy named Shakespeare. A little cricket in Oxford after that. Nothing you'd probably be very interested in."

"Oh yes I would," he insisted—as it involved a game with a ball.

"Really? Well, in that case I'm glad we're not going home."

He smiled at me. Something else was hanging fire.

"Do we have to, like, fly there, though?" he said, a bit timorously.

"No," I reassured him, rubbing his fluffy head. "It's only fifty miles. We'll drive. I love driving in Britain. Particularly with your grandmother in the car. I can really make her crazy. I'll show you how."

THREE

Baseball on Valium

"You know, James. It's a *most* unusual man who gets married to a woman one day and then takes his former mother-in-law on the honeymoon the next. By the way, dear, are we lost?"

This was two days after our adventures in hospital and I reflected on this ironic turn of life Mum proposed as we were banged along a narrow farm road between the ancient hedgerows of the empire in a car meant for Hertz Gold members half our size. To complicate matters, as I carefully pointed out to her, some idiot had placed the steering wheel on the wrong side of the car, and every now and then, just for kicks, flying through a thatch-roofed village that looked like a postcard from Willie Wordsworth, I swerved to the right side of the road and enjoyed the jolly sight of villagers yanking leashed dogs and small children out of our path and my former mother-in-law, seated rigidly beside me up front, reflexively lurching forward to grab the dash and slam on a brake pedal that wasn't there. It was more fun than a grown man should probably legally be permitted to have while crossing a foreign country.

We'd been to Stratford and Warwick and were now headed generally in the direction of Oxford—the "dreaming spires" where the New English Bible was written, the brothers Wesley launched Methodism, Edmond Halley predicted the return of his comet, Lewis Carroll wrote *Alice's Adventures in Wonderland*, and the MG motor car was invented. For our purposes, though, Oxford was where Jack had been invited to learn about the ancient game of cricket at a distinguished private school for boys called Summer Fields. My good friend and golf pal Charles Churchill once served as senior master at the famous prep school, teaching classics, coaching cricket, and building the nine-hole golf course largely through the offices of forced schoolboy labor. Summer Fields produced Harold McMillan and actor Patrick McNee and has, among other things, been accused of being a breeding camp for Eton old boys. I frankly couldn't wait to see what the old boys would make of a true public library card–carrying Red Tide Socialist like Mum, and vice versa.

As usual where I was concerned, though, the QM was cheekily having me on, as the Brits like to say—this bit about marrying one day and taking my former wife's mother on the honeymoon the next. The simple truth was, Wendy and I were married almost *three* whole days before I abandoned her and ran off to parts unknown with my son and former mother-in-law.

Jack's mom, to clarify (probably far more than you really want to know) had been happily remarried for almost three years, but, owing to the complexities of modern life, I'd only returned to a state of wedded bliss in the backyard seventy-two hours before Jack and I were scheduled to embark with the Queen Mum for the Continent. It was either postpone the wedding or delay the trip we'd been planning since the days of *Goodnight Moon*, and we'd simply opted to do neither— Wendy, my tolerant new bride, would simply join Dodsons Minor and Major for part of the sojourn through Italy and Greece. As I on more than one occasion reminded the Queen Mum, who attended the service and kept a civil tongue in her mouth despite the reverend's rather reckless invitation to skeptics in the congregation to give voice to any worrying doubts, the way our honeymoon had evolved was, I'll grant, a tad unconventional in the Martha Stewart sense of wedded bliss. But on the other side of the ledger, despite our big mistakes and small transgressions in life, we were now officially one big happy extended family linked by children and matrimonial histories, and the older I got the more I realized nothing in life really works out quite the way you expect it to anyway so you might as well try and relax, take another slice of cake, and try your best not spill the fruit punch all over the front of your rented tuxedo.

Besides, another reason for this extended field trip, it seemed to me,
though I didn't dare let on such allegorical thinking to my traveling
companions, was to show young Jack that even if you had no idea what
untidy things the world was going to throw at you as you rambled
down the road of life, you simply needed to keep your chin up, faith
strong, and feet constantly moving forward. Even an old pink agnostic
could hardly disparage that working philosophy—in fact, Mum had
pretty much said those very words to me in the aftermath of a divorce
that seemed to take both Jack's mom and me by surprise. Half a decade
had passed since that difficult time and now life had taken an unexpected turn for the better. Jack's mother and I were once again great
friends and now I had a wonderful new bride to boot—even though
summer would be mostly over before I saw her pretty face again. I
looked forward to a long and prosperous married life with spunky
Dame Wendy and dearly hoped she would enjoy a fine and comforting
summer until we met again and, since we're somewhat on the subject,
would remember to water the ruinously expensive border plants I'd in-
stalled in the yard a week before we departed, lest they wither away in
my absence and present grounds for immediate legal annulment.

"This may be an unusual honeymoon," I vollied sharply back at the
QM, "but it's certainly no picnic. By the way, we're not lost. This is
only a picturesque shortcut to Oxford I know like the back of my hand.
So shut up, with all due respect, madam, before I give it to you."

A laugh came from somewhere in back where Jack was wedged in
with our luggage and the last of the Baudelaire children's awful adventures. I glanced in the mirror and saw his cute oval face smiling at
me above the final pages of his book. Considering what an Ealing
comedy film the past few days had been in greater London, it was terrific to see him smiling and laughing again as the elderly hedgerows
flew past.

The great thing about motoring in rural England is, unless you're
either from someplace in South Carolina or a total dolt, you can never
really get lost because there's always a helpful roundabout approximately every seventy-five meters along the road, which means you can
conveniently go in circles for as long as you care to before having to
make a serious commitment one way or another. Also, the English are

big on village signposts. *Spotted Dick,* the sign will suddenly proclaim, pointing sharply to a field of drowsy sheep. And sure enough, just two miles over the hill, beyond the sheep and seventeen more roundabouts down the lane, there it lies, cute little Spotted Dick. Home of peat huts and contented sheep and not much else.

I had high hopes for Oxford because we'd already found our way to Warwick Castle and beautiful Stratford on River Avon with decidedly mixed results. Warwick Castle, to briefly review, is said to be the finest Medieval castle in England, a most attractive place, with high fortified walls and dramatic towers, secret passages, a nifty dungeon, a functioning drawbridge, a moat that could seriously use some water, and a general air of Medieval hostility that enriches one with a vivid sense of history and gives a chap the irresistible urge to take up arms and slay a Frenchman.

Despite my unvoiced worry that he might react to the place with a revulsion similar to what he felt for the hokey London Dungeons, Nibsy absolutely adored Warwick Castle, suggesting the real McCoy is more interesting and tolerable than a bad imitation any old day. Even better, the afternoon we came calling there, a Medieval country fair occupied the castle grounds, complete with strolling minstrels, guys in felt hats and funny tights, lusty wenches in poorly laced-up bodices, knights in clanging armor, crude games of chance, archery exhibitions, shuffling monks, and an official court rat catcher named Ned. Jack lost a few queen's sovereigns trying to knock over some dusty alchemist's bottles with his Pedro fastball and Ned the Royal Rat Catcher, a whiskery sort with a roving glass eye, caught me admiring the handsome costume details of his traveling wench's period-correct bodice and wondered if I might wish to volunteer as a hay-stuffed dummy for the archery exhibition. I politely passed on the opportunity.

The next day, though, Shakespeare's hometown was a major disappointment—a picturesque English village overrun with tour buses transporting retired Missourians. It was there, as we killed time before the evening performance of *Hamlet, Prince of Denmark,* and Mum and Jack nibbled sandwiches and cooled their heels under a festival tent with a chilled glass of vino and a warm lemon Coke respectively, that I snuck off to a pay phone in the performance hall lobby and dialed the

American Embassy in London, hoping to get the lowdown on a genuinely worrisome item Mum had seen just that morning in the *Times*.

According to the paper, the terrorists who bombed the American embassy in Kenya had just been convicted and sent to prison in leg irons, prompting the American government to issue a "strong" travel advisory against American citizens going to Africa for the "foreseeable future." That was just our rotten luck, and I could only imagine Jack's mom's reaction when she got wind of this unsettling news, confirming her darkest worries about darkest Africa. First it was teenage suicide camps in Gaza, now Kenyan crackpots. For weeks, too, I'd been quietly waiting and hoping to hear the all-clear given to Americans who wished to travel to mainland China, where the downed spy plane incident was still stirring up anti-Yank passions many months after the fact.

The embassy operator connected me with a guy named Chet who claimed he was a senior foreign travel officer but sounded more like a lonely ace about to give up and hurl himself beneath the wheels of a Piccadilly bus. I sketched out a rough outline of our hopeful freewheeling caprice to Europe and maybe Africa, Egypt, and China and wondered if Chet had any helpful travel advice to render vis-à-vis these destinations.

"What exactly do you do for a living?" Chet asked as if he were jotting it down on an official form that would be faxed straight to Colin Powell's desk.

I was caught off guard by his question. "I write stuff," I replied without thinking too much about it, frankly.

"What sort of things?" he demanded in a slightly skeptical tone.

I hesitated for a moment, wondering if I was legally obliged to reveal how I made my daily crust to some guy who sounded like his favorite light reading was the obituaries. I was half-tempted to tell him I was either a presidential speechwriter or a Lake District poet.

"Golf tips. Gardening manifestos. The occasional exploitative book about traveling with my friends and family."

"I see. And your son. What exactly does he do?"

I glanced across the sunlit plaza where Jack was now throwing his crappy sandwich at geese gliding in the lovely River Avon, just outside the festival hall tent.

"The usual things a ten-year-old boy does," I replied truthfully. "Right now he's throwing egg mayonnaise at ducks."

"So, he's *not* a journalist?"

I was beginning to get a mental picture of Chet sitting in a damp corner of the embassy basement, alternately reading personal ads in *Bare Bums of the Baltic* and trying to do the crossword puzzle thoughtfully mailed to him each week by his widowed mother in Poughkeepsie.

"No," I answered.

Chet abruptly placed me on hold. You'd think, on the cusp of a new millennium, the embassy of the greatest country on earth could afford better canned music than Tony Orlando and the golden hits of the Bicentennial decade. After a few indeterminate minutes of idle woolgathering on my part, Chet came back on line.

"So I assume the context of your visits to these places is recreational rather than professional in nature?" He picked straight up where he'd left off. Perhaps he'd simply had to use the john.

"That's correct," I answered. "After knocking off Europe and Greece we hope to see the black rhinos of Africa and moonwalk along the Great Wall. Basically, boys just want to have fun."

He didn't seem to get my Cyndi Lauper joke. Perhaps *knocking off Europe* hadn't been the best way to describe our travel hopes.

"I see. Well, I'm afraid Africa, Egypt, and China aren't places we're advising *any* Americans to go at the present," he advised somewhat lugubriously. "In my opinion, given their acute political instability, it would be highly unadvisable to proceed to those places at the moment, especially with a child and no familiarity with the regions in question. I trust you've never been to Africa or China?"

"No. But I've seen a lot of movies about them."

"I'm not at liberty to say much more than perhaps you should seriously consider holding your trip off until the fall. Check back with us again, if you like. Any other places I can help you with?"

"How about Oxford? Any violence in the streets reported there?"

I hung up and went back to where Mum was now enjoying a nice preperformance gin and tonic near the summer Shakespeare Festival's outdoor stage. A cotton scrim had been drawn behind her and someone was obviously rehearsing a play mere feet from where she sat. I plopped down in a plastic chair, waving for the waiter, and Mum asked what I'd learned from the embassy. I told her the news wasn't one bit encouraging—our prospects for wandering the world like Odysseus and Telemachus were dimming as rapidly as the approaching English dusk. If I hadn't known better, I added, I'd have sworn there was an international conspiracy to make me look like a boob who promised the world but delivered only an inedible egg mayonnaise sandwich.

"Don't take it personally," she said, trying to console me. "The world was pretty awful in my day, too. It comes and goes. Why don't you just take it a day at a time and see what evolves."

"Besides, you're such a complete imbecile," a woman's voice accused acidly from the far side of the curtain—as I say, mere feet from where we sat. For a nutty second, I could have sworn that, Lady Macbeth–like, I was hearing voices from beyond more than just a curtain.

"That may be," a man's voice replied. "But you chose to marry me, Hortense. You bloody well should have known . . ."

Mum smiled. "I don't think *that's* Shakespeare," she said.

"Domestic comedy," I agreed with relief. "Probably some lesser known Pinter."

This tense exchange, though, was followed by a sudden jarring pistol shot, followed by a heavy thud where something or someone struck the stage floor beyond our view—though the curtain creepily billowed. Mum and I both jumped a foot in our plastic chairs just as Jack came strolling back with more egg on his hands than his face, which suddenly went ashen at the sound of unexpected gunplay.

"What was *that?*" he demanded, checking up.

"Murder mystery," I quickly explained. "Probably early Agatha Christie."

"Relax, Lamb," Mum assured him, patting a nice empty chair beside her and remembering how he detested loud noises of any kind. "It's just a silly old play. They're rehearsing next door, something I'm grateful we won't be seeing."

That was pretty much what I thought about *Hamlet, Prince of Denmark*—a silly old play that never fails to set my teeth on edge. But it was Mum's favorite play, and since we were in pretty Stratford-upon-

Avon along with half the retired population of Missouri, I was determined to keep an open mind, see what evolved, and give that timeless
whiny twerp Hamlet, poster boy for modern dysfunctional males
everywhere, a chance to show me something new.

"Does this play have any, like, shooting guns in it?" Jack thoughtfully inquired as we filtered into the grand performance hall and found
our seats in the plush orchestra section. Brother, what a house! I tried
not to think about what these bucket seats had set us back and focused
instead on the positive. They'd be absolutely sensational for catching
a couple hours of valuable nap time in.

"Of course not." Mum, visibly excited, patted his thigh pertly.
"*Hamlet*, dear, was written four hundred years ago. There *weren't*
firearms in those days."

"Oh good," he said, breathing a sigh of relief, settling in and prying
open his program.

"Just a few dagger stabbings and a little poison in the ear," I leaned
over and assured him fondly. "Nothing you can't handle."

With that, the lights went down and the Danes came forth.

An eerie mist rose and mysterious figures appeared on the stage. I
thought how peculiar it was they were dressed more like Nazi storm
troopers than Medieval Danes and carried what appeared to be, golly,
modern military assault rifles. A moment later, the ghost of Hamlet's
murdered father, the king, appeared and the palace guards began firing
at will—an earsplitting fusillade of gunfire that wreathed the stage in
acrid smoke and sent Jack and me and half the audience diving for
cover beneath our seats.

The Queen Mum, I must tell you, wasn't one bit pleased to discover
we'd paid a king's ransom for a "contemporized" production of *Hamlet,
Prince of Denmark*. The only thing a true overeducated Scot detests
more than a false bargain is some young peckerwood English director
fooling around with the Bard of Avon. For our part, Jack and I simply
wanted to get the heck out of the place before more heavy artillery was
rolled out and the shooting match resumed.

"Oh, what villainous slander men do! What chipped-tooth son of
a drunkard's mongrel, what pretentious foul-breathed lump of worm
meat made this unholy mess?" Mum muttered beneath her minty

breath as we fled the performance hall shortly after the second act, trying to remember where we'd left the car in Shakespeare's birthplace. It
was somewhere near the spot, I recalled, where a brass placard more or
less explained where he got his first poor mark in English literature and
told his unhappy parents it was really much ado about nothing—he
planned to drop out of school, go off to London Town, find a decent
waiter's job, and maybe try his hand at acting—that old Winter's Tale.

Actually, to be fair, these weren't the Queen Mum's exact words.
Her exact words were "Dreadful. Simply dreadful. Someone ought to
be truly ashamed of themselves for staging that atrocity."

For a change, she didn't mean me, either. With a daughter of the
Red Tide Clyde, I've learned, you basically have to read between the
lines and interpret various subtle facial tics. She looked like Chet
sounded. But as we fled over the hill toward the ancient river town of
Oxford, where no travel advisories had yet been posted, taking a shortcut I knew like the back of my hand through the lovely countryside
that would lead us (at most) only twenty or so kilometers in the wrong
direction, I thought there might be yet another valuable life lesson for
Jack in the aftermath of this comic little tragedy by the tranquil River
Avon. Sometimes when you least expected it, things really *did* turn out
dramatically differently than you hoped and *paid* for. But there was always a bright side to be found if you looked long and hard enough to
find it. For once, it was nice to think, we were all in complete agree-
ment about William Shakespeare's most famous play.

Early the next morning, before cricket got underway at Summer
Fields, Jack and I put on our walking shoes and hoofed with our baseball gloves down the busy Banbury Road into the world's most famous
college town, which may or may not have been named for a shoe or a
bunch of cattle crossing the River Cherwell.

After the unplanned thrills of late, I decided a nice dull walk into
a sleepy college town to buy a new book for Jack and find a place to
pitch the ball might be just the thing to settle both our nerves and buy
me time to try and figure out what the heck we were going to do about
Africa, Egypt, and the rest of the world who didn't seem to want us.

Jack must have been thinking along the same lines because we'd barely gone a block before he apologized for taking his grandmother and me on an extended tour of two London hospitals and "freaking out," as he put it, at Stratford-upon-Avon.

"What are you talking about?" I said, carefully taking his arm at the crosswalk where the words *Look Right* were helpfully painted in emergency-technician yellow to help prevent unthinking foreigners like us from being knocked down or run over by a vegetable lorry. But Jack, being Jack, an American *and* a born dreamer, naturally looked left. "I should apologize to you for managing to find the world's only performance of Shakespeare with machine guns."

"That's okay," he said, as we finally skedaddled across the busy thoroughfare and fell in line between some interesting college students wearing more face metal than some African tribes. "I guess I probably shouldn't have been so worried."

That may be, I said to him, but worrying about stuff was simply part of growing up. Worrying about stuff, someone said, I told him (though a bit worryingly I couldn't for the life of me remember who), is a true sign of sanity because only the mentally unbalanced never worry about anything at all. The trick, or so it seemed to me, was to figure out what sort of things were *worth* your time worrying about and what things it was utterly pointless to give more than a passing thought to. Worrying about how to get safely across the street in Britain, for example, seemed a perfectly fine and useful thing to worry about because worrying made you pay attention to the pedestrian warning that was plainly painted at your feet.

Worrying about how much metal to insert in your face when you get to college, on the other hand, to cite an example at hand, was utterly pointless because if you did that your father was simply going to cancel the check to the college and lock you in the basement until you turned forty.

Besides, as I pointed out to Jack—hoping not to worry the lad or anything—worrying about certain things was a thoroughly natural process because he and his somewhat bossy older sister hailed from a long and distinguished line of world-class worriers. Both his grandfathers were dedicated worriers, as was his mother back in Maine and the Queen Mum back at our new temporary home, the Galaxy Hotel. For example, right this very minute, I explained to him, the Queen Mum was sitting in her hotel ostensibly reading Trollope but, in fact, quietly worrying that I would get us lost on a silly hike into Oxford and cause Jack to miss a swell lunch with the other boys at Summer Fields School. You can take the school superintendent out of Maine, it was pretty clear, but not the school superintendent out of the Queen Mum.

"You don't seem to worry much," Jack remarked.

I laughed and thumped my ball glove, looking around to see if I could spot a vacant college lawn where we might work on his fastball. It worried me a little that we hadn't seriously thrown the ball since leaving America.

"On the contrary, Boss. I worry about *everything*. You just don't see it."

"Really?" This revelation seemed to please him somehow.

"Yep. You have no idea." I gave him a random sampling of my on-going roster of active parental worries, probably enough minor mental anguish to keep a decent psychoanalyst comfortably employed for the next twenty years or so. To begin with, any time my children left my sight for more than two Greenwich Mean minutes, I worried that something unpleasant might happen to them that would make me kick myself for the rest of my natural life. In no particular order of significance, I also worried about the furnace going out in the dead of winter, the old Volvo breaking down for good, the dog dying, drought withering my flower gardens, a killer asteroid flattening our house, and finally getting too old to pitch for the Red Sox, even in short relief.

"When you were little," I added in the sudden spirit of candid revelation, "I used to worry about flying on airplanes. Not because I was afraid of dying if the plane crashed, mind you. But because if I died in a plane crash you might remember Barney the Dinosaur better than me. Crazy, huh?"

"Golly, no." Jack thumped his glove. "But I would have remembered you, I'll bet."

"Maybe so, maybe not. Maybe you'd have thought your old man was fat, purple, and sang really dopey songs."

Jack chortled but quickly grew thoughtful again. "Did you worry about stuff when you were, like, *my* age, too?" Now he sounded like a pint-sized Jungian analyst.

"Oh, that was the *worst* time of all," I admitted, "in terms of worrying. You wouldn't believe the stuff I worried about. It worries me just to remember that sort of thing."

"Really? Like what?"

I gave him a second sampling, from my exhaustive personal archives of childhood worries: eating radioactive snow and dying slowly from some horrible disfiguring disease, looking at a solar eclipse I'd been warned not to look at and going blind as a fruit bat as a result, getting beaten up by Randy Farmer, not having a bomb shelter in our backyard.

The list, I explained, was basically as long as your arm. I worried about losing my library books, being bitten by a poisonous snake, not making shortstop on the Pet Dairy baseball team, my father mysteriously failing to come home from a business trip, and being framed for a murder I didn't commit and being cruelly sent to the electric chair even though I was clearly innocent and only ten. I saw a lot of old Jimmy Cagney and George Raft movies in those days. That worried my mother.

"What's a bomb shelter?"

I explained that when I was about his age American television was full of scary reports that the Russians might drop an atomic bomb on America any day now. People like our neighbor Mr. Sullivan were hurriedly building bomb shelters in their backyards, but we didn't have one in ours. I worried myself sick about that. If the Russians dropped a bomb on South Carolina, our neighborhood in particular, I figured, we'd all be turned to monkey dust while Mr. Sullivan would be sitting safely inside his bomb shelter eating Snickers bars and watching *Bonanza*. The walls of his bomb shelter were rumored to be two feet thick.

"Wow. Did you ever see it?"

"As a matter of fact I did. Talk about a letdown."

One day, I explained, Mr. Sullivan went to the hospital to have his gallbladder removed and my mother asked me to transport a tuna casserole across the street to his wife Elma. After I delivered the goods, I snooped around behind the Sullivan garage and found myself peeking in the door of Mr. Sullivan's famous bomb shelter.

"What did you see?" Jack was enthralled.

"Just some old camping gear and nudist magazines and a bunch of empty Baby Ruth wrappers lying on the floor of a damp cinder-block hole in the ground. It was more Hobbit hole than bomb shelter, I'm afraid. And not a very nice Hobbit hole at that."

Jack, punching his glove delightedly, laughed again. "What's *that*?"

"Black-and-white pictures of overweight naked folks playing volleyball. A nudist is someone who loves to take their clothes off in public places but probably should seriously ask themselves why."

"No," he said, still laughing, still punching, "I mean a *Hobbit* hole."

We stopped dead in our tracks on Broad Street, not far from the famous black iron gates of Balliol College, founded by a lord as part of his holy penance to the Bishop of Durham for being drunk and disorderly in 1264. What a gorgeous gothic pile of brick and stone it was! Perhaps Nibs the Lost Boy would matriculate there himself someday, after his old man successfully worried about him through the perilous straits of middle and high school!

"You've never heard of a *Hobbit*?" For some reason I thought for sure he'd heard of Professor Tolkien's famous furry folk from Middle Earth, because we had several dog-eared copies of the book and it's companion trilogy gathering dust on the shelves back home in Maine.

"No, sir," he answered, glancing around at the dreaming spires as if we might see one at any moment.

"Well, let's correct that problem right now," I proposed, and shoved him gently in the direction of Blackwell's Bookshop down the block. Baseball and worrying could wait for the moment. The magic of Middle Earth beckoned us.

As we walked down the street, I explained to him that my father had given me a copy of *The Hobbit* just prior to my first trip to Europe in 1976, the year of gas lines and the Bicentennial garbage can, as I affectionately looked back on it. Tolkien, a professor of ancient languages at Merton College, Oxford, wrote the book as the prelude to a large trilogy called *The Lord of the Rings* which he wrote prior to that at the height of World War Two. His youngest daughter, if I recalled correctly, hadn't been able to understand the fairly complicated plot twists and characters of the trilogy, so he penned *The Hobbit* later to make the trilogy a little more understandable to her and other young readers.

"Neat. What's it about?"

"About two hundred pages."

Jack gave me what laughably passes for a threatening look in him—bunched eyebrows that make him look a little like a constipated eaglet. He was such a perfect straight man for my brand of humor, and I happily hoped we might to go on like Hope and Crosby for many years, if not decades, to come.

As we approached Blackwell's, I gave him the rough plot line of Professor Tolkien's famous tale of questing Hobbits and magical wizards, thinking how I could probably do with a refresher course myself, almost exactly a quarter century since my last proper visit to Middle Earth.

"Look," Jack proclaimed suddenly, halting before the large display window at Blackwell's. It took me a senior wizardly moment to realize what had him so worked up and beaming like a Hobbit about to sit down to his sixth meal of the day.

But there in the shop window sat, of all things, a huge display of Professor Tolkien's various works—everything anybody could ever wish to know about the creatures of Middle Earth! There were dozens of new Tolkien books on display, various "collector's" editions of *The Hobbit* and the famous *Ring* trilogy, gilded gift boxes, leather editions, a Tolkien *Bestiary*, an official encyclopedia of *The Lord of the Rings*, Tolkien's unfinished tales, biographies of the creator—you name it, it was there.

"I think they must have made a movie out of it or something," Jack interpreted from the explosion of bright-covered Tolkien-belia.

"Really?" For an instant this news worried me a little bit. I mean, honestly, it's such a cliché to say the book is always better than the movie, but in this case, considering the epic involved, what would Hollywood do with Professor Tolkien's Middle Earth? Some things, it seems to me, are best left to a boy's imagination. Even one pushing fifty.

"Can we get a copy *The Hobbit*?" Jack piped up right on cue, I'm happy to report.

"Absolutely," I said, opening the door to Blackwell's for my son, as an elderly lady with a full bag came trundling at us. Jack promptly shifted to the side and held the door for her to pass, good Hobbit boy that he is.

"Such a nice lad," she said, smiling cheerfully at him and then me.

I smiled back at her, thinking how she'd taken the very words from my mouth.

The afternoon at Summer Fields was just what the doctor, or maybe Professor Tolkien himself, would have ordered. After lunch in a great hall that could have served for a working model of Harry Potter's Hogwarts, Jack loped off with a pair of eleven-year-olds called Harry Peel-Yates and Marcus Gibson for a spin around the Summer Fields nine-hole golf course, then moseyed on to the school's vast cricket fields to watch a bit of the important term-ending match against the rival Cheam School.

I took in the cricket match, too, from a discreet distance where a number of Summer Fields parents were sitting on folding chairs on the sidelines near a regal blueblood who'd brought a pair of Jack Russells to watch her son Tony "bowl" his final match for Summer Fields. Tony was finishing up and heading straight to Harrow, she explained, sounding a little like the woman behind the curtain at Stratford-upon-Avon—the one wielding the service revolver, I mean to say. The dogs were staying put with her, she explained, and Tony's father was on business in South Africa.

"I'm sorry to have to ask this," I said to her, "but can you tell me an approximate score?"

Frankly, as usual where the game of cricket is concerned, I was stumped. The truth is, I've watched cricket matches off and on for donkey years with various British sporting friends and frankly still have yet to figure out what the hell is really going on. I know it involves the throwing of a ball and hitting it with a stick, and thus I feel that I'm naturally predisposed to enjoy and appreciate the ancient game and all the excitations it elicits in fully grown Anglo-Saxon people. Yet mostly it appears to me to be a pastime where guys dressed like ambulance attendants stand around for hours and sometimes days on end aimlessly waiting for some other guy who can't seem to throw the ball more than ten feet without bouncing it on the dirt, to try and knock over some skinny sticks guarded by yet another guy dressed in hospital whites holding some kind of poorly made baseball bat. The ball is dinky and painted red, a precautionary measure, I gather, so somebody drowsing in the outfield—wherever that is, exactly—can see the sucker coming at their face in case the guy with the bat actually hits the ball, which only seems to occur about every other hour or so, between breaks for tea and hard biscuits and maybe a helpful slug of French brandy.

Whoever said cricket is a game created by the English who, not being a particularly spiritual people, invented it primarily to give themselves some conception of eternity, was probably really onto something, though I personally think Robin Williams's characterization that it is merely baseball on Valium is a wee bit on the uncharitable side. I mean, the British are also mad about soccer, a game where there's usually far more interesting action going on up in the spectator bleachers than on the field itself. We latter-day colonists, on the hand, prefer our sporting events to be a lot like the wars we choose to fight— mindlessly violent, reasonably brief, with lots of good video for the eleven o'clock news.

"One hundred six to nine," her Ladyship kindly informed me, smiling tolerantly, patting one of her Russells on his intelligent brow; he appeared to have a far better grasp of the proceedings than I did, a problem I immediately compounded by foolishly asking how a point, per se, was actually scored in cricket.

"Oh, it's quite simple *really*," she replied as if any fool should be able to fathom it, and launched into a perky if inscrutable monologue that went on for the next ten minutes and involved, if I recall properly, the signing of the Magna Carta, something about Indian independence, "stumps" and "bails" and "errors on the wicket keeper," and so forth, until my colonial eyelids began to shut involuntarily and I nearly fell off my stool into the grass.

Luckily at this point my good friend Charles Churchill came back from walking his elderly labs Mashie and Niblick on Summer Fields's adjoining playing fields, where, I believe, they alone—the dogs, I mean—possess fouling rights that also date to the Magna Carta. Charles was an institution at Summer Fields, something of a real life Mr. Chips. The only son of a British Army general who spent the first eight years of his life in India, Charles, a Cambridge Classics graduate who did his national service by commanding a platoon of Gerkas, showed up for a job interview at beautiful Summer Fields outside of Oxford one day in 1964 with three dogs and a cat in his small car and never left the premises until he officially retired in 1996. Among other things, Senior Master Churchill coached several champion cricket teams, built the school golf course, and founded the annual Summer Fields teddy bear tea. For years he also chaperoned numerous squads of top English schoolboy golfers on exhibition tours of America and was a complete English gentleman of the links in every good sense of the phrase, a chap who would charmingly lift the contents of your wallet in a heartbeat, and not think twice about buying you a consoling pint of ale afterward with your own folding money.

"Oh, hello, Charles," trilled the mother with the Jack Russells. "I'm just telling your American *guest* here all about cricket."

"Jolly good," Charles said. "Does he get it at all?"

I felt like a disreputable child no one was willing to speak to.

"Very little, it would seem."

"Pity. But I think his boy Jack is getting the hang of it, down in the practice stumps. Gibson and Peel-Yates are making quite a batsman of him, I daresay."

"Oh, lovely."

Up in the school garden, meanwhile, the Summer Fields rose was in full bloom and tea and sandwiches were being served on bone china. That's where I discovered the Queen Mum a short while later palely loitering on the soles of her sensible flat shoes, sipping Earl Grey with a man who turned to me and reflected somewhat wistfully through his brown teeth, "These were unquestionably the happiest days of my life, Summer Fields. But you might not have known it if you read this. Here. Have a look at this. *Devastating,* don't you think?"

He thrust a faded blue examination form at me which dated from the dark ages of the early 1960s.

I wouldn't say he doesn't try, began the summary by the Summer

Fields Classics teacher Charles Churchill perhaps followed to the institution, *but the results are negligible. He understands 'au frond' nothing, however simple. The truth must be faced that his IQ is low and it would surprise me if he ever reached by normal career a sufficient standard in the subject.*

I handed it back to him with a sympathetic smile.

"I know how you feel. One man's Classics class is another man's cricket match, eh?"

"Touché," he agreed.

"I often think," boomed another old Summer Fieldsian fondly over his china cup, standing much closer than I realized, "that there's *really* only one decision in a boy's life that matters at the end of the day."

"Really, Clive? And what exactly do you mean by that?" demanded the chap who'd managed to make a small fortune in the City despite his low IQ and embarrassing marks in Classics. He sounded either baffled or annoyed, hard to tell which.

"Whether one goes *up* to Oxford or *down* to Cambridge, of course."

I saw a prim superintendent's smile appear on Mum's handsome Glaswegian face and feared the Red Tide Clyde was about to roll over this poor unsuspecting Thames aristocrat. As an honor grad of Glasgow University, she already had Jack pegged, I think, for some fine institution in the Holy Land—that's to say dear old Scotland. Purely for my purposes, as I've gently conveyed to Jack on several occasions on the golf course, Saint Andrews University would suffice quite nicely as a venue of higher matriculation if it comes down to that. Having the Old Course within mashie niblick distance would sure make parents' weekend all the more special.

"So where exactly has our lad gotten off to?" Mum wondered demurely, glancing around and sipping her tea. Disappointingly, I guess, she was hell bent to be on her best socialist behavior.

"Last I heard," I said, "he was trying out for the Summer Fields cricket team. Before we know it he'll probably be running up to Oxford or trotting down to Cambridge." It was worth one last shot, to see if I could get the Red Tide rolling. But she would have none of it and simply smiled at me as she would any youthful offender caught in the act of penciling blue words on the bathroom wall.

"Damned fine decision!" boomed the Thames aristocrat, showing us his teeth.

I found Jack a little while later. He was dressed ridiculously in kneepads and Summer Fields helmet, guarding a wicket and wielding a mean cricket bat as Marcus Gibson flung a hard red cricket ball into the dirt at his feet. Jack's face was flushed, his hair thoroughly disordered. He swung repeatedly at the bouncing ball, striking only about every third or fourth pitch, assuming that's what they're called.

Frankly speaking, I still didn't get the point of the game, but Jack looked like a boy perfectly delighted to be lost in the fields of British summer, suddenly having the time of his life.

Harry Peel-Yates's father was a peacekeeper in Bosnia, and Marcus Gibson's family had, of all things, a place in Maine. I learned this near dusk when Jack and I hopped a stone wall behind the Galaxy Hotel after supper and wandered out to find a place to throw the baseball we'd intended to throw earlier in the day, before Professor Tolkien and cricket entered Jack's life.

"Dad," he asked, "would you ever want to go to Summer Fields?"

I replied that it was an awful nice school but I would probably look ridiculous in the tiny blue corduroy shorts the boys were forced to wear there.

Jack rewarded me with his second good chortle of the day, another reason to be glad we'd ventured there.

"I'd kind of like to go there," he admitted. "It's kind of like a real Hogwarts."

I said I knew what he meant but that his mother would dearly miss him, as would his old dog and his two cats, his best buddy Andrew, the director of the chapel choir, his travel basketball team, and a certain adorable little girl named Bethany Bellnap.

He nodded, and the bright smile vanished as quickly as it had come. He punched his glove.

"Dad," he explained after a moment, "Bethany and I aren't going out anymore."

"You *aren't*?"

Jack and Bethany Bellnap, in fact, so far as I knew, had never actually physically "gone out" together. My son was speaking in the peculiar idiom of Woodside Elementary School, describing a somewhat passive social convention in which the agreed parties in question merely expressed a heightened public interest in each other's person and politely circled each other like a pair of chaste but curious young peacocks.

Bethany was a pretty little girl who'd shown up at Woodside the previous autumn and quickly attached herself to Jack and his best pal, Andrew Tufts, and for the balance of the school term the three of them had been inseparable, until Jack's older sister, Maggie, stirred the pot of intrigue by revealing to the world at large, and me in particular, that Jack and Bethany were officially an item.

Confused? I certainly was, to begin with. "Going out" turned out to simply mean they "liked" each other, which was apparently the accepted protocol until they moved on to the next level of intimacy at middle school: asking to be dropped off together at the movie theater— at which point, I extrapolated, they would be considered "engaged" and headed toward an actual first kiss or holding hands.

It was all very sweet and—I dearly hoped—totally innocent. In any case, fittingly enough, Jack and Bethany had just capped off the school year by playing two of the adorable Von Trapp children in the school's spring production of *The Sound of Music*.

I was genuinely surprised then to hear of this new development and wondered when this parting of hearts had taken place. After all, I hadn't heard a whisper of gossip from the original pot stirrer, Jack's sister, Maggie, who normally keeps a sharp ear to the ground.

He sighed heavily. "After the play she told me she wanted to go out with Joey Di Lombardo. I didn't tell anybody but I guess she did."

"Did you do something to make her mad or hurt her feelings?"

"No, sir. Nothing. Honest! It's weird. One day she was like she always is. The next day she wouldn't even speak to me. I don't know what happened! She told Kelsey McIntosh that I was a geek."

I nodded, thumping my mitt. Obviously pretty Bethany Bellnap had ditched Jack in favor of a more popular kid, a story as old as the elementary school hills. Joey Di Lombardo was not exactly a scholar but arguably the school's best little athlete. She'd clearly traded up in a play for greater popularity, leaving Jack in her dust.

We found a grassy spot near the River Cherwell and began throwing the ball back and forth. The dreaming spires were growing dark beyond the trees, but we still had ten or so minutes of decent light left. Jack's pitches at first looped into the turf, but then they began to pick up accuracy and velocity. I could see him focusing and relaxing, gaining a bit of his pitcher's rhythm.

"For what it's worth, I'm sorry about Bethany," I called to him from my catcher's crouch on somewhat dodgy knees. "She's making a big mistake, Nibs. Maybe she'll realize that."

Don't count on it, though, I thought but wisely didn't share with him. She was obviously quite an adroit little social climber, young Miss Bellnap.

"Thanks. It's okay, I guess," he said, then wound up and threw a ball into the dirt, proving it obviously wasn't. I could see how this had really been eating away at him, which placed his anxiety about leaving home, the troubled flight, and the rest of it in a revealing new light. It was probably going to take Jack weeks to get over the trauma of his first bruised heart. It was probably going to take his old man much longer than that.

"Trust me when I tell you, Boss, there will be lots of other pretty girls in your life," I said, attempting to perk him up, tossing the ball back to him. My pitch lamely bounced in the dirt but he neatly one-hopped it; Joey Di Lombardo might be a better athlete than Jack, but not by all that much.

"Did anybody ever, like, dump you when you were my age?" he wondered, possibly still thinking of our conversation about worrying on the road to Blackwell's that morning.

"Oh yeah," I assured him, catching a pretty good pitch and looping it back to him. I told him about Della Hockaday, a pretty girl I gave a Beatles record to shortly before Randy Farmer threatened to beat me up if I ever set foot in her yard again. Della kept the record and told me to scram.

"Did Randy Farmer ever beat you up?"

"Nope. It was all bluff. By the way," I said, "none of those other

worries came to pass, either. I made shortstop on the Pet Dairy baseball team and didn't go blind by looking at the eclipse. I wasn't bitten
by a poisonous snake or framed for a murder I didn't commit. Best of
all, my father always came home from his business trips and the Russians never did bomb South Carolina the way Mr. Sullivan expected
them to."

"Cool," he said, as if this news made him feel better already. Knowing Jack, pretty soon only *I* would be carrying a grudge against pretty
Bethany Bellnap for calling my son a geek and giving him unexpected
heart pains.

"So all that stuff you worried about never happened?"

"That's right. Most of it, at any rate. Of course I did eat radioactive
snow and it made me pee electric green for a couple years. But other
than that, no problem."

We threw for a few minutes more and suddenly it grew too dark to
go on, at which point we walked back to the Galaxy through the fragrant summer darkness, swinging hands like we used to do when he
was small and chatting about what a great idea coming to Summer
Fields had been and what a really swell game cricket was, though honestly I only understood about half of what we were pleasantly talking
about.

FOUR

A Brief History of Mum

I had a surprise for my traveling companions. We were going to church. But not just any old church or any old service—evensong at King's College Chapel, Cambridge.

After cricket at Oxford, church at Cambridge would probably seem like a night at Maxim's, or so I predicted to the Queen Mum as we rolled into the second most famous college town in Britain, across the tranquil River Cam, the sun-dappled bend of water that produced several of Britain's greatest Romantic poets—Milton, Wordsworth, Coleridge, and my own personal favorite, that timeless inspiration to intellectual party animals everywhere, George Gordon, a.k.a. Lord Byron.

"When *was* the last time you went to church?" I pleasantly needled the stubborn Scottish agnostic beside me. "In case lightning strikes the building, I may need to know for insurance purposes."

"I think the wheel had just been invented," she replied thoughtfully, rising effortlessly to the bait. "Or maybe fire had just been brought indoors. It was one of those two."

King's Chapel, our afternoon's destination, owed its existence to King Henry VI, the same pious monarch who inspired Shakespeare to write *three* separate historical plays that nobody who prefers to have a paying audience performs anymore. Sometimes called the "Royal Saint" due to his gentle manners and highly refined religious disposition, Henry became monarch of both England and France as just a ten-month-old baby, when his famous father, Henry V, the brilliant military tactician and stump speech-maker whose army wiped out six thousand Frenchmen at Agincourt (and whose play I dearly wish we'd seen at Stratford) prematurely expired. Henry the son, alas, is probably best known by historians of the monarchy as the indecisive chappie who lost his throne on three separate occasions, presided over the bloody Wars of the Roses between the houses of York and Lancaster, and was running neighboring France pretty much the way you would expect any eight-year-old to run a large foreign country when a young peasant French girl named Joan from a backwater called Domremy suffered an ecstatic vision in which, among other things, she claimed that the Virgin Mary had personally instructed her to drive the English and their revolting eating habits forever out of France.

Within twenty years Henry would lose France, but on the plus side of the ledger he built a swell church that required him to only demolish half of a quaint Medieval hamlet on the banks of the Cam. On the Feast of St. James Day, July 1446, having leveled several village blocks that included a couple competing churches and a popular fish and chips hangout, Henry laid the ambitious foundation stone of King's Chapel and mandated to his personal master mason to create an "incomparable temple of Christian worship" that would stand a thousand years and be so extraordinarily beautiful it would eventually make Christopher Wren weep with envy when he finally saw it. Among his crowning touches, the Royal Saint instituted a mandatory daily afternoon choral office called "evensong" designed to "deepen yeoman faith" and keep most of the village roughnecks safely off the streets and either piously kneeling in church or covertly drinking in the pub, which may or may not have given rise to the concept of Happy Hour and Housman's famous toast that *Malt does more than Milton can/To justify God's way to man.*

"Excuse me, Dad." Jack interrupted this spiel. We were seated in a front-row pew of the magnificent church, adjacent to the choir loft, waiting for the famous King's Chapel Choir to enter, within a few yards of a famous ornately carved chancel screen that elegantly depicted Saint George slaying the dragon. I could swear that from where I sat somebody had whimsically scratched *Henry Eight thinks Annie Boleyn is a hottie* into the wood of the priceless Medieval screen, but perhaps I was simply allowing my jester's mind to run away with me. The church, in any case, was packed with congregants and I was reading quietly to Nibs the Lost Boy from a nifty printed history of King's and its founder that I'd picked up at a gift shop selling various college rugby shirts and beer mugs and other Cambridge knickknacks on nearby King's Parade, where drinking pubs now outnumbered praying churches five to one. "Was he the guy who was in *Winnie-the-Pooh?*"

"You're thinking of Christopher Robin, son. He built the house at Pooh Corner. Chris Wren built Saint Paul's Cathedral in London. They're birds of a different feather, Boss."

I resumed the tale, placing my own larkish spin on an otherwise pretty gruesome ecclesiastical history in hopes of keeping my own worried laddie faithful and smiling. The roof was barely on Henry's dream church, I explained, when the Earl of Warwick massacred the Lancastrians up at Northampton, deposed Henry, and declared a fellow named Richard of York protector of the English throne. Richard's rule was terribly short-lived, though, because Margaret, Henry's angry wife, escaped to Scotland and returned a short while later with an army of burly unshaven guys in wool skirts carrying pickaxes. They killed Richard the Protector at a village called Wakefield and thoughtfully gave Henry back his lost throne—*Here's your crown back, mate. Do try and keep both hands on it this time, eh?* Richard's son Edward, wouldn't you know it, promptly asserted his claim to the English throne as Edward IV, recaptured poor Henry, and stuffed him into the Tower of London, where he stayed until the Earl of Warwick had a major falling out with Edward over something as trivial as the proper way a gentleman wears a codpiece during evensong and trounced King Eddie's troops at another village, called Edgecote. Edward subsequently fled to Flanders, at which point Henry took his throne back for the *third* time, but, alas, only briefly. A year or so later, Edward returned from exile to Flanders with a large army of Flemish guys who thought the English were a bunch of tea-sipping sissies who didn't know how to wear a proper codpiece, killed Warwick, defeated Queen Margaret, and sent poor old Henry back to the Tower for good. It probably came as a relief to him when somebody finally had the decency to murder him in his prison cell at the Tower in 1471, leaving behind a lot of bloody history but one really swell church building and a choral tradition un-matched anywhere on the planet.

"Boy," Jack said. "English history sure is *complicated*." He tilted his head back and gazed upward at the amazing vaulted ceiling that re-duced Chris Wren to tears. "But this place is pretty cool."

He was right on both counts, I agreed, craning back in the pew to take in the spectacular marriage of stone and stained glass that soared to a meeting point in an unforgettable fan vault floating far above our heads—a magnificent place, you have to grant it to the old boy, but alas one the Royal Saint never got to see finished, which seems a true pity. When Goethe described gothic architecture as "frozen music" this sort of thing is clearly what he had in mind.

"You two had better pipe down," Mum suddenly whispered along the pew, giving us the woolly eye because the Sunday afternoon serv-ice was about to get underway. King's famous choristers had swapped their Eton suits and top hats for ecclesiastical red robes and, with a sweeping fanfare from the booming pipe organ, began to proceed with a stirring rendition of "Old Hundredth."

We all dutifully rose and began to sing along with them, some of us obviously better than others. Back home in Maine, Jack was some-thing of a fading boy soprano star in the chapel choir of St. Paul's Epis-copal, but here he was just another steadily improving alto voice in the crowd, though you wouldn't have known it to look at him. The sound of the choir was so startlingly ethereal, it first appeared to positively hush him with awe and admiration. Then he quickly recovered his confidence and began belting out the famous old hymn in a manner that would have made Gil Peterson, his delightfully crusty choir-master, very proud indeed. Somewhere in his travel gear, Jack was transporting across international boundaries a medallion from the Royal Academy of Church Music, the governing Anglican music au-thority that apparently regards King's College Chapel as its spiritual Carnegie Hall. He'd been given it for completing his first year of ad-vanced sacred choral study, which probably would have made the Royal Saint happy to know he was in attendance.

For her part, the Queen Mum followed the optimistic words of "Old Hundredth" in the hymnal but, so far as I could ascertain, chose not to try and sing. It didn't surprise me one bit, however, to see her dip a hand into her vast carryall, withdraw a wadded Kleenex, and discreetly dab a leaky eye with it.

At this point you may be musing on the gentle irony of an old Red Tide Agnostic Scot advising her rambunctious Episcopalian charges to pipe down in the front pew of a high Anglican church, moreover getting all dewy and damp-eyed over a hundred-year-old hymn in praise of a divine entity she wasn't convinced even existed.

The truth is—and I here fully expect her to bash me over the head with the collected works of Bertrand Russell for saying this—Mum was one of the most spiritually advanced, if inwardly private, people I'd ever known. Her personal history was almost as complicated as England's, but at least her take on organized religion was fairly commonplace among Britons of her generation.

Growing up in war-riddled Glasgow, her father Alec, an officer of the British Linen Bank, had run the city's cathedral Sunday school for a time and Kate had obviously had a thorough grounding in the Gospels and the spiritual traditions of the Church of Scotland. But then a devastating world war came along and she lost both her parents at a relatively young age to disease and found herself basically on her own in a world where nothing made much sense except studying chemistry and falling for a brilliant electrical engineering student named Sam Bennie, son of a Paisley deacon, whom she eventually married (by civil ceremony, on a windy day in Toronto) after immigrating to a new life in Canada.

Fifty years later along whatever spiritual path she was quietly treading in good sensible shoes—and lest she give me a good solid crack with the collected works of George Bernard Shaw, I wouldn't dream of trying to interpret the fine print on the Queen Mum's personal contract with the Almighty on matters of faith and spirituality—but by every outward visible indication she was one of the most genuinely kindhearted, functionally "Christian" and disgustingly upright individuals I'd ever known. She knew the Bible better than most theologians and could be safely relied upon to always choose the path of Presbyterian righteousness when meting out justice to truant eighth graders, channel-surfing with her grandchildren, or selecting market vegetables and mitten yarn.

In sum, from what I'd been able to ascertain over many long years of pleasantly harassing her on the subject, the gist of Mum's complaint against any organized religion was the irrefutable evidence that kings and potentates and small-time despots of almost every stripe throughout history (Henry's saga being a prime example) never hesitated to employ "divine right" as a convenient excuse to steal, burn, pillage, and plunder their neighbor's plot on behalf of a "God" that appeared, at best, to be dangerously uninvolved, absent entirely, and maybe just nodding off for the afternoon in the hammock.

Suffice it to say, as a result, if I read her correctly, Mum had grave doubts about His or Her general fitness for keeping up with the demands of being Supreme Creator of the Universe, which I suppose isn't quite the same thing as flatly insisting He or She simply doesn't exist, especially without any hard scientific data one way or another to back up the various competing claims. Ever the humane scientist, she was, to her everlasting credit and almost a fault, deeply respectful of dissenting views within her very own household, including my own brand of dirt road transcendentalism, which meant we'd enjoyed not a few lively theological debates over gin and tonic on the summer evening porch back home.

Anyway, as sweet irony would have it, "Old Hundredth" was the hymn she chose to play at her husband Sam's funeral one snowy day in March, and it didn't surprise me one bit, given her own complicated ecclesiastical history, to glance down the pew and spy the old girl (whom I confess I love as much as my own mother but, let's face it, am dearly thankful to God in his firmament I never had for a school principal) giving her eyeballs a brisk no-nonsense swipe with wadded Kleenex.

Jack didn't seem to notice this because, as I say, he was utterly transfixed by the supernatural sound made by sixteen boy sopranos and one booming chapel organ with four thousand pipes. Evensong at King's Chapel has been widely described as one of the most sublime audiovisual experiences on earth, and that certainly proved to be the case with us. After "Old Hundredth," the King's Choristers gave a simply breathtaking *"Magnificat"* and *"Nunc Dimittis"* followed by an unforgettable Purcell in G and Byrd's rapturous anthem *"Laudibus in*

Sanctis." As if that weren't enough for one blissful afternoon, the whole place finished up collectively on its hind legs with a rousing version of "Immortal, Invisible," my own favorite hymn and the very anthem sung at both of my parents' funerals, the unexpected surprise of which nearly reduced *me* to a puddle of old-fashioned Anglican tears.

"Forsooth! Methinks these old pagan conch shells hath heard the angels sing!" even the Queen Mum felt compelled to admit as we filtered out the great double doors of King Henry's extraordinary church into the lengthening afternoon shadows of the Great Lawn and turned in the direction of the smoothly flowing River Cam without thinking where we might be headed next.

It was just past Midsummer's Eve and there was talk of pagan bonfires out in the country, but I hoped to shortly steer us off to an early dinner at Brown's, maybe hoof out for a brief tour of the town, and locate a safe spot for a little pitching practice before dark.

Actually, to be fair, these weren't the Queen Mum's precise words on the subject of King's evensong. She actually just sniffed, dabbed her eye one last time, tucked away her tissue for the next trial of life, and said primly, as we stepped out of the Royal Saint's chapel, "That was very nice, James. Thank you. I enjoyed that." But as I've said before, you can always read between the lines of a sentimental Red Tide Scot.

We moseyed down to the river's edge and discovered fleets of narrow boxy wooden boats floating past us in the lazy current of the Cam, bearing whole families and lovers with picnic baskets along in a bucolic tableau that looked like an Arthur Rackham illustration from *The Wind and the Willows.*

"Dad, can we go row one of those awesome boats?" Jack suddenly got all worked up, pointing to a family of noisy Italians who didn't appear to have a clue what they were doing and were in grave danger of toppling into the river, to their joyous delight. My kind of tourists, unafraid to make complete peckerwoods of themselves.

"Those are called *punts,* Lamb," his grandmother corrected. "And you don't really row them. You pole them."

She glanced at me a bit anxiously.

"Have you ever done that sort of thing?" she wondered, ever the de facto voice of good Christian reason and logic. "I understand it can be kind of tricky."

"Nope," I said, feeling the kid in me come surging forth. "But that'll only make it more fun. C'mon, Nibsy. Let's go live like Lord Byron."

Mum refused to get into the boat. Perhaps she thought it undignified for a woman of her age to be seen doing a half gainer in front of complete strangers.

"Oh no, no, *no*," she hooted after I extended a hand to her from our rented punt, on the shore near the romantically arched stone bridge in the village millpond where other families were piling into boats and chaotically banging into each other. The Millpond marks the beginning of a particularly fine stretch of the river popularly called "The Backs," where beautiful gardens and lush lawns belonging to Cambridge's six oldest colleges brush up against the river's edge.

Mum retreated rapidly for the safety of the bridge, withdrawing her camera and trilling over her shoulder, "No, no. You two go and have a nice time getting wet. I'll just see you off and then mosey around a bit and document your return on the river."

The attractive young woman who shoved us off had a lovely smile and cotton-candy pink hair. I wondered if she was a student at one of the town's colleges. "International Trade Law at Magdalene," she answered briskly, patting a soggy green cushion in front where I was instructed to plant my bottom. Jack, all hands agreed, would take first crack at poling us down the river.

"Right you are. Off you go now. Mind the arches." And with that, she sharply booted us into the swirling current and chaos of other boats.

The current took us straight into one of the bridge's stone arches, and the swirling water turned us sideways against the bridge. A familiar gray head craned out above us; it was Mum, looking gently worried as usual.

"Are you two . . . okay?" she demanded from above.

"Doing fine, thanks," I assured her cheerfully, then whispered quietly to Jack, "Need some help, Boss?"

Poling a punt was clearly harder than it looked, and I didn't want him to get discouraged before we even got underway. At this rate, though, we weren't even going to get out of the crowded Millpond, much less down a lazy river, before nightfall.

"No, sir. I can do it," he replied, grunting and breathing heavily as he gamely struggled to gain mastery of the long, unwieldy, and surprisingly heavy hardwood pole. I trailed a lazy hand in the water and realized the river was only a few feet deep. Then I noticed that our punt even came with a name, printed on a moldy green brass plate on the bow. So I leaned over—damn near tipping us into the drink, I regret to say—and saw it was called *Childe Harold.*

I braced a foot against the ancient stonework and Jack dug his pole into the rocky river bottom and between us we eventually levered our craft in the currents, falling in rank behind a pair of listing punts bearing pairs of guffawing teenagers. As we disappeared beneath the arch, I glanced up quickly to see if the Queen Mum was "documenting" any of this awkward beginning and thumped my head on the mossy underside of the bridge.

"Dad," Jack said, catching his breath as we finally began to glide along, "where exactly does this river go?"

Massaging my head, I thought about it for a moment and admitted I didn't have the foggiest notion where the River Cam went, though I guessed it might flow into the Thames or some other large river and ultimately, one supposed, find its way to an estuary by the sea. If all roads lead to Rome, all rivers eventually lead to the sea. Besides, as I pointed out, all old market towns of any size had some means of reaching the sea, the source of life in ancient of days, the pathway to other worlds.

"So where are we going after here?"

Under the circumstances, this was a perfectly reasonable question for him to ask, though I silently dreaded trying to answer it. Now that Nibs was clearly feeling better and showing few if any lingering effects of our trip's tumultuous start, we could proceed apace to wherever the treasure map in our heads said go.

That was the good news. The bad news was, I hadn't properly conferred with Jack's mother on the new international developments yet, but Africa, Egypt, and China now all looked problematic at best. I didn't want to dash Jack's hopes (not to mention my own) until it was entirely necessary, though, so I did what any self-respecting parent does. I stalled for time.

"I was thinking," I thought out loud, "that we might just wander down to a hotel I know in the New Forest before we let Mum go on her own off to Scotland. It's probably England's nicest country hotel. After the Edward Lear, Chewton Glen will seem like Buckingham Palace. What do you say?"

"Great," Jack grunted from aft, obviously absorbed in the yeoman task of keeping us off the banks or out of the way of other punts wobbling to and fro around us.

"The New Forest is magical, you know."

"Really? What do you mean?"

I explained that it was not only the setting for Lewis Carroll's *Alice's Adventures in Wonderland* but also a place where wild and domestic farm animals had roamed free of any restraint, protected by royal decree, since the days of William the Conquerer.

"That means you're likely to wind up with a shaggy two-thousand-pound highland cow standing in your bedroom—or on the green where you're putting your golf ball." I explained how this very thing happened to me once while playing golf with my friend Martin Skan, who owned Chewton Glen with his wife Brigge.

"Oh, *cool.*"

"By the way," I added, "there's a swell little par-three course on the grounds at Chewton Glen."

"Really? Could we play it?"

"Sure. I'll call Martin after we get off the river and see if he can take us. Can't promise, though. It's high season down that way."

Jack fell silent, obviously concentrating on his poling. Our punt slipped along past several other struggling punts; the boy was clearly getting the hang of it. If he didn't go up to Oxford and become the next J. R. R. Tolkien, maybe he'd at least come down to Cambridge and be a punting romantic poet.

"Is the New Forest anywhere near King Arthur's grave?"

I explained that Arthur's grave was out at Glastonbury, in Britain's West Country, a hundred or so miles west of Chewton Glen. That wasn't exactly in the direction we'd talked about going—assuming mainland Europe was our eventual port of call—but then again we were making this expedition up as we went along. Jack was a huge fan of the Arthurian myths, as I'd been at his age, and I happened to belong to a famous old golf club out that way in North Devon but had never taken the time to see Arthur's grave, an omission it would be nice to rectify.

"Would you like to go find Arthur's grave and see the Glastonbury Tor?"

"What's that?"

"An ancient signal hill. Some legends say it's where the Holy Grail is buried. It's supposed to be one of the most spiritual spots in the world."

"Oh yes, please, could we?" he answered quickly and enthusiastically.

"No problem," I allowed drowsily, shutting my eyes and enjoying the ride. At least we had the next two or three days properly sorted out. I'd worry about the rest of the world come Wednesday or Thursday. For a few moments, I think, I actually dozed off, trailing a hand in the timeless Cam.

"Dad," Jack spoke up a little farther along, "why was Grandma crying in church?"

"I'm sorry?"

I opened my eyes and blinked at the shore, not certain if I'd heard him correctly. I gazed upon a cute elderly couple reposing together on the sunny bank behind Trinity College, flat on their backs, faces turned to the blue British sky. They looked either very peaceful or very dead.

"Grandma was crying in church. Didn't you see her?"

"I did. But I didn't think you did. I think she was just overcome by the majesty of it all, Boss—the music of the choir and the spectacular architecture. Also, that first hymn was the one she had played at your grandfather's funeral."

"I thought she was an agnostic. They don't believe in God."

"An agnostic is simply an irreligious person who stays away from church religiously."

There was thoughtful silence over my shoulder; he obviously

didn't seem to get the drift of my little ecclesiastical funny, so I clarified it a bit.

"Jack, an agnostic is a person who hasn't made up their mind if
there is a God. They remain to be convinced one way or another. They
have doubts about God."

"Do you think that's, like, good or bad?"

"Sometimes doubts can be very useful. A famous English poet
named John Donne said that doubt is actually the voice of God in our
conscience—causing us to ask the important questions. By the way,
Donne wasn't just your mother's favorite poet. He was also an Anglican priest."

"Cool. Did he go here, too?" He meant, obviously, Cambridge.

I admitted that I didn't know. For all I knew he might have gone
up to Oxford and played cricket for Master Charles Churchill instead.
Jack failed to get the joke, or maybe his mind was still up in the clouds,
so to speak.

A sudden giddy burst of teenage laughter interrupted us.

A larger chauffeured punt bearing three young couples overtook us
and glided rapidly past, its occupants in beautiful formal attire, drinking wine and horsing around as we approached another of the town's
famous arched bridges. The chauffeur was wearing a tattered Dicken-
sian top hat. He nodded politely across the water at us at then cried,
"Careful, miss!" as one of the young women attempted to stand up in
the craft and raise her glass to us as an arch of Clare Bridge rapidly approached.

"Hello, *Childe Harold*!" she trilled in very upper-crust English.
"Would you care to follow us to a lovely lawn party?"

"Sit *down*, you silly cow, or you'll put us all in the filthy river!" One
of the tuxedo boys seized her roughly by the waist and pulled her on
top of him just as a sharp edge of the bridge's bottom passed overhead.
The chauffeur looked relieved; the boat dissolved in gales of laughter.

"Why did she call us Childe Harold?" Jack wondered, smiling after
them as he ducked and we followed their punt beneath the arch.

"That's the name of our boat," I explained to him, adding that our
punt was named for a poem by a famous Cambridge poet named
George Byron who originally dreamed of going up to Christchurch,

Oxford, to play cricket but settled instead for going down to Trinity, Cambridge, and writing tortured epic poems.

"He probably would have felt right at home in the punt with a bunch of tipsy tuxedoed undergrads," I said, noting that when Byron was a student at Trinity College the institution supposedly refused to allow him to keep a pet dog in his dorm room, so he went out and found a trained bear which he kept on a leash—just to tweak the administration's nose, or so the legend went.

"Did you like his poems?"

"Not at first. But they grew on me. Poetry is like that. You start reading it out of curiosity or because some stern educator like the Queen Mum makes you do it. Next thing, you're bloody hooked on the stuff."

I explained that Byron was a pretty odd duck, all things considered, the clubfooted son of a broken-down spendthrift military man and a domineering Scottish mother with aristocratic pretensions, who published a slim volume of verse called *Hours of Idleness* which brought him instant literary fame and enough money to embark on a two-year pilgrimage around Europe that resulted in the writing of "Childe Harold."

"How do you know all this?"

"I took a bunch of poetry courses in college trying to get around one trigonometry course and accidentally fell in love with reading Romantic poets."

I glanced back at Nibs and smiled, only to see his handsome face dinted with a gentle, perplexed frown. Jack, I remembered, was already a large fan of poetry. The Queen Mum and I had both been funneling him the stuff since he was knee-high to a trundle bed.

"Why was that so bad?"

"I guess it wasn't," I amended. "There wasn't much of a job market for aspiring romantic poets when I graduated in 1975. So I became a newspaper reporter instead."

"Whatever happened to Byron?"

"Not pretty, I'm afraid. He wound up in the papers, too."

I explained how Lord Byron went on to savagely attack the literary establishment of his day and developed a persona for himself one of my college professors called the Byronic Hero—courageous, reckless, irresistible to women, and hopelessly doomed. He shocked London society by flaunting several affairs with married women, enjoyed a well-publicized liaison with his half sister, made a disaster of his brief society marriage, never wearied of shamelsssly promoting himself to the *Times of London,* and finally visited the plains where Achilles fell and swam the mythical Hellespont before dying of a fever in a grim Greek backwater called Messalonghi while waiting to fight a battle against a Turkish army that never showed up. He wasn't even forty years old.

"Wow," Jack said, as if Byron's life exhausted him almost as much as poling down the Cam did.

We'd reached the Bridge of Sighs and I decided it was time to turn around and head back upstream if we wanted any hope of dinner and a little pitching practice before dusk. Besides, Mum would be getting anxious, worrying that we'd somehow gone to sea.

I suggested to Jack that I take over the poling duties because he frankly looked a little tuckered out and I'd been doing nothing but brooding about my failed career as a British romantic poet for the past half an hour. He reluctantly agreed to swap ends of the punt as he eased us toward the grassy bank.

Everything was dandy as a Wordsworth couplet until I attempted to climb back into the punt with my heavy pole in hand. I'd scarcely gotten one foot into the boat when the damned thing eased offshore a few feet, leaving me briefly suspended above the timeless River Cam with a foot, as it were, in two places. At the last second, though, I jammed my pole into the rocky bottom and attempted a doomed Byronic leap for the shore, actually managing to get both feet planted on the grassy bank before sliding pathetically back into the water.

Several passing punts erupted in laughter and a man on shore thoughtfully helped me climb out of the river.

"Dad," Jack said, unable to stop grinning after we successfully re-launched *Childe Harold,* "do you think I could, like, fall into the river, too? It really looked fun."

At first I glared at him, thinking how that would mean we *both* had to change pants in order to go find supper. But then I remembered

someone's poetic injunction that man is the only one of God's creatures who can actually laugh at himself—or needs to—and that the
unofficial motto of our Byronic summer pilgrimage to God knows
where was "Boys just wanna have fun." I told him to go ahead and
jump in the river if it would make him feel any better.

He did, and clearly savored the experience, though the moment he
spotted the Queen Mum worriedly hovering on top of the stone bridge
by the Millpond, he wondered if I thought she might be angry with us.
I noticed she was aiming her camera directly at us.

"Nah," I said to him as we both waved and gestured to our soaked
pants. She made a disapproving face and recorded the moment for pos-
terity or the author's flap of Jack's first book of epic poetry, whichever
came first.

"See?" I said to Nibs, "she's standing up there thinking how clever
she was not to get into this boat with us. Scots hate to be wrong about
anything, son—God, history, or even casual boating."

FIVE

The Magic Forest

I took a second shortcut down a narrow road I knew like the back of my hand through the New Forest, from Lyndhurst to New Milton, and got us briefly lost for the second time in six days. Fortunately, the forest was lovely, dark, and deep and soon there was a friendly round-about that permitted us to go pleasantly in circles until I could get my bearings, at which point we followed a helpful signpost to *Spotted Dick* and soon came upon a charming thatched-roof village straight from Thomas Hardy, where a Scottish highland bull was standing in the road frowning at passing motorists. I knew we'd arrived.

"Oh my *gosh*." Jack jolted upright in the backseat when he saw the great shaggy beast in our path, momentarily abandoning Bilbo and his loyal gang of dwarves in Mirkwood. "I thought maybe you were joking about the farm animals being loose. What if you hit it or something?"

Slowing to a friendly crawl and easing past the big horned fellow, I conceded that it would be bad for the cow, but probably far worse for the car and its owner. I knew from previous motoring experience here-about that people who were foolish enough to knock over the live-stock paid a rather dear price to the gentle folk who inhabited this enchanted wood. Their eyes could be put out by glowing poker irons, their limbs hacked off by rusty broadswords! At a very minimum their driving licenses were confiscated by the local constabulary and their heads placed in public stocks where farm animals could uses their faces as a salt lick and locals could heave rotten cabbages at them.

Nibsy's eyebrows shot straight up, his sweet blue eyes widened in alarm.

Mum demurred, reaching round to pat Jack's knee. "James, don't exaggerate. I think you only have to pay a fine or something, Lamb."

"That's true now. But you should have been here back when Billy the Conquerer was running the New Forest. In fact, weren't you?"

Mum smiled tolerantly, as if she would dearly miss my barbs as least as much as my driving among the hedgerows of the empire. The truth was, as it says somewhere in the Book of Ecclesiastes or maybe the *Better British Motoring Guide*, all good things (and motorways) must come to an end, and in less than a day's time Jack and I would be dropping the QM off at her pal Ann's place in Heathfield and setting off as officially unchaperoned mates down the lane to Glastonbury. Personally speaking, I was sorry to see this moment arrive because Jack simply adores his agnostic Scottish granny and I find traveling with the old girl to be about as much fun as a bloke can possibly have with his former mother-in-law and still avoid jail time. All joshing aside, as she's steadfastly proved though good times and bad, year in and year out, through one tedious Republican administration and Super Bowl after another, Mum may be the bane of eighth-grade boys everywhere but she's basically as loyal a friend as I have on this earth, a treasured adviser, possibly the closest thing I have left to a mother or at least a good gin-drinking pal, and I fully intend to get to my hind legs and say these nice things about her when the U.S. Immigration authorities haul her in for her deportation hearing.

As we followed a signpost to Chewton Glen, I gave my traveling companions a snippet or two of local lore I'd gleaned from Martin Skan during the memorable golf outing where the highland cow nearly trampled my nerves and ruined my putting stroke.

The New Forest lies along the Hampshire coast, and it's only there in all of Britain since early Medieval times that wild and domestic farm animals have been permitted to roam free of any restraint on the rough theory, supported by royal edict and the point of a sword, that a shaggy cow the size of a Volkswagen, or a wild pony reputed to have descended from the herd that swam ashore when the Spanish Armada sunk in the English Channel, instinctively knows where it really wants to be. Sometimes that's wandering safely in the village fields; sometimes in the vicar's veggie patch. Often it's in the middle of the lane, amusing and shaking up tourists.

In fact, there's nothing remotely *new* about the Forest, sections of which were cleared for settlement and agriculture long before the Normans arrived. William the Conqueror officially decreed the area as a game preserve in 1079, and the rights of its human inhabitants promptly became subservient to those of the Forest's animals. Thus fences were forbidden and a forest dweller caught disturbing any sort of critter—shooting it dead with a crossbow, say, calling it unflattering names, you name it—could indeed legally have his eyes put out or hands lopped off on the spot by order of the Crown. Subsequent ruling monarchs who were slightly less dotty about hunting than the Normans eventually restored the rights of New Forest humans, but a patchwork quilt of feudal and modern laws developed which governs the mystical woods to this day. The Forest boundary, for example, is called a "perambulation" and landowners there still hold obscure rights to ancient practices such as peat cutting ("turbury"), firewood collection ("estover"), and allowing one's pigs to root for acorns and beech masts ("masting"). A landowner or esquire of the rank of knight or baronet was sometimes called a "verderer" or "keeper of the forest," and from Elizabethan times onward, guys like my friend Martin Skan, who'd turned Chewton Glen from a run-down regency mansion into England's finest country hotel, were obliged to protect the magical forest and its woolly inhabitants, even if it meant they were terribly late for a tee time.

Other nifty but essentially useless tidbits of New Forest lore I'd picked up from Martin over the years included the fact that the timber used to make British warships, including Admiral Nelson's HMS *Agamemnon* and most of the Trafalgar fleet, came from New Forest, and somewhere in the Forest—though I had yet to actually find it—was a famous stone reputed to be the spot where William the Conquerer's son, rambunctious Rufus, was "accidentally" shot and killed by a bolt to the heart from a crossbow that glanced off a stag during a hunting party. (Most historians suspect it was a political assassination carried out by Henry, his dull but somewhat more stable younger brother.) Also somewhere around—though I wasn't sure where, given all the confusing trees—was a mystical specimen called the Knight-wood Oak, measuring more than twenty five feet in circumference, where knights loyal to the king often made their oaths of fidelity. According to the legend, the tree was standing when King Arthur formed his round table and chivalric code, though most egghead archaeologists and spoilsport arborists insist that claim is so much folkish hokum, little more than a pile of fresh New Forest cow doo on the road.

Still, it makes for a nice, diverting yarn and I shamelessly relayed it with as much romantic savoir faire as I could muster, in order to distract my companions until we rolled into the grounds of pretty Chewton Glen.

"How come you know so much about this place?" Jack wanted to know after we hastily stashed our stuff in a handsome guest room, borrowed a couple sets of the hotel's golf clubs, and hustled straight for Martin's delightful parkland par-three course, the only golf either of us was likely to get in for a while unless we decided to loiter around England and maybe the New Forest for the balance of the summer.

That prospect, as I admitted to Jack somewhere about the eighth green, where he was putting out and I maintained a wary eye for intruding cows, had no small appeal to me, frankly speaking, because after a handful of business trips to the forest I'd grown so deeply smitten with the atmosphere of the place and its ancient ways I sometimes fantasized about packing up our whole family and shipping us there for the length and breadth of a standard British summer. T. E. Lawrence did that once upon a time with his brood, ditto Janey Austen. They found inspiration and a kind of magic in the splendid isolation of the New Forest.

If we ever wound up doing such a thing, I assured Nibs as we finished up the game and retreated to the hotel's beautiful stone terrace to have a cool drink and wait for Mum to come down from her guest room and rendezvous with Martin and Brigge Skan for an after-dinner refreshment, we would probably have to bring along all our dogs and cats, my garden tractor, and a couple hundred books because, if I planted myself here, I wasn't certain a visiting verderer like me would ever be able to leave again.

"Could we bring Mum, too?"

"Oh, we'd *have* to have her. She's the only one who gets the point of my jokes."

"I get them." He sounded a bit hurt.

"You laugh at my jokes," I corrected him. "And for that yeoman loyalty, you should immediately be promoted from page to knight-in-training." I glanced about the crowded terrace. "If we can ever find the Queen Mum again, I'll personally suggest that in her good hairy ear."

I was frankly a wee bit worried about Mum. Several minutes had passed since she was last glimpsed in public, and I suddenly feared that the floral elegance of Chewton Glen might be chaffing her good socialist values the way, say, the dreary Edward Lear made me genuinely regret ever reading "The Owl and the Pussycat." The place, after all, was crawling with well-bred aristocrat types out for a weekend frolic in the Forest, and for a worrying moment I pictured the Queen Mum up in her beautiful guest suite writing Maoist slogans on the Sloane Square wallpaper or plotting how to short circuit the electric tea kettle and discreetly burn the place to the ground.

A waiter appeared to take our orders. Jack ordered his usual pint of Coke and I ordered a couple goblets of fine French chardonnay in anticipation of Mum's arrival.

"Look, Dad," Jack said with visible pleasure, pointing to the darkening golf course we'd just left, where perhaps a dozen small rabbits had now emerged to feed around the greens. "Just like in *Alice* . . ."

Earlier somewhere out on the course, as we scuffed along half an hour ago, I had explained to Jack that Charles Dodgson, the Oxford mathematics don who created *Alice's Adventures in Wonderland* under the name Lewis Carroll to amuse and entertain the precocious daughter of his friend the vicar of Christ Church Oxford, used the New Forest as a setting for the classic tale he put on paper the same year the American Civil War ended. Alice Liddell, the girl for whom the story was written, was buried not far away in a New Forest churchyard—another magical spot I hadn't quite discovered yet.

"I'll tell you something else pretty interesting," I said now. "You might have a closer connection to those rabbits and this place than you realize."

I explained that an amateur genealogist doing some snooping around in our family's tree recently phoned me to say she thought there was a chance we might related to this same Reverend Dodgson, based on the fact that the surname appears in our early family records. She theorized that those immigrating Dodgsons dropped the g from their name intentionally after the end of the American Civil War, either to protect family lands from being confiscated by occupying federal forces or perhaps as the result of a simple clerical error in a country courthouse.

"Cool. Do you think it's true?" Jack wondered, sounding as if he really hoped it so. The *Alice* book had been one of his favorite childhood stories, and the Disney film based on it probably his all-time favorite kid video.

"Could be," I said, explaining how my father's family burrowed rabbitlike back to the founding of the colony of North Carolina, a family tree that would have given the Knightwood Oak a run for its money. Somewhere in the thousands of tiny names inscribed on its limbs might be a genuine link to Lewis Carroll. History was funny that way—at worst, fiction agreed upon; at best, someone else's account of what really happened, as they say. There was probably no way to know for certain if it was true. But the messages of myths and stories, I proposed, were far more revealing and frequently truer than the bare facts at hand. It really didn't matter if we were related to Alice Liddell—we were surely her American cousins of the spirit.

The waiter returned. He put down two goblets of chardonnay and I picked up one and tasted it. The wine was delicious, with a hint of wood and lemon in it. If Mum didn't show her sober superintendent's face soon, I'd be forced to finish mine and drink hers as well.

"Cheers," I said, lifting my glass to Jack. "By the way, nice playing out there. Sorry we're having to miss a whole summer of baseball *and* golf."

"Cheers," he replied. "That's okay. We can play golf and stuff when we get back."

I smiled at him and started to say how wise he was beginning to sound, how grown-up he appeared to be getting. But that would only have served to embarrass us both, so I mentioned another family connection to lovely Chewton Glen instead, something even more substantial than Lewis Carroll. When my father was a boy about Jack's age in North Carolina, among his favorite books—a tale that made him yearn to someday set off and see England the way we were doing—was a bestseller called *Children of the New Forest,* the adventures of the brave Beverley children during the bloody English Civil War, the struggle that resulted in English monarchs being stripped of their "divine right" to make war or mayhem and the establishment of a republican commonwealth form of government.

"Your grandfather always said that book was one reason he became a newspaperman," I said, pointing to the main building of the hotel, where the lights had begun to come on. "And that book, Nibs, was written in *this* house."

Jack's eyes widened. This news flash seemed to really impress him.

"Dad . . . ," he said, after a moment, as if this revelation spurred another kind of thought, "did you ever, like, want to be anything other than a writer?"

I nodded and gave him a short list of things I really wanted to be before I stumbled into a career of having to eat my own words. To begin with, about age five or six, I seriously committed myself to the life of a working cowboy—punching cattle all day, saloon fights at night, getting the pretty girl in the end. Then we moved from Texas back to the Carolinas, where my father was from, and I decided my true life's destiny was to play shortstop for the Washington Senators.

"Who were they?"

"A major league baseball team that soon packed up and moved to Texas and renamed themselves the Rangers. Just my rotten luck."

Professional juggler, point guard for Dean Smith, and playing backup guitar for the Beatles all preceded my dedicated ambition to win the U.S. Open, meet Arnold Palmer, move to France, and marry a beautiful dark-haired French girl with exotic underarm hair. By then I was nineteen and reading *far* too much Ernest Hemingway.

"French girls in those days," I carefully added, "all had hair under their arms. That's how you knew they were authentically French."

"Wow," he said, taking a slug of Coke. Then he announced surprisingly, "I think I want to be a writer, too."

"Really?" I smiled at Jack. He reminded me of both his grandfathers in so many subtle and unmistakable ways. He had Sam Bennie's questing brain and my father's ease with the world. Most of all, he loved a rousing good yarn—so I guess the apple didn't fall far from the family tree and any career path was possible at this point. Oxford scientist. Cambridge poet. Maybe even Red Sox shortstop.

"Funny, I remember when you wanted to be a stage magician. Make rabbits appear from a hat, pianos disappear, that sort of thing." I didn't want to say it, but that seemed like half a minute ago, to me.

He glanced at the lawn, where rabbits had appeared magically on the grass.

"I remember that," he admitted a bit wistfully, then looked at me and smiled. "Do you think there really is such a thing as magic?"

Ah, the skeptic Queen Mum side of him was revealing itself, too! I picked up Mum's wine and sipped it, having given the old socialist biddy time enough to powder her face and make herself known to nice Conservative Party folks on the terrace.

"I don't know. But let me tell you something that happened right up there," I said, pointing to a set of mullioned windows standing open in the evening light of a stunning room tucked beneath the rafters of hotel. "It was probably the most magical thing I ever witnessed. Your mom saw it, too."

I explained how Jack's mother and I had come to Chewton Glen at the end of what had been, as I looked back, a critical moment in our ten-year marriage—at least that's how I'd thought of our week of wandering about England during the height of bluebell season six years before.

We both knew in our hearts that our marriage was quietly unraveling but we seemed helpless to save it. This was mere months before we separated, I explained to him, a terribly confusing time for everyone involved.

"Where was I?" Jack wondered. I noticed he wasn't drinking his Coke or watching the rabbits. I had his full and undivided attention.

I said he was back home in Maine with Grandma and his sister, oblivious to what was about to happen to all our lives, probably asking the Queen Mum to rewind *Alice in Wonderland* over and over on the VCR.

Chewton Glen was the final stop on our trip—and our marriage, too, as it turned out.

"Your mom and I had just reached that room and set our bags down when something extraordinary happened." A beautiful white dove flew straight through the window and perched on the bed's newel post.

"Holy cow," Jack said.

"Holy *bird*, you mean. Then again, come to think of it, I guess the cows around here are kind of holy, too."

I explained to him how the spectacular critter just perched there calmly staring at us—first at me, then his mother, then me again—for a minute or two. Maybe it was three or four minutes. Then it flew straight back out the window and was gone, fluke of nature or a messenger from the gods. I still wasn't certain which.

"I don't really know if it was magic, but I suppose I wanted to think that it was a sign of some kind, like the dove that brought old Noah an olive branch to tell him his ordeal on the ocean was nearly over."

I sipped Mum's wine. It was delicious. I might have even said *magical*.

"We could have used an olive branch about then. In any case, magic or not, I chose to believe it was a messenger who'd been sent to tell us to keep faith and life would eventually get back on track again. It did, of course—just not the way I thought it would."

"I never heard you guys arguing much," Jack revealed, as if it might be of some consolation to me now, all these years after the split.

"You're nice to say that. Your mom and I still worry about how that time—the things we did or didn't do—affected you."

He shrugged, glancing off to see if the Queen Mum was anywhere afoot yet.

"I was really mad at you both for a long time," he admitted over the edge of his glass. "Almost *all* of the third grade."

"You're probably still a little sore. No one would blame you."

"I'm not mad. It still makes me kind of sad, though. I wish you two hadn't gotten divorced."

"Ah, but you like Scott, don't you?" Scott was Jack's new stepdad. Initially, Jack had given Scott a pretty hard time. But I sensed a growing friendship between them, which was good for all parties concerned.

"Oh yeah," he said, as if that much should be pretty obvious by now. "How about Wendy?"

Since we were having an unexpected heart-to-heart, this seemed as good a moment as any to take a sounding on my new wife of less than a fortnight.

"Wendy's great. You guys seem to still like each other a lot—you and Mom, I mean. I know you like Wendy, too, or probably *love* her, I mean."

"I do love Wendy," I agreed, tempted to trot out some chestnut about second marriages being like second chances because they let you learn from your mistakes and get on with things, more or less exactly what the Queen Mum had advised in the aftermath of the divorce. For an old pink agnostic, she sure kept the faith.

"Will you always love Mom?"

"Of course."

His mother and I spoke nearly every day of our lives about the affairs of our children, arranging pickups, swapping the latest gossip, sharing every mundane and thrilling detail of their lives; we'd recovered an important equilibrium and were now an extended family that had its ups and downs the same as every big and somewhat complicated American family. But nothing could change the past, as far as I was concerned. I loved the memory of my marriage to his mother because she gave me the one thing I valued most in life: fatherhood.

Naturally, I didn't say all of this to Jack, sitting there on the fragrant, shadowy terrace of the hotel where the beautiful winged creature mysteriously appeared and had told us—at least me—*something*. This was simply my take on our last good night as man and wife, and his mother would certainly have her own interpretation of events and their meaning. I encouraged him to ask her about it.

"Yeah. Maybe I will," he replied, then knocked off the last bit of Coke and gave me a modest smile that said he was okay with how things had worked out. Maybe he was just putting on a brave face à la the Beverley children of the New Forest. Only time would tell.

I waved the waiter back over to order Jack and Mum both refills. The terrace was clearing out; the summer night was no less magical but a good bit cooler.

"You and Wendy don't have wedding rings yet," Jack pointed out.

"True, Tonto."

Wendy and I had this idea of trying to find a couple old rings somewhere along the road when she joined us in Italy, I revealed. Maybe they would just cry out to us from some dusty alley along the Appian Way, give voice or appear the way the dove in the upper room had, like magic.

"What's all this about magic?" A pleasant English voice floated toward us across the darkened terrace stones.

It was my former golf buddy Martin Skan, hotelier *extraordinaire* and New Forest verderer come to convey his friendly proprietary greetings. Brigge, he apologized smoothly, was still inside entertaining their dinner guests and hoped we might see her before we slipped away in the morning.

I promised we would and then said, "I was just telling Jack about a magical time his mom and I spent here once in the spring. The bluebells were in bloom and a perfect white dove flew into our bedroom upstairs."

"I remember it well," Martin said, shaking Jack's hand. "I also remember that while your mother enjoyed the pool and spa, your father and I played golf over at Brockenhurst and an angry member complained that your father's shouting ruined his chance for a par." He laughed charmingly.

"It was the damned cow's fault. He wouldn't move and let me see the hole. By the way," I added, "we saw the same old fella standing on the road this afternoon—the cow, I mean. I think he was looking for a game, or maybe an American golfer to terrorize."

"They're everywhere, I'm afraid, shy of the spa pool. But one grows rather fond of the beasts," Martin mused, taking up a chair next to Jack. "It's part of what makes life in the New Forest such an adventure. Magical things *do* happen here, Jack. As perhaps you've now seen."

On that note, I prompted Martin to tell Jack the rather magical story of Chewton Glen's transformation from the dowdy regency manor house where Captain Frederick Marryat wrote *Children of the New Forest* into England's most distinctive country lodging. *Gourmet* magazine, I'd just read somewhere, had recently designated Chewton as the finest country hotel in the world.

Martin was just finishing up the tale, wouldn't you know it, when the Queen Mum suddenly charged into view. She was decked out handsomely in a classic evening dress, wearing sensible black flats and an unaccountably happy expression on her face. Perhaps she hadn't been busy scrawling militant union rally slogans in the hotel guest book after all.

I introduced her to Martin and presented her with a fresh glass of wine, which the waiter had thoughtfully deposited only moments before her arrival.

"Are you with these lads for the entire journey?" Martin inquired, hovering a moment more before returning to join Brigge and his dinner guests.

"Oh no," Mum explained, "I'm bound briefly for Scotland after a small visit with a friend in Heathfield. Then I'm taking my granddaughter, Jack's older sister, Maggie, on a little tour of Prince Edward Island."

"They're doing the Anne of Green Gables party tour," I amplified. "The entire country has been placed on high alert."

"He's a tart one," Mum relayed to Martin.

"How very odd. The offended member in Brockenhurst said exactly the same thing."

The hotel man in Martin couldn't help inquiring if her guest room was satisfactory. He had her placed in the Colonel Beverley Suite.

"Oh, perfectly lovely," Mum trilled like a schoolgirl on bank holiday. "I believe I could be happy here for a *very* long time."

They chatted pleasantly for a moment and then Martin bowed and left us, winking and cheekily admonishing me to come back again soon with whichever wife or mother-in-law I cared to bring along. They were all very welcome at Chewton Glen, he said.

Jack asked if he could go hang out with some boys he'd seen down on the golf course near the croquet lawn. I looked over but saw only a navy curtain of midsummer night and realized that the older I got, the better my eyesight used to be. But I could still see that beautiful white dove on the newel post.

"How are you feeling, Lamb?" Mum inquired gently, examining him more closely.

"Fine. Great," he chirped, showing us his chipmunkish front teeth. "Why?"

She glanced at me and smiled. I glanced at him and smiled. Perhaps he could tell we were both relieved that there were no obvious lingering effects from our strange odyssey down the rabbit hole of London's medical system or, for that matter, the sad thing that happened in a boy's life half his age ago.

"Just checking," Mum said gently, patting his arm.

He put down his scarcely touched second cola and loped off into the dark. I watched him vanishing, still not seeing the boys he meant but hearing their voices somewhere off toward the woods.

"He seems fine to go on." She pronounced simply, sounding like the tough but tenderhearted school authority that made her forever our Queen Mum.

I said I thought so, too, not so much wondering *where* we were going after King Arthur's grave but already missing my personal Fabian Socialist adviser wherever the spirit was leading us.

"Thank you, James," she said primly. Then, unexpectedly, she lifted her wineglass to make a toast.

"To your health and safe travels. This has been *most* enjoyable."

"Thanks," I said, touched her glass with mine, and then cranked over and kissed her on the cheek. I think she actually blushed, although with a Red Tide Scot you can never be too certain.

"I'm thinking of letting Jack drive across France," I announced brightly, hoping to rev her up at least one last time for the road. "Maybe Italy, too. I bet nobody there will even notice."

She only smiled at me as if it were a gift to be simple.

"Well," she said with a sigh, "the gods protect young children and old fools. Where will you go after Glastonbury, dear?"

"Haven't a clue," I admitted. "That's half the fun."

SIX

An Older Hill

Afternoon was drifting pleasantly into evening again when Jack and I finally set off for the summit of Britain's most sacred hill. This was two days later, or the day after we bid the Queen Mum a fond adieu for Scotland. That same morning at Ann's place in Heathfield, while our freshly washed duds were being tumble dried, I phoned my buddy Chet in the basement of the American embassy just to see if by chance the world had improved its disposition during the previous six days. I caught Chet just as he arrived at work, a little out of breath and sounding as if he'd fallen off his bicycle while crossing Trafalgar Square.

"What's the travel situation in Kenya?" I put to him straightaway, thinking how I dearly wanted to go on that East African safari we'd booked and partially paid for. The refund deadline loomed and I had exactly one day to decide if Africa was a calculated risk I was willing to take.

"No better than when we spoke last week, sorry to say. In fact, all but essential embassy staff are being temporarily sent out. We're on highest alert over there." The travel advisory to American tourists was still in effect, he said, and probably would be until Thanksgiving.

So I asked about China with a slumping heart.

"Oh, *much* worse than before. Looks like the reds are planning to keep the bloody reconnaissance plane. Old hands haven't seen it this dodgy since Nixon and pingpong."

He wondered if we'd considered Sweden. I inquired instead about the Holy Land and Egypt. He laughed ruefully and pointed out there had been two suicide bombings in Gaza just that week alone. Sharon was threatening to close the West Bank. Egypt, meanwhile, was cracking down on Shiite fundamentalists. A nasty backlash was expected. Even the *Germans* weren't going there for the moment.

"India?" I asked weakly. I'd always wanted to see India—the ancient Ganges, Charles Churchill's birthplace, skinny guys coaxing lethal cobras from baskets, pretty girls wearing diamonds glued to their foreheads. Plus, I really liked nan bread.

"A significant upsurge of Hindu nationalism. Ongoing instability on the Pakistani border with Kashmir. Potential powderkeg, I'm afraid."

He sounded like a man reading a really bad weather forecast. Meanwhile, our personal forecast for traveling around the world appeared more unpromising by the hour. I was scheduled to phone Jack's mom and bring her up to speed on our progress, if you want to call it that, and could honestly now report to her that it appeared the ancient world would soon be sending us home to Maine, probably in time for Jack's birthday. That would undoubtedly be music to her ears. Though she put on a brave face about the expedition, she wasn't exactly thrilled about us going all the way to the other side of the world just to climb up the Pyramids or hoof along the Great Wall.

"Anything *else* I should know?" I almost hesitated to ask this before I conveyed to Chet our new international cell phone number and politely invited him to reach out and touch us if anything in those corners of the world suddenly changed for the better.

"England just lost a critical test match to bloody South Africa, seventy-nil," he related dejectedly. "It boggles the mind, quite truthfully."

For a moment I had no idea what he was telling me. Had a new Boer War broken out? Then I realized Chet was a devoted cricket fan. He sounded fully prepared to shoot himself in the temple before lunchtime.

Oh well. *Bloody hell,* as the Brits like to say. We still had Arthur's England, and Jack was now thankfully smiling almost ear to ear. Perhaps we'd at least make Paris on Bastille Day and a little bit of Italy, too—hook up with Dame Wendy, scout for cheap wedding rings in Firenze, eat some terrific pasta, then go home and mow the lawn. Amazing how rapidly a summer vacation can vanish in no time flat.

Legend has it that the Glastonbury Tor, our day's objective, which rises a couple hundred feet in the air on a pretty Somerset meadow a mile or so from the center of the famous ancient town of the same name, is the center of King Arthur's Isle of Avalon and the holy site where Christianity first came to Britain, possibly brought by Jesus himself when he visited England as a little shaver in Nike trainers.

That rather outrageous suggestion, which flies in the face of most biblical scholarship, as we learned that morning while wandering through the town's crowded High Street en route to Glastonbury Abbey's ruins and the Tor itself, turns out not to be quite as loony as it sounds.

According to a book I excavated from a pile of dusty tomes in an alchemist's shop selling healing crystals and magic potions, the nearby Mendip Hills were long ago mined for lead by the occupying Roman invaders, and one of those mines was reportedly owned by none other than Joseph of Arimathea, the well-to-do merchant said to have been related to Mary and in whose family cave, according to the Gospel of Matthew, Jesus' body was placed following his crucifixion.

During the period of time between his Nazarine youth and the beginning of his adult ministry, the locally held theory goes, when little or nothing is known of Jesus' travels and activities, the savior of mankind accompanied his wealthy relative on an inspection tour of family property in Gaul, a road trip immortalized, among other things, by poet William Blake in the "Glastonbury Hymn," sometimes called "Jerusalem"—"And did those feet in ancient times/Walk upon England's mountains green?"

Furthermore, after Christ's death and ascension, Joseph supposedly brought the chalice used by Christ and the disciples at the Last Supper and either buried it for safekeeping somewhere on the Glastonbury Tor itself or hid it in a local well, then planted a tree sprouted from the crucified Christ's crown of thorns, which bloomed thereafter only around Christmas, on the site of an abbey that was soon built by Christian monks, who aimed to convert the local pagans.

According to a later legend that grew out Joseph's early adventures, the lost chalice or so-called Holy Grail eventually became an object of obsession for Britain's first Christian warrior, an early sixth-century tribal chieftain called Arthur, who beat the invading Saxons into retreat, drove the Scots back to their homeland, subdued the Pict barbarians, and eventually instituted peace and civilized behavior on the bloody southwest peninsula of Britain by convening twenty-eight "knights" around a symbolically circular table. For what it's worth, he later starred in a big Lerner and Lowe West End musical with the eternal Bobby Goulet.

Anyway, Glastonbury's High Street was a spiritual gas, a teeming New Jerusalem of curiosity shops and spiritual boutiques catering to the evolving spiritual pilgrim in every traveler. After checking into the George and Pilgrim Hotel off the High Street and setting off to investigate the ruins and locate the mystical Tor, rural American bumpkins that we were, we repeatedly got sidetracked from our prescribed destination by fascinating joints peddling everything from crystal therapy to herbal healing, Wiccan poultices to green tea enemas, how-to books on the Pagan lifestyle, holistic cancer treatments, Buddhist love trace candles, Tantric sex manuals, Jamaican voodoo—a human jamboree of mystical possibilities, enough New Age *crap* to send Shirley MacLaine fleeing to a Dominican nunnery.

Sacred stones, tarot cards, dowsing rods, numerology charts, and Nostradamus day planners were just the tip of the Aquarian iceberg. One shop was selling Druidic planting guides, vegan soil starters, and a mysteriously cloudy liquid in a small blue bottle enigmatically labeled "Pearl of Real Mother's Milk," purporting to cure "almost anything."

"That's excellent for signs of visible aging," the nice lady clerk behind the cash register offered up, spotting me handling the merchandise. I was discreetly trying to determine the source of the mystery fluid, picturing a cottage industry for stay-at-home pregnant mothers.

"What kind of real mother?" I asked as casually as possible.

"I believe it's marmot or mink," she answered, deftly sacking up someone else's New Age goodies. "But it's absolutely *brilliant* on nappie rash."

A few paces farther along the sidewalk, in a nifty shop specializing in "important mystical writings," vintage American comic books, and sacred African tribal drums, I wasted ten minutes on another little tome revealing invaluable gardening secrets, like how to conjure helpful "spirits" and attract garden gnomes who would thoughtfully keep an eye peeled for mold spot and grub worms. Meanwhile, Nibs the Lost Boy got lost through a curtain of Woodstock love beads. I heard tribal drumming in the near distance, and a short while later found him squatting in a back room filled with gigantic African war drums.

"Dad, can I get this?" he called out over the din. I could only make out the top of his head and a pair of blurry hands. He meant the instrument he was pounding on—a gigantic African bush drum that probably would have required a couple buffed Watusi warriors just to cart it out of the shop.

"Absolutely not," I said, realizing someone had to show some New Age fiscal restraint. I suggested, as an alternative, some astrologically tuned jelly beans from the mystical candy shop across the street.

"But we ship anywhere," prompted the clerk, a small unshaven man with a large Adam's apple, who suddenly appeared as if by a poof of smoke at my elbow.

Back on the sidewalk, a billboard festooned with fliers announced the formation of a new Women's Lunar Chanting Circle, an upcoming seminar in determining "personal lei lines in the New Millennium," and a special Shamanistic fertility lecture scheduled for that very evening at the village hall. So many gods. So little time. The Museum of Pagan Heritage was also offering a special exhibit called "The Burning Times" to commemorate the fiftieth anniversary of the repeal of Britain's Witchcraft Act.

Down the hill near the cathedral and abbey ruins, just past the Museum of Pagan Heritage, a sizable crowd of tourists had gathered around a dude costumed remarkably like the court jester in my beloved oil painting back home. He and his buxom Medieval wench were harassing their audience for volunteer recruits willing to participate in a "Fool School." Several small children bravely stepped forward as volunteers, as did two blushing moms and three smirking teenage girls. Naturally, Nibs wanted to do it.

"Go for it," I encouraged him, offering to hold his mystical jelly beans without eating too many of them. I promised to get a snapshot of him being a young fool on our brand-new digital camera (which I had yet to figure out how to operate).

"No. I want us *both* to do it."

"Oh. Right. Forget it, Slick."

Jack waved his hand and the jester and his wench came over grinning like the fools they were.

"Excellent!" the jester bellowed, patting Jack stoutly on the back, then yanking him rudely by the collar toward the other willing rubes. He leered at me. "The king could use a big strapping bloke like you!"

I demurred. "No, thanks. Dodgy knees and other signs of visible aging, I'm afraid. Besides, I'm holding the beans and the camera."

"C'mon, *Dod*," he brayed in my face like a Medieval drill sergeant. "It's ver-ry liberating to play the fool. We need a strong back and a weak mind! Chances are the only thing you'll break, Charlie, is wind!"

The crowd laughed; it was tough to tell which of us they thought was potentially the bigger fool.

"Would someone kindly volunteer to hold this gentleman's candy and camera?" the jester petitioned the crowd, which was really more like a mob.

"I'll be happy to hold them," offered a sweet little old lady standing beside me. Thus, against my better judgment, I found myself standing over with the blushing moms and smirking teens and Nibs the Lost Boy.

"My name is Tom and this lusty wench is called Pamela," the jester began, clearing his throat. "We're here to train you for service to the Crown as professional fools. Any questions before we get started?"

I raised my hand. "Yes. May I go to the bathroom?"

"Oh, a joker," Tom declared, grinning slyly. "I like that. The bigger they are, the harder the fall I always says." The crowd chuckled loyally.

"Very good," he continued, ignoring my plea to pee. "Now, pupils. The cardinal rule of being a successful professional fool is to learn how to make any and every person laugh. Especially the king. Thus you will be schooled in the ancient arts of juggling, japery, tumbling, and generally falling down and making a complete arse of yourself . . ."

The thing was, I really did have to go. No fooling.

For the next ten minutes or so, we practiced juggling rings and small leather balls, which of course I was fairly accomplished at because, not to boast or anything, I've juggled one thing or another, including golf balls, after-school schedules, and overdue monthly bills, since I was knee high to a busty wench. This talent didn't go unnoticed by Tom the Fool, who paired me up with the school's smallest person, a tiny girl named Becky, who had no clue how to juggle but admitted she had to pee, too.

While Medieval court music played from Pamela's boom box, we were tutored in the arts of tumbling, balancing brightly colored sticks on our heads, walking on stilts, making disgusting faces, and forming a human pyramid with *you know who* anchoring the base. At one point, the blushing mother who'd climbed on my back slipped and the pyramid collapsed in a heap on top of me. The crowd let loose a volley of laughter and I nearly let loose a stream of distilled Coca Cola. From beneath the pile, I looked about to see if the nice old lady had caught our japery on camera but couldn't, alas, spot her.

Finally, we were shown how to take absurd "falls" and simulate comic injury, the kind of brainless slapstick humor you see in old Charlie Chaplin films and presidential press conferences. Tom and Pamela ran through an impressive repertoire of violent slips, gaffes, and spills: sprawling on the turf from an accidental sock to the nose, reeling from a carelessly flung elbow to the eye. Tom displayed how to leap and click heels in the air, then landed with a flatulent splat on his rump, rolling his dazed eyes comically. Pamela followed this bravura performance with an impressive trip and spill like a rag doll, hopping absurdly to her feet before falling backward in a heap of dress and mussed-up hair. The mob applauded vigorously, loving every dopey minute of it. Then, unfortunately, it was our turn. Fool School's "final examination," as Tom the Fool put it, was to "caper and fall convincingly to the delight of the king and his audience."

Historically speaking, I'm gifted in the art of unexpectedly falling. The Almighty gave me two sorry knees and one really bad ankle for expressly these purposes, and I've entertained hundreds of complete strangers for decades by abruptly doing violent headers down public stairways, witlessly stepping into civic potholes, and performing impressive somersaults, ludicrously tripping over my own shaky wheels and spilling into innocent store displays, you name it. But could I manage to do it on command, with a critical audience no less?

Nibs and I watched as the blushing moms and smirking teenagers went first, self-consciously executing modest little rolls and tumbles for which, as the audience applauded, Tom the Fool and Pamela ceremonially rewarded them with roguish bear hugs and a pinned-on badge that read *I'm a Certified Fool.* My small tumbling mate, Becky, went next, performing a pretty fair cartwheel that stirred up the crowd, followed by Jack, who did an even more spectacular cartwheel, fell backward, and sprung to his feet in a manner that would have impressed a talent scout from the World Wrestling Federation.

I was still scanning the crowd for Granny Smith and my new digital camera when Tom cleared his throat and wondered if I planned to caper and fall or simply stand there like a witless fool all day.

I decided a simple, dignified rodeo-style click of the heels in midair would probably suffice nicely, so I jogged a bit and leapt gracefully into the air, in a manner of speaking, managed to touch my heels, and then landed on my traitorous left ankle, which promptly buckled like a two-dollar beach chair and sent me sprawling into the crowd. I felt a surge of pain and heard something ripping apart that turned out to be the seam of my safari shorts.

"That was awesome, Dad," Jack said, helping me limp on down the High Street a few minutes later, after I'd been pinned and officially designated a *Certified Fool,* and for my trouble been disgustingly kissed on the mouth by both Tom and Pamela. Truth be told, my dignity was probably more wounded than my ankle, but it suddenly came to me that something vital was missing.

"Yikes. The camera!" I exclaimed, stopping dead in my tracks. I looked the length and breadth of the High Street but no Granny Smith was visible. The crowds had dispersed and even Pamela and Tom were nowhere to be seen.

"By golly, I think we've been royally snookered," I declared, wondering if the three of them could have been in cahoots, victims of a ruse straight from the pages of *Oliver Twist*.

"She even took my jelly beans," Jack said, echoing the sentiment.

Frankly, I wasn't certain what to do about this development—go find a village beadle and report grand theft by a grandmother, make a beeline for a new pair of pants at the George and Pilgrim, or venture on to the abbey ruins and write it off as just another adventure gone askew in a summer that seemed to be going nowhere fast.

Since we were already at the abbey's entrance, I suggested we go inside and find King Arthur's grave and see the Glastonbury thorn tree, until I could decide on the proper plan of action.

Moments later, as we waited in a small line to purchase tickets for the cathedral grounds, however, a well-dressed older gent who appeared to be a dentist coming home from a Rotary luncheon approached us and handed me a printed piece of paper, a flier of some sort peddling heaven knows what—some miracle healing unguent made from crushed ram's testicles, or notice of an all-night warlock sing-along party.

"If I may say," the man said, with an avuncular smile, "why are you here? He certainly *isn't*."

I asked whom, exactly, he meant. But then again, I was a newly certified fool.

"The one who is coming again to save you from your sins purely by the grace of God."

"You mean Arthur the once and future king?"

His handsome face flinched. I glanced at the flier and Jack, baffled, stared at me. The flier announced that the end of the world was at hand. There was the usual supporting verse or two from the Book of Revelation and a rather crude sketch of people writhing in the flames of hell.

"King Arthur is only a myth," the man said with grave sympathy. "A mere child's fable."

Considering all the emotional garbage I was wrestling with at that moment—anger over my stolen camera, annoyance with my sorry aching ankle, embarrassment at my radically ventilated shorts—I'd probably have been wise to politely shrug off the well-dressed doomsayer and simply leave well enough alone. Even a fool, says Proverbs, when he finally falls silent, can be considered wise. It's not that I don't take biblical prophecy seriously. On the contrary, I have no doubt whatsoever that we will find a way, more likely sooner than later, to do ourselves in as a functioning species. I just maintain hope that the end won't come before either my kids produce cute bouncy heirs or the Red Sox at least find a way to beat the Curse of the Bambino.

"You know," I admitted to him with a sigh, starting down a path I was probably certain to regret, "I like children's fables. In fact, I like them quite a lot. I love legends and myths, too. I read somewhere that the Latin root of myth means 'truth.' "

"That's strictly your interpretation, friend. Not God's. When I was a child, sayeth the Lord, I spake like a child. When I became a man, I put away childish things."

Apparently he spoke on behalf of the Almighty, or at least an authority somewhat higher than the Glastonbury Lunar Chanting Circle. I was tempted to point out to him that it was *Saint Paul* who said the bit about giving up your toys, in Corinthians, but who was I to split scriptural hairs? Where was the Queen Mum when I needed her most?

"If I may ask," he continued smoothly, before I could get a word in edgewise, "do you practice an active faith in our lord and savior Jesus Christ?" He made it sound more like a veiled threat than a simple question.

"I practice all the time," I replied. "Someday I hope to get pretty good at it."

It seemed pointless to try and explain to him that my son and I followed the Anglican tradition and that the older I got the more I saw traces of the good lord beneath every rock, which probably really made me more of a dirt road transcendentalist.

He didn't appear to find my snappy comeback particularly amusing— but, heck, who was joking? Guys like him give Christianity a really bad name, it seems to me, hectoring fallen sinners who've inadvertently split their pants and just want to find their way home at the end of the day. Jack, for his part, looked utterly buffaloed by this unexpected exchange.

"If *that's* true," the man persisted, like an amorous pit bull trying to seduce a leg, "then you know Holy Scripture says the hour is short before your children rebel and all worldly empires cease. Sons will murder their fathers in their sleep, brothers, mothers will weep in lamentation, towers will crumble to dust! The wrath of the Lord will be upon the land, cutting down the unrighteous children like a mighty turning sword."

I saw Jack's eyes widen with alarm. Oh, great, I thought. Just when my sweet lad is smiling again along comes the Grim Reaper in a JCPenney suit. Next thing we'll be seeing the insides of the King Arthur Medical Center.

"Jack," I said calmly, peeling off one of the queen's ten-pound notes and noticing that the line had moved on without us. "Why don't you go get us a couple tickets for the abbey? I'll catch up with you inside the ruins."

He hesitated, looking the man over with genuine wariness.

"It's okay, Boss," I assured him, smiling, patting his shoulder. "I'll be right there."

I waited until Nibsy was safely out of earshot and then turned back to the man in order to speak to him as a child, or at least on behalf of one.

"My son and I are trying to go around the world," I explained to him without much preamble. "We've had kind of a rocky start, to be honest, but the general idea is to somehow show him that people are basically the same wherever you go. If it's all the same to you, I'd prefer him to see that the world's goodness far outweighs the bad. After all, it's his world to inherit—even if he doesn't murder me in my sleep."

"Oh, how nice," he said pleasantly, as if I'd just announced I hoped to join the Glastonbury Optimists Club.

"Every man is a divinity in disguise, a god playing a fool," I gave him my favorite quote from Emerson for no good reason other than I knew it would bunch his theological shorts. The Queen Mum would probably have been very proud of me.

"So you think of yourself as a god . . ."

"Far more of a fool. Certified, actually." I proudly showed him my new lapel button.

He smiled but didn't appear really amused. "Sounds to me, friend, as if you place your faith entirely in *this* world and reject any idea of a spiritual reckoning . . ."

On the contrary, I heard myself reply with a sigh, wondering what on *earth* I was doing wasting valuable sight-seeing time with Jack and perfectly good oxygen arguing with a modern-day Medieval doomsayer! Every day brought a spiritual reckoning of some sort to somebody—a doctor's frightening opinion, a jury's sobering verdict, a sudden event that peels back the veil of the ordinary to reveal some unlikely spark of the divine. The luckiest among us, it seemed to me, I pushed on with the faith of a mustard seed, suffered some kind of epiphany that reminded us that faith is the only thing that gets us through a troubled day with anything resembling a sense of humor.

I quoted Muhammad the taxi driver. "God wants to see laughter in your eyes. That's basically why my son and I are trying to see the world. To meet people, see the sights, and have a few good laughs. Besides, I've always wanted to see King Arthur's grave. Is it really neat?"

"I see." He gave a curt nod, obviously failing to convert me, edging away as if he suddenly feared I might attempt to convert *him* to my loony optimistic brand of dirt road transcendentalism. "In that case, good luck. By the way, brother, I believe your commando shorts are torn."

"Thanks," I said, handing him back his doomsday tract and going on in the abbey door where Jack had left an admission ticket waiting, revealing far more of myself than I'd intended to.

Inside the cathedral grounds, I found Jack standing beside the famous thorn tree, reading about it from a glossy brochure. I'm no expert on sacred trees or anything but it looked more like a young mulberry tree to me.

"Hi, Dad," he said. "Was that guy back there, like, angry or something?"

"I think his intentions were honorable, Nibs. Everybody has a viewpoint. He just didn't realize he was dealing with a couple certified fools."

Jack smiled, obviously relieved, and I hoped the unsettling encounter would slip out of his agile mind as quickly as it had occurred.

We didn't need any repeats of Greenwich Hill at this point in time. He glanced at the famous thorn tree and frowned a bit.

"Do you think Joseph of Arimathea really planted this tree? I mean, it looks kind of small for a tree that's supposed to be, like, two thousand years old."

I consulted our walking map to make certain this was the exact tree in question. This was it. But it did look kind of, well, puny for such an old sacred tree.

"Maybe it's just a story or myth or something," Jack theorized, touching a leafy branch, willing to extend it the benefit of the doubt, or at least suspend his disbelief.

"Could be," I agreed, but pointed out that no less than the Queen of England had a sprig of the tree placed on her breakfast tray every Christmas morning, to signify Britain's original connection with Christendom. I also filled him in on what I said to the obnoxious doomsayer about "myth" meaning truth, adding that in my view stories told by the fire are often more helpful than simple facts reported in the newspaper. If nothing else, they revealed how people before us dealt with the same challenges of life. That was why, for this summer at least, we were skipping the news and chasing the myths.

"By the way," I said as we set off deeper into the ruins, "in King Arthur's day the gods always protected fools. That would be us, Boss."

We wandered through the Lady Chapel and eventually came to a spot marked by stones on the ground believed to contain the remains of Arthur and good Queen Guinevere. Jack plopped his knapsack on the tufted grass and my old catcher's mitt slipped out. I picked it up, thumping the leather.

"Want to throw some? Nice open place . . ."

He glanced at me with deep surprise, then around the vast and rolling lawn of the ruins. The place was immaculate, green, hushed as a New England burying ground—exactly what I hoped my own lawn would someday be with the proper application of time and enough Scotts seasonal fertilizer. Only a few gray-haired tourist sorts were poking about the ruins, none of them, alas, the sweet old bitty who swiped our new four-hundred-dollar camera.

"Sure."

"We can use King Arthur's grave as home plate."

"*Really?*"

"I don't think he'll mind. Just keep your fastball out of the dirt."

Nibs took his glove and went one way and I limped the other, crouching behind the famous grave.

After we'd made a few tentative pitches back and forth, Jack ventured, "Do you think King Arthur is really in here or is it like the thorn tree?"

"I don't know. Kind of neat to think he might really be buried here, isn't it? One popular legend says that Arthur will come back someday when Britain needs him most. On the other hand, it might just be some guy called Kevin or Dudley lying here. I mean, not even Grant is buried in Grant's tomb. But that doesn't mean Grant wasn't a real guy."

Nibs caught my return throw and stood placing his fingers on the ball's stitches, apparently thinking about this dichotomy between myth and reality, perceived truth and ancient wisdom. In the brief interval while I waited for him to wind up and throw, I saw a stout and matronly figure approaching us from the abbey entrance. For a crazy moment, I thought it might be the Queen Mum coming back. The sun of western England was sinking at her back, but she was clearly waving and hooting. Oh great, I thought—nabbed by the myth police . . .

It took me a moment or two before I realized who she was. None other than Granny Smith!

"Mercy! I've been hunting for you two *everywhere*," she declared, flushed from her slow-motion sprint across the broad cathedral lawn. She presented me a plastic sack which contained my camera and Jack's jelly beans.

"Someone said you might have come this way and I'm so glad I found you!" she said, chattering pleasantly on about how she'd stepped inside the High Street porcelain shop to momentarily check out figurines for her great niece's upcoming baby shower and came out a half an hour later—only to discover the Fool School had ended and we'd vanished on the bricks of old Glastonbury.

"I felt so bad," she confessed, beaming at Jack, "I went and filled your jelly bean bag, honey. I hope I got the right kind."

"Yes, ma'am," he said, plunging an obliging hand in and taking out a palmful.

I thanked her for her kindness, thinking as I did how just when you're about to give up on the world at large something really nice like this happens to restore your faith in absolute strangers.

"Isn't this place simply beautiful?" she said, still puffing, glancing around.

The summit of Glastonbury Tor at sunset seemed as good a place as any to officially break the bad news about our trip around the world. It wasn't going to happen the way either of us hoped and expected it to.

"Jack," I said without preamble, after we'd climbed the two-hundred-foot hill with our ball gloves still in hand and sat down to catch our breath on a tilted stone outside the crumbling fourteenth-century tower. "I think Africa's out of the picture—and probably Egypt and China, too."

For once, I wasn't fooling around. He knew that and looked shocked and disappointed, maybe even a bit betrayed, his young face warmly lit by the midsummer sun's retreat somewhere out over Wales.

"Dad . . . *why?*"

I explained about my secret consultations with Chet from the embassy, the trouble and violence in all those places, the travel advisory placed on Kenya, the suicide bombings in Gaza, the continuing diplomatic dustup over the downed American spy plane. His mother, I said, would be worried sick if I hauled him into harm's way, and I wasn't entirely convinced it was a risk I was willing to take, either.

"But I'm *fine* now," he protested. "I'm sorry about the hospital! It won't happen again. Really . . . I *want* to go to Africa."

I patted his bare knee, attempting to put a cheerful face on the fact that what he didn't know could really hurt him in this world. "I know. But it's not about what happened in London or on the plane. It's about being realistic and smart and . . . safe."

He got up and walked around the Tor to where a scraggly band of rough travelers had occupied the entrance doors and interior space of the ancient watchtower. A young man with long braided hair was playing an unintelligible song on a wooden flute while a woman sat in the lotus position on the trampled earthen floor of the tower, head tilted back, eyes shut, lips moving in silent meditation. A few feet away, a toddler and a three-legged dog played in the dirt.

I got up and walked around the tower, only to find Jack sitting on another stone, staring due east. He'd taken a ball out of his knapsack and was silently fingering it. Obviously thinking the situation over.

"I can fly," he said as I sat down beside him.

"I'm glad to hear it. But Africa's still not possible."

I held out my upturned glove asking for the ball. He deposited it in my glove and stared glumly down the hill at the elderly couple that was trudging up to take in the sunset. They were carrying a blanket and a bottle of wine, probably going to make out like a couple young druids.

Then I noticed something funny about the ball, which was one of two balls we'd brought along with us. Jack had printed names of the places we already visited on the leather skin, the way travelers used to plaster destination stickers on their luggage. I suppose it was one boy's way of charting his progress through the world.

"Here . . . catch," I said and tossed the ball gently up into the air. He stuck out his glove and caught it without too much problem, or enthusiasm.

"Now you can write Glastonbury on the ball," I said.

He shrugged.

"Are we going home?"

"Do you want to?"

"No, sir."

"I don't either."

For what it was worth, I said, we could still go kick up our heels in Paris on France's birthday, maybe catch the beaches of Normandy on the way, scope out the south of France and dip into Italy for a few meals, and maybe hop over to ancient Greece to see whatever there was worth seeing—a bunch of crumbling temples and stuff where half-dressed heroes and gods used to hang out while making mortal man's life a real hell. For what it was worth, the island of Crete was also supposed to be very cool, the edge of Western Civilization, where Minos put the half-bull monster in the palace labyrinth.

"Really?" This news seemed to revive a bit of interest in the mysteries of an older world, pushing on with the pilgrimage to who knows where.

"Yep. Might be a myth-take we'd both regret to take our ball and just go home at this point."

Nibs thumped his glove and turned and gave me another of his laughably threatening eaglet looks, trying hard not to laugh, then allowed the faintest smile to indicate he got my dopey pun.

"But what about those shots we had to get for Africa?"

Months before, each of us had a series of painful (and expensive) vaccinations against a host of horrible Third World diseases most people in America never give a passing thought to.

"Well, I suppose it means there's no chance we can catch malaria or yellow fever anywhere we go from here."

He was silent for another moment.

"What's *that* way?" he asked simply, nodding toward the eastern horizon, which had turned several lovely shades of evening purple now. Swallows or field sparrows or blood-sucking bats of some kind whirled madly overhead, and the ancient druid lovers were nearing the top of the famous grassy signal hill; I could hear them pleasantly murmuring about breaking open the wine and who would get to be first on top in the pagan starlight.

"Holland, I think."

"What's in Holland?"

"Windmills. Wooden shoes. Heineken beer. Tulips. The canals of Amsterdam. Anne Frank's house. Gouda cheese. Jan Vermeer. Really cool stuff. I went there once."

He nodded and gave his glove another thump.

"Can we go there?"

"Sure. You might really like Holland."

I really didn't. But that was another story. This was more Jack's trip than mine, anyway. I was just pleased to keep on keeping on, wherever the good road took us.

"Okay," he agreed.

And with that, we set off for Holland.

SEVEN

Dutch Treats

Hot, tired, and cranky from two hours of sitting with my knees beneath my chin on a creeping high-speed express train from Hoek van Holland to Amsterdam that was supposed to take only thirty minutes, I left Jack temporarily in charge of our bags, with his nose safely plugged into the pages of *The Hobbit*, outside Amsterdam's busy Central Station, while I plodded off to change some British sterling into Dutch gilders for a tram ride out to our hotel in the Museum District. While boys were busy being boys on the thrilling North Sea crossing that morning—watching *Spy Kids* in the ferry movie theater, playing pinball, heaving wads of bread dough at shrieking gulls off the ship's poop deck—Wendy, our Houston Control person back in Maine, had gone on the Internet and managed to locate and book us a room at a hotel called Des Filosoofs somewhere around the Vondelpark, Amsterdam's biggest public park, not far from the Rijksmuseum, and then thoughtfully phoned us on our brand-new international cell phone to convey the good news that we didn't have to go panhandling for a cheap room in the drugs, sex, and rock-and-roll capital of the Western world, the way I had to twenty-five years ago when I first came to Amsterdam.

"Don't move from this spot," I instructed Nibs as he settled down on top of our bags in front of the crowded station. "And please don't speak to any strangers. You'll learn soon enough that this ain't Kansas, Toto. Or even merry old England."

When I returned with a pocket full of Dutch currency a few minutes later, wouldn't you know it, he was chatting amiably with the two female Canadian backpackers who'd sat directly in front of us on the monotonous train ride. They had matching buzzcuts and *Death Rules* tattoos and spent most of the excruciating interval in a passionate clutch, which poignantly reminded me that Jack and I could probably do with a brush-up conversation about amore's endless varieties of expression.

"Are you guys here for the rock festival?" the tougher-looking one asked me pleasantly, reaching for her friend's hand as I walked up.

" 'Fraid not," I admitted. "Just hoping to catch the Vermeers, say howdy to Anne Frank, and sample the beer."

"Awesome weed here," the shorter one provided helpfully, snorted, and winked at Jack. "And it's legal."

Nibs returned her smile, apparently having no clue what she meant. We promptly bid them adieu and stepped into a taxi queue where a beautifully dressed woman who looked remarkably like Jack's elementary school choir teacher, Barbara Larson, presented him with a glossy brochure about some kind of local attraction.

"Are you to be here long, sir?" she inquired, smiling at me.

I said no, probably just long enough to hire a couple bicycles and pedal around the Venice of the North for a bit. I started to go into how I'd rolled into town twenty-five years ago and managed to have a pretty awful time due to circumstances beyond my control, and always thought Amsterdam probably deserved a second look because my dad had wandered through the city on his way home from World War Two, liked the beer and loved the Rembrandts. Then I remembered that I sometimes run on at the mouth with complete strangers and didn't bother to explain any of this.

"Well," she said, pointing to the brochure Jack was holding and staring at with more than casual interest, "we have the most modern facilities in all of Amsterdam and our beautiful shopping store is open twenty-four days a day. I do hope you'll drop in and browse awhile. We have lovely escorts, too."

Escorts?

"Thanks," I replied, politely relieving Jack of the brochure. It turned out to be a flier for Amsterdam's leading sex club and twenty-four-hour porno super store. A tram pulled up and instead of waiting any longer for a taxi to appear, I hurriedly shoved Jack onto it.

The Venice of the North, as it's been called, of course, is renowned for its permissiveness in all matters of intimate human social congress, famed for a deep commitment to religious and political tolerance of every stripe, the legacy of a mighty great seagoing power which tossed off the yoke of Spanish religious oppression in the late 1600s and made a fortune in flogging tulips and cheese and other civilized commodities to the rest of the world, prompting a civic flowering in the arts that made Holland the envy of Europe during its so-called "Golden Age."

That was then. This was now. I attempted to convey this contextual background to Jack as we rattled out through the colorfully Bohemian Leidseplein toward the more sedate Museum District and adjacent Vondelpark, but being almost eleven years old he was far more interested in what the Canadian girls were planning to do with weeds and what the Barbara Larson of Holland was peddling back at the train station.

I explained the Canadian party girls were planning to smoke their approximate body weight in marijuana and the woman who looked like his favorite schoolteacher was peddling dirty pictures and sex for hire. Both things were perfectly legal in Amsterdam, the international fun capital of Dead Heads everywhere.

"You mean you can buy sex in a store?" He sounded flatly astonished or morally offended—hard to tell which.

"A window is more like it."

On the theory that honesty is the best policy and the realization that this was probably as good a time and place as any to have a frank floor discussion on a couple subjects that were maybe even a little overdue, I clarified how the good citizens of Amsterdam believed taking mind-altering drugs was a person's God-given right, and they would rather have the junkies out in the open than lurking in dark alleyways mugging tourists. For that reason there were cannabis stores on almost every street corner. As for sex, I plunged ahead, you could hire the sexual services of a woman the same way you hired a bicycle for an afternoon's ride, and there were even a couple neighborhood blocks devoted entirely to the peddling of human flesh, the largest red light district in the world. For what it was worth, I amplified, reaching for some kind of historical coda, these were direct legacies of Amsterdam's seagoing prowess and social permissiveness, too.

"Dad," he said with a sly smile, sensing my modest discomforture. "You don't have to be embarrassed. I *know* about drugs and sex."

"Really? I'm not embarrassed."

"Well, you're kind of red . . ."

"That's only because I'm sore at you for talking to strangers at the train station, Boss. If you hadn't done that, I wouldn't be so embarrassed that you probably know more about sex and drugs than I do."

Mind, dear reader, I'm no dirt road prude. I love sex as much as the next red-blooded American male. Sex with the woman you love, as our Canadian neighbors on the train would no doubt corroborate, is a beautiful thing indeed.

But as I hoped should now be perfectly obvious to Jack, sex in Maine was one thing and sex in Amsterdam was something else entirely. In a nutshell, sex in Maine involves a complex mating ritual of monosyllabic communication and years of no body contact whatsoever between potential consenting pairs, followed by prolonged periods of critical mutual scrutiny—seeing if your prospective mate can, say, tear down a chainsaw or bait a decent hook completely barehanded at the height of ice fishing season, that sort of thing. If everything clicks and you're not particularly picky about small stuff like the love of your life missing fingers or visibly having more gum than teeth, you romantically go off together on the back of a borrowed snowmobile to an unheated shack near the Canadian border at the height of a January blizzard to snuggle under an old LL Bean blanket and see if one thing leads to another. Assuming you don't freeze to death, you're officially ready to move on to the next stage of intimacy in Maine: holding gloved hands and telling naughty French Canadian jokes. It can take years of this sort of thing before a prospective suitor sees or touches anything resembling human flesh. And people marvel that the population of Maine is actually shrinking.

Sex in Amsterdam, on the other hand, simply involves picking up a handy brochure as you arrive at the central train station.

"Do you think maybe we could see the red light district or something?" he wondered innocently. Or not. "That might be kind of weird. I'd like to tell Andrew about it."

"Maybe so, after we see the Vermeers and Rembrandts," I replied, then artfully noted that the Dutch invented oil painting and were probably the greatest landscape painters of all time. Among other things, I added, hoping to elevate the conversation to a higher plane, they developed something called chiaroscuro, which meant the interplay of light and shade, a revolutionary concept in landscape painting.

"Cool," he pronounced and, budding artist and young man of the world that he was fast becoming, glanced out the tram window to see if there was anybody else who looked like somebody he knew from back home peddling Dutch landscapes or smut clubs on the sidewalk.

Our room in the basement of the elegant Hotel des Filosoofs, which is apparently Dutch for "The Philosophers" but sounds like a toddler trying to speak French, was a black-and-white affair named in honor of Zen Buddhism: twin beds with stark black-and-white bedspreads, a jolly black Buddha statue nailed to the wall, blinding white walls, a jet black phone, even a black-and-white checkerboard shower curtain.

Speaking of chiaroscuro, Jack loved the place on sight, but alas, I wasn't in that stark two-tone monk's cell of a room a full Amsterdam minute before I felt the walls creeping in on us and panicked like a color-blind Buddhist locked in Father Rembrandt's basement. We had to either get out until darkness fell or else trek back upstairs and ask the friendly woman on the front desk for the Karl Marx Suite done up in pretty Soviet Army red. She'd wondered, as we checked in, if we were maybe in town for the big organized protest against Amsterdam's liberal drug laws. The protest, she explained, was a popular backlash due to the city's recent alarming rise in theft and petty crime. "Families from all over the Netherlands have come here this weekend, you see, to say enough is enough, eh? If everybody has *too* much, darling, nobody has anything. You know what I'm saying?"

I'd nodded dumbly, while Jack fiddled with another brochure, trying to digest the philosophical gist of her argument, which I think I agreed with.

In any case, it was too late to visit the Rijksmuseum so I suggested to Nibs that we grab our baseball mitts and make a beeline for the Vondelpark for a little exercise and throwing practice, after which we could go grab some authentic Dutch grub in the Leidseplein and watch the passing parade of party animals and protesting families into the night.

Down the leafy residential street off the busy Overtoom we went, tossing the ball back and forth and horsing around like a couple Little Leaguers on the lam. Jack kept glancing up at the quaint narrow Dutch row houses and I tried to remember why it was I'd found Amsterdam so disagreeable way back in the year of the Bicentennial garbage can. I'd just dropped out of graduate school because I was still puzzled and angry at *somebody* beyond belief that my girlfriend Kristin had been killed, so with my father's blessing (and the copy of *The Hobbit* he gave me for the road) I'd taken off with my golf bag to wander the Old World the way Kris and I had talked about doing many times, perhaps thinking that would give me some much needed answers, or at least some time and space to try and figure things out. After having my golf bag swiped on a train from the south of France, I'd stopped off in Amsterdam en route to Scotland, hoping to see the Rembrandts that had so delighted my old man thirty years before me—only to discover that the Rembrandts had gone to Paris for an extended exhibition. Short on funds, I billeted for two long nights in a grim five-floor walk-up off the Leidseplein where the walls made worrying noises and someone kept shouting angrily in German. I left town on an early morning train in a heavy September downpour, not having spoken to a soul in the Venice of the North.

"Hey, Dad," Nibs thoughtfully interrupted this pointless woolgathering, "have you ever heard of Roy G. Biv?"

Rog G. Biv, I thought. Was he, like, I dunno, some lesser-known Dutch landscape painter or possibly a filosoof? Maybe he was a firebrand in charge of the big family smut and drug protest?

"Sorry, Boss. Haven't a clue."

Jack smiled, snagging a pitch and side-arming the ball back to me, more Ripkin than Martinez. A woman pushing a perambulator paused and stared at us from across the street.

"No. It's an acronym for the visible light spectrum."

"Oh. Right. How stupid of me."

He explained that each letter of *Roy G. Biv* corresponded to the name of a primary color that was visible when light radiated through a standard glass prism. The primary colors were red, orange, yellow, green, blue, indigo, and violet. Hence Roy G. Biv.

"Get it?"

"I do now. That's pretty useful information to have."

Maybe our brief talk about the Dutch Masters and chiaroscuro had him thinking about a career in art. Wait till he got an eyeful of Jan Vermeer's *Lady in Blue* and the maiden pouring milk at the Rijksmuseum. As I looked back on that crazy time in my grief-addled odyssey, I recalled that those paintings had unexpectedly been the one positive aspect of my strange brief passage through town a quarter century ago, perhaps explaining why I'd been more of a Vermeer fan than a Rembrandt guy ever since.

"For example," he said, "when you see your favorite color green, do you really know what you're seeing?"

"A park?" I ventured, wondering if the quiet residential street we were scraping along would in fact lead us into the famous Vondelpark, which appeared to be on the other side of a seriously imposing iron fence that seemed meant to repel a cavalry charge. Through the thick green foliage, though, I saw lots of people lolling about on the grass— lying on blankets, petting dogs, wandering along stone paths, throwing Frisbees, and doing whatever urban Dutch people do on a perfect late summer afternoon.

"Well, what you're really seeing is the *absence* of all the other colors. Or maybe I should say it this way—all the other colors absorb the light except green, the color you're seeing, which reflects its light back to you. That's why you're seeing green."

"No kidding."

I thanked my son for the highly useful knowledge and told him he really was my father's grandson after all, a font of unexpectedly helpful details of life. For example, if I may digress a bit, I fondly recall the time he helpfully informed me during a lull in the action at Fenway Park, as I prepared to go find the public facilities, that a recent comprehensive study by the American Toilet Manufacturers Association had determined that the first stall in any public rest room accommodation is on average fifty to seventy percent cleaner than the adjoining toilet stalls, which really gives a bloke something to think about before he picks a seat. You can never get enough of this sort of travel wisdom, I find.

The park, I noticed, wasn't getting any closer. But I saw a woman suddenly come out of a handsome brick church and decided to see if someone in there could tell us if there was an entrance anywhere ahead. I loped up the steps of the church and yanked open the heavy wooden door and discovered a young man seated at a computer. He blinked at me and I smiled like a lost Nebraskan at him.

"Excuse me," I said, speaking slowly, in case he didn't understand the queen's English, "does this street lead into the Von-del-park?"

"We have no public rest rooms," he said curtly, in very good English, continuing to tap keys pertly.

"I don't want a bathroom, thanks," I replied. "I just wanted to know how to get into the park."

"That is the Vondelpark, yes," he said irritably, nodding briskly toward the frothy vegetation beyond the fence across the street. *Tap, tap, tap* went his keys as I palely loitered, looking around to see if there was anybody else in the room who might be either willing or able to help us. There was nobody . . . although I did suddenly see a familiar face. She was on this guy's computer screen, of all things, hectoring some chump about stiffing his landlord out of apartment rent. Judge Judy was also in Amsterdam that afternoon, via the Internet, prompting me to think, not for the first time, what a strange and unexpected place this world your children and mine will inherit has become thanks to rampant media technology, a global community that seems weirdly smitten with America's most dubious achievements. I'd recently read in the *New York Times*, for example, that a particularly virulent group of Middle Eastern terrorists are seriously addicted to Hollywood action films and the kind of American talk show where the guests usually wind up hurling chairs at each other. They worship Sly, Arnold, and Steven Seagal. For what it's worth, they also fancy Pizza Hut, MTV, and Britney Spears—but then again, I guess, so does Bob Dole. They apparently just don't like the other annoying things we (and Bob) stand for as a collective free people—the right to free and unfettered expression of dissenting talk radio stations, the constitutional right to choose your own religion and pizza topping, and so forth.

"Yes?" The *Judge Judy* fan glanced up and frowned at me. He seemed intensely annoyed to discover I was still with him. Perhaps it was almost time for *Oprah*.

"Hi," I said. "I'm sorry to be such a pest. If you don't mind me asking, how do we actually get *in* to the park?"

He released a lengthy, exasperated sigh.

"There is an entrance just ahead. This is a computer store, if you please."

"Oh. Right. Sorry. I thought it was a church."

"No. We are a *private* computer store."

Oh well, I thought as I slunk away, *at least I've finally spoken to the locals*.

Back outside, I found Jack waiting and staring worriedly up at one of Amsterdam's adorable leaning row houses, which appeared to be about to topple forward into the street and was actually shored up with large wooden poles.

"Whoa," he said, pointing to it, "Look at that . . ."

I used the opportunity to explain that Amsterdam was an engineering marvel built on a marsh reclaimed from the sea, protected by a series of friendly dikes, which were not to be confused with the girls on the train, which not only explained why there were dozens of pretty canals but also why so many of the houses tilted one way or another. As I recalled from my previous lonely wanderings about the Venice of the North, which lies something like ten feet below sea level, that's why so many structures had gigantic oversized windows in them—more glass, less weight. All that marshy ground underfoot was also why wooden clogs had been cleverly invented, so Dutch farmers wouldn't sink in the muck.

"Cool," Jack said, having learned something from me for a change. "What's that big hook for up there?"

He meant, of course, the colorful block and tackle jutting from the gabled roof lines of roughly every other house along the block.

"Oh, those," I said nonchalantly, resuming our walk toward a gate where, indeed, I saw young people on bikes rolling out of the Vondelpark. "That's where they hang annoying foreigners who ask where the public rest room is located."

The blood drained a bit from my Lost Boy's cute little face. His mouth fell open in shock. Someday, I was sure going to miss being able to pull his leg so easily.

"Nah, I'm joking," I said and quickly explained to him that those hooks were really how the ever-industrious Dutch folks got baby grand pianos and designer sofas and stuff to the upper floors of their quaint little buildings.

Amsterdam's largest park, when we finally got into the place, was crammed with sun worshipers of every stripe, every possible gender and voter registration, a true People's Republic of personal lifestyle choices and commendable Dutch egalitarianism. There were *so* many people loafing about doing nothing, in fact, we had to walk the length of the darn thing just to locate a decent grassy patch where nobody was sunning, smoking, sleeping, making out, drinking designer water, listening to a Walkman, talking on a cell phone, writing a manifesto, or plucking on a guitar. Finally, between a group of sunbathers with their tops off and some older teenagers playing soccer, we found sixty feet of unoccupied grass near one of the park's larger ponds, not far from a stage where some sad long-haired dudes, who looked as if they came directly to Amsterdam from my old college dormitory, were tuning up electric guitars for some kind of early evening rock concert. I half expected to see the Canadian backpackers toking up for the show.

Instead, I crouched and thumped my mitt.

"Start easy. Remember your papa is aging by the minute," I said to Nibs, still feeling the pain of my foolish leap in Glastonbury.

He grinned and looped an ineffectual pitch into the dirt. The ball struck me on the shin and, jeez, really hurt.

"Very funny. A little harder than *that*, if you please. Hit the mitt, Pedro. Not me."

"Sorry."

The next throw was a strike, pertly snapping the leather. I saw an older woman watching us with gentle bewilderment from a nearby folding chair, knitting something beneath a cloud of frizzy gray hair, perhaps wondering what a bizarre new way of loafing we'd imported to her country.

Another pitch hit the target. The ball went back and forth several times, each time getting faster and stronger. Jack always threw better when he was loose and happy, and he seemed very loose and happy now. Perhaps he was looking forward to sleeping in our bleak Zen Buddhist monks' cell back at the Filosoofs.

"Can I try a fastball?"

"I thought that was a fastball."

"No, I mean a *really* fast one . . ."

"Okay. Just remember the lessons of Zen and successful dinner speaking. Less is more. Nice and easy."

He wound up and threw another fine pitch that sharply popped the leather and tingled my hand. Move over, Pedro Martinez. Nibs the Nasty is on his way to Pawtucket.

"What exactly *is* Zen?"

I explained to him that Zen was a form of disciplined meditation practiced mostly in the Far East and parts of Cambridge, Massachusetts, that stressed that consciousness was genuine but material objects weren't, therefore it was pointless to get upset when something didn't go your way. People who practiced Zen aimed for satori or sudden enlightenment, and a good friend who taught Zen was always quoting Zen Buddhist sages who said peculiar things like cracked objects were how the light got in. Not knowing was knowing. Losing the way was finding it. Good pitching will always beat good hitting—and so forth. Or maybe I was thinking of Earl Weaver.

"So forget trying to hit the mitt and you'll throw a strike. That's the message, Ace."

"Right."

He made a beautiful windup and threw the ball four feet over my head. I turned in time to see the ball bounce twice on the grass, skitter across part of the gravel footpath, pass between two couples lollygagging on a blanket, and roll up to a bare-chested dude reposing on a bath towel by the edge of the weed-choked pond. It bumped into his shoulder gently and stopped.

Jack immediately loped after it. As he approached, though, the sun-bather sat up and removed his Walkman earphones, picked up the ball and tossed it into the shallows of the pond.

I couldn't believe what I had just seen, so I started that way, too. Jack looked completely flummoxed by what had happened, uncertain what to do next. I walked straight past him toward the bearded dude, who'd safely clamped his Walkman back on and lain back down to boogie.

"Excuse me," I said to him. "that was my son's ball . . ."

The man, who was probably ten years younger and forty pounds lighter than I, opened his eyes, glared up at me, and then closed them again.

I used the toe of my Maine-made boat shoe to politely nudge his shoulder and he opened his eyes a second time, shielded them with one hand, and lifted an earphone with the other.

"Hey," I said, hoping it was an honest mistake on his part. I mean, maybe he'd never seen a baseball and thought it was, I dunno, a new kind of doughnut with laces somebody had thrown to the ducks. "That was our baseball you threw in the water."

He said something sharply to me in Dutch. It sounded like *Your sister makes great homemade pickles. I wish she would loan me her unicycle Tuesday.* Dutch basically sounds like a made-up language to me.

The woman who had been watching us a few minutes earlier hap-pened to be making her way out of the park, with her chair and knit-ting. She overheard this confusing exchange and helpfully paused and straightened me out. "He said you should not be playing that sort of thing here. This is a public park where people are resting."

I stared at the woman in disbelief. She smiled sweetly at Jack. The man put on his earphones and lay back down, ignoring me for a third time in less than one minute. Then he opened his eyes and glared bale-fully up at me.

"Go away now," he said in unmistakably clear English.

Jack was watching intently to see what I would do next. The older I get, the more I really do aspire to practice the principles of spiritual tolerance and good humor I preached to the well-dressed doomsayer outside Glastonbury Abbey. But looking down at this coconut oil–coated creep it was tough to tell if there was really a spark of the divine in him or if he was merely another totally absorbed Dutch bung hole getting a suntan. Thus, I stood there for a lengthy moment trying to decide what Judge Judy would do in this situation—whether to simply ignore his arrogant rudeness and go on our transcendental way or give in to the impulse to pick up this scrawny dude by his Walkman wires and toss his scrawny butt into the pond after our baseball.

I decided on an approach Judge Judy might well have approved of, and calmly said to the lady, "Would you kindly tell our friend here I wish I had a pair of real Dutch wooden shoes so I could put them on and kick him in the head?"

Jack, loyal boy that he is, laughed at this solution. The lady smiled, too, but shook her head. "I can't tell him that. He will call a policeman if you are not careful. You see, there are many rights here."

"Oh. Right. Rights. I forgot."

Suddenly, the proprietor's words back at the Filosoofs took on fresh relevance. *If everybody has too much, darling, nobody has anything, eh?*

"C'mon Jack," I said, deciding to listen to the angel of my better self after all, or at least be filosoof-ical about the bizarre encounter. I searched the pond for our ball and spotted it bobbing a few yards offshore in a flotsam of discarded plastic bottles and other garbage collecting in the scummy shallows. Without further ado, I marched directly into the pond and picked it up, wondering if my next stop ought to be a local clinic for a shot of antibiotics, or at least a nice long boiling shower back in our black-and-white Buddhist accommodation.

"Why did that guy do that?" Jack wanted to know as we exited the park and angled back down the empty residential street so I could at least change out of my squishy boat shoes for supper. We were passing the adorably leaning house again.

"I don't know, Boss," I replied, hoping there might be a useful little lesson in this episode for us both. I just wasn't entirely sure yet what it was.

I placed my arm around his slim shoulders and pointed to the poles holding up one side of the tilting house. "They always say you should put yourself in somebody else's place," I said. "Maybe his house fell over and he has to sleep in the park or something."

*   *   *

In honor of Jack's mother's thirty-ninth birthday, which was the next morning, a Friday, I proposed an ambitious final day exploring the Venice of the North: a morning bike ride around the famous inner ring of canals, followed by an evening boat ride through them. Along the way we could hunt for an unusual birthday gift to send Jack's mom, take in the Anne Frank House, maybe even sneak a naughty peek at the red light district so Jack would have something interesting to tell Andrew Tufts about when he gŏt home from the road. I decided we would save a visit to the Rijksmuseum and the glorious Vermeers for last.

"Awesome," Jack enthusiastically agreed. We were having breakfast on the Philosophers' pretty sun-splashed porch. "But can we maybe get something else to eat on the bike ride?"

Dutch breakfast—plain yogurt, dull brown muselli, a hard-boiled egg, a chunk of aged Gouda, and cold toast—didn't seem to agree with Jack very much.

"I haven't pooped since England," he confided in a low voice. "I think it's this food or something."

"Right," I said, putting down my napkin and pushing back my chair. "We'll find a market and get some nice juicy prunes. That'll fix you up."

Jack hadn't been on a bike since about fifth grade, but I hadn't been on one since Gerry Ford was falling down the steps of Air Force One. Whoever said you never really forget how to ride a bike clearly never tried riding a rental bike in Amsterdam.

To begin with, on any given day, half a million people ride bikes through the narrow streets of the city, most of them at breakneck speed, ringing these annoying little handlebar bells—*ching ching*—that warn pedestrians, unsuspecting tourists, stray animals, and visiting rubes like me to stay bloody well out of their way or else.

Jack seemed to grasp this Darwinist principal of bike travel right off the bat, zooming effortlessly ahead with little or no visible difficulty into a stream of commuting bikes flowing handsomely over an arched bridge into the Central Canal Ring and along the picturesque Singel-gracht. I trailed farther behind with each passing minute, furiously pedalling the tiny bicycle I'd been issued in a hopeless effort to try to catch up with him, desperately trying to remember exactly which gear was which, while keeping my only known son on the planet safely in view.

In the space of just three or four blocks, regrettably, I nearly got flattened by a tram and was furiously honked at by several passing motorists, a couple of whom stuck their heads out of their windows and said things that didn't really sound like, *Hey, Lumpy, welcome to Amsterdam!*

Even worse, a bus ran me up the curb into a crowded sidewalk café where some nice people were just having their morning caffe latte and reading the newspaper. This embarrassment was followed by a small pileup I guess I caused at a green traffic signal near the Prinsengracht when I thought I spotted Jack waiting for me just up ahead and confused my brake handle for my gear handle, abruptly screeching to a halt and nearly doing a somersault over my own handlebars onto the pavement. This prompted an angry flurry of *ching ching*s and several more Dutch Reformed greetings and a worrying crunch of metal somewhere behind me. I pedaled away as quickly as I could on my tiny bike.

"Sorry to hold you up," I said, panting dangerously, when I finally caught up to Nibs near the Anne Frank House. I noticed that Anne's house wasn't yet open but the admission line already stretched nearly a block in length. "I think that guy gave me a bike meant for Hobbits."

"Really? You can have mine if you want . . ."

"Nah. I think I'm getting the hang of it. Short strokes. Avoid gears."

I glanced at the queuing line—a two-hour wait, easily—and pulled out the folding street map which was already soaked with my sweat.

"Let's go look at the Nieuwe Kerk. I think it's . . . *that* way."

We pedaled down the Raadhuisstraat to the Spuistraat, which I challenge even any sober visiting American tourist to pronounce properly, crossed several charming arched canal bridges, and came to the largest outdoor chessboard I'd ever seen.

"Dad, can we play?" Jack was reigning ten-and-under chess champion of Bowdoin Day Camp. I hated to have to admit to him that his old man didn't have a clue how to play chess. It was one of those things like learning the constellations or the metric system or dating

Sigourney Weaver that I simply hadn't gotten around to yet in life. Besides, there seemed to be eight or nine guys waiting in line, ready to take on the winner. We could be there until nightfall.

"Maybe we'll buy one of those little travel chess sets and you can teach me," I proposed to him.

"Great," he agreed, looking as if he'd barely broken a sweat in the Dutch heat and traffic turmoil. I, on the other hand, was nearly an exhausted, nervous wreck.

On we pedaled to even more congested Dam Square, where we briefly parked our wheels on the steps of the Nieuwe Kerk and slipped inside to take a quick peek at Amsterdam's second parish church, if only to make sure it hadn't been transformed into a big computer warehouse or art cinema. Golly, what an interior! The carved pulpit looked like the prow of the *Golden Hind,* and some unseen prodigy was practicing Bach on the church's magnificent pipe organ, giving us a private concert and a vivid sense of why, as someone said, pipe organs really are the most powerful things on earth that don't blow up and kill people.

Suddenly, I remembered that I'd failed to lock our bikes. The clerk back at the rental shop had been very clear on this subject. People swipe bikes in Amsterdam, apparently, the same way customers help themselves to toothpicks in southern barbecue joints. I guess they feel it's their *right.* Sex-related crime might be down, but bike theft remains something of a growth industry in the Venice of the North.

Anyway, I was relieved to see we hadn't become just another petty crime statistic, and we decided to push on through the square and pedaled around a corner, crossed another quaint canal full of garbage, and found ourselves back by the city's busy Central train station, trams and bicycles flying madly in every direction, car horns bleating, more unwashed backpackers arriving to do fun things their parents would mercifully never hear a peep about.

"Dad, can we get some lunch?"

"Sure. Let's go over there," I said, pointing across the urban mayhem to a quieter district that turned out to be on the edge of Amsterdam's infamous red light area. I didn't quite realize this at the time, though, because that part of my street map had fully disintegrated through the body sweat of my hip pocket.

We pedaled rapidly across the wide square, dipped down a narrow street crowded with pedestrians, turned a corner or two in search of a decent-looking café, and suddenly there it was—everything you wanted to know about the human anatomy and several things you didn't.

"Please keep up," I called sharply over my shoulder to Nibs as we pedaled past a gauntlet of neon sex shops and the famous madams in their boxy curtained windows. Fortunately the tourist crowds here were so thick we had to keep our eyes on the road lest we flatten some Shriner from Ocala and his wife.

"Hey, Dad, what's *that?*" Jack called out excitedly, pointing to something huge and pink sitting in a window display where a group of retired geology teachers from Cleveland were posing for a group photo.

"I think that's the world's largest plastic vagina, son."

We pedaled rapidly on, crossing over a narrow canal, passing the famous Hash Marihuana Hemp Museum, slipping over into a mercifully duller neighborhood, and soon found ourselves smack dab in front of Rembrandt van Ryn's old *haus*, leaning romantically over the River Amstel, which some American hicks really think is named for a famous American light beer.

The queue there, alas, was almost as long and slow-moving as the one at the Anne Frank House. But we stopped anyway, so I could catch my breath and try and get my bearings and figure out how the heck we got to the Rijksmuseum. If I recalled from the map that had fully disintegrated in my pants, all we had to do was follow the Amstel south for a bit more and then hang a left on the next canal, whose name I couldn't begin to pronounce . . .

We did this and came out, suddenly and rather magically, onto the Magere Brug, Amsterdam's most charming wooden drawbridge, supposedly named for two sisters who lived on either side of the River Amstel. A few minutes later, we were standing amid gorgeous cut flowers and luscious fruit bins in the busy Albert Cuypmarkt, the famous outdoor marketplace where the locals buy everything from kumquats to bike locks.

"Maybe we could send Mom flowers for her birthday," Jack suggested, after we safely locked our bikes and set out to explore the various stalls and funky shops on foot.

"I don't think flowers will keep," I said to him as we wandered into a junk shop cluttered with heaps of really swell stuff—an English diving suit, lots of old Victorian street lamps, plus an impressive array of Medieval weapons and chain restraints that probably went over big with the Amsterdam sex club crowd.

"Maybe she'd like her very own crossbow," I suggested, hefting a dusty implement of death to my shoulder and taking imaginary aim at the bearded guy leaning on a bridge railing.

"Yeah," he agreed, "or *this* . . . !" He held up a mace which appeared to have vivid traces of dried human blood on it, perfect for the lady executive intent on breaking through the corporate glass ceiling—or, as in Jack's mummy's case, the papal intrigues of the college administration where she worked.

We poked around in that place for the better part of an hour, I must admit, carefully considering various kinds of hooked daggers, hammered body armor, matching fencing masks, and a really nifty Norman helmet that would probably get Jack's mama noticed straightaway at the next annual meeting of the college's board of governors.

"I think we're probably thinking of ourselves instead of her," I finally had to say. "Maybe we can find something she'd like better at the museum gift shop."

"Okay," Jack agreed, reluctantly putting back a gigantic broadsword he'd been swinging with both hands. It looked large enough to lop off multiple heads. "But can I get this?"

It was the Glastonbury Watusi drum problem all over and I could just picture us trying to get that medieval death instrument through customs or onto an airplane. So I said what any reasonable parent would have said.

"We'll discuss it at lunch."

At a crowded café in the nearby Rembrandtplein, Jack ordered a Coke and a grilled cheese. The waitress brought him a hamburger and a flagon of brown beer. I ordered a Heineken and the daily special asparagus omelet. She brought me a ham sandwich and a ginger ale. Perhaps there was a slight problem with translation—or maybe it was simply that Amsterdam wasn't a whole lot friendlier than I remembered it being.

"I'll eat yours," Jack cheerfully volunteered, so we swapped plates and beverages.

I thanked him and admitted to him that Amsterdam's charms were beginning to wane on me ever so slightly. In the morning, I proposed, perhaps we should mosey on down the road in the rental car Dame Wendy had thoughtfully reserved us and see what other trouble we could get into in the rest of the Old World.

"Sounds good," he agreed, biting into my former sandwich. "Which way do you want to go?"

"I don't know," I said. "You pick. This is your trip."

"What's north of here?"

I thought for a moment and came up with Norway, Denmark, Viking ships, attractive blond Swedish golfers, front doors painted a cheerful blue, Lutherans, and reindeer. Personally, I would have loved to have gone that way. I understand the food is supposed to be world class in Stockholm, wherever it was from here.

"What about east?"

That way, I said, more or less, is Germany: the famous Rhine River, tasty sausages and good beer, the rainy streets of Berlin, dusky-voiced cabaret singers, the old Third Reich, Brandenburg's Gate, and Bach's cantatas. If you went far enough that direction, I guess, you ran smack dab into Mother Russia and the boys in the Kremlin. Wouldn't *that* be something to tell good old Andy Tufts back home?

"Oh yeah," he agreed, knocking back the last of his ginger ale. "So what's, like, south of here?"

Belgium and France, I replied. Chivalrous knights, the tapestry at Bayeaux, the beaches of Normandy, the streets of Paris, Brie cheese, good wine, great bread. A theme was definitely emerging here. You can never have enough of a good time in France, I pointed out. Besides, we had a hotel reservation there for Bastille Day.

"Let's go that way," he said, as if there really weren't much of a decision to make after all.

"You sure? This is *our* trip. We can go wherever we want, Boss . . ."

"I know. But I'd like to see France. Isn't Wendy meeting us there?"

"No. That's Italy in two more weeks. Frankly, I've lost track of time. I think you'll like Italy. For one thing, if they get your lunch order screwed up, it won't matter a bit. The food is unbelievable and the women are really beautiful. But don't take my word for it. Or tell Wendy I said that."

After lunch, we pedaled to the Rijksmuseum to see the Vermeers.

But wouldn't you know it, all thirty-two of Vermeer's famous paintings housed there had recently been shipped to London for an extended exhibition at the Tate, yet another sign from the gods that it was time to vacate the Venice of the North for a second time in less than thirty years. Talk about déjà vu, man . . .

Luckily the Rembrandts were back in town, so we checked them out in the vast, empty, echoing corridors of the Rijksmuseum and then hoofed on to the Van Gogh Museum to see the artist's bedroom at Arles and other stuff the tortured man painted before he completely lost his mind and at least one ear. Jack was keen to see *Starry Night,* but the painting on display turned out to be only a replica of the original, which is apparently kept at a museum somewhere in Manhattan.

"Dad," Jack whispered as we stood looking at it anyway. "I have to go."

"I know," I agreed. "It's no fun looking at a replica."

"No. I mean . . ." He lowered his voice and glanced furtively around. "I have to *poop!*"

"Really? That's wonderful!" I declared, probably a little louder than I should have in the somewhat crowded gallery. Our taxing bike ride had done some good, after all.

While he was busy in the museum bathroom, I checked out the peddler's stall in front of the museum and found a nice silk scarf with *Starry Night* silk-screened on it.

When he appeared a few moments later, smiling like his old unburdened self, Jack agreed with me that his mom would probably love it.

The guy who took back our rental bikes, on the other hand, wasn't pleased with what I'd allegedly done to his bicycle.

"This bell is broken, you will have to pay for it," he said, flicking a bell that didn't make a sound.

I explained to him that I'd never even tried the bell. Several of his irascible countrymen, on the other hand, hadn't hesitated to use their nasty little bells on me, I pointed out.

"You will still have to pay for the bell," he said, quickly writing out an additional thirty bucks on my Amex card receipt. He ripped it off and presented it to me with a grunt.

While this unpleasant exchange was taking place, Jack was busy performing farewell figure eights on his bike in the little courtyard where a couple lanky Dutch guys were working on other bicycles. I got the feeling he hated to give up his wheels.

"Hey, Nibs," I called to him. "Time to go, son. We've got to get a move on if you want to take a boat ride."

"Yes, sir," he called back, doing a valedictory loop around the court-yard.

As he passed the chaps on the bench, I heard one of them remark, "Mind your father, you little snot-nosed shit. Turn in your bike *now*."

Jack stopped and got off his bike, looking a little startled. He walked past the men and handed his bike to the clerk, who *ching*ed the bell, grunted satisfactorily, and pushed it away. Then Jack came over to where I was standing and trying to decide if I'd had about enough of a city where people apparently have too much of everything, except perhaps civility to strangers.

Talk about déjà vu, it was the Vondelpark incident all over again. This time, regrettably, I chose not to listen to the angel of my better self. I walked over to where the two guys were sitting fiddling with bikes.

"Hey, Slick," I said calmly to the one who'd spoken to Jack. "Why don't you apologize to my son and then we'll all be best friends again."

He glanced at his buddy and laughed. Both of them smiled as if they couldn't believe what a bung hole I was to propose such a silly thing.

"I was joking him, man," he allowed, glancing with smirky indiffer-ence at Jack, who was visibly on guard. "I guess he can't take a joke or something?"

"He probably can," I admitted pleasantly. "But I probably can't."

I waited a moment more and added, as nicely as possible, "Better yet, why don't you stand up and shake his hand. That way he'll know it's coming from the heart."

"Dad," Jack said, "it's okay . . ."

The guy thought about it a moment, staring worriedly up at me. After a few more moments, he tossed away his cigarette and stood up, limply putting out his hand to Jack.

Later that night, as our tram was rumbling past the noisy Leidseplein onto the Overtoom, carrying us from our boat ride through the canals back home to Des Filosoofs, Jack yawned and leaned into my side.

"Dad," he said drowsily, "what would you have done if that guy at the bike shop hadn't stood up and apologized to me?"

"I don't know," I admitted—though, in fact, I did.

I replied that I sincerely hoped I would have had the intelligence to shrug it off and walk away. That would be the civilized thing to do, under the circumstances, what the smarter man would do. Regrettably, in this instance, though, I'm afraid I probably would have helped the jerk to his feet and "encouraged" him to do the right thing. Fathers are human, too, and this one still didn't practice everything he preached.

"Do you *like* Amsterdam?" he wondered sleepily, as we jolted down the darker Overtoom.

"Not particularly," I confessed, yawning myself. It was way past our regular bedtime back home in Maine. Next time I came to Holland, I added, I'd probably stick to the countryside, where a rube like me belonged.

"Tell you what. Let's go visit Belgium and see what's there."

"Okay."

EIGHT

Good Beer

A fascinating item in the *International Herald-Tribune* caught my attention. A famous Trappist monastery located on a tributary of the River Schelde just outside the ancient Flemish capital of Ghent was hauling a large Belgian commercial poultry company to court seeking compensatory damages for alleged improper disposal of its chicken wastes.

The pending suit claimed, among other things, that nitrate levels from chicken manure runoff had contaminated the area's local watershed so severely that the sacred tributary water monks had relied on for over three hundred years for brewing was being "significantly and dangerously altered in taste and composition." The monastery's somewhat hip-sounding abbot summed up the nature of the complaint: "We view this as a serious threat to both our livelihood and our spiritual heritage. If we do not undertake some kind of legal action on behalf of the water, our product may begin to taste, well, a little *different*."

Reading this, I sipped my Belgian ale and considered how, as beers went, this one really was a superior brew—as dark as Tennessee molasses, fruity and full bodied yet peppery, as interesting as I'd ever tasted. I'm no expert on ale, mind you. When it comes to drinking beer and picking presidential candidates, I simply know what I like, and this one simply had that elusive extra *something* that made you think of, say, Al Gore down on the farm feeding the chickens and talking to himself about lock boxes and the unsigned Kyoto Environmental Accords.

"Did you realize," I remarked to Jack, who was busy writing in his journal and watching a Belgian garage band performing a loud but earnest cover of Bob Dylan's "Knockin' on Heaven's Door" at a crowded festival café in the square, "that *this* beer is older than the United States?"

He glanced at me skeptically, his pale eyebrows arching over his Coke and lemon.

After Amsterdam in the sun, Ghent in the rain had been a marvelous surprise. Two or so hours before, hoping to make it to beautiful Bruges (said to be the best-preserved Medieval city in Europe), we'd rolled through the ugly industrial suburbs of this famous nine-hundred-year-old Belgian river city, the windshield wipers on our cozy Volvo hatchback flapping energetically, only to discover a gorgeous old stone center city with a fairy-tale ornate town hall, dark cathedrals, intersecting bottle-green canals, charming neogothic row houses, and a thriving shopping district full of people bustling around in the rain over a cobbled square full of white tents with a dozen separate beer and food vendors beneath them and the aforementioned garage band tuning up on stage.

"You won't find a room, I'm afraid, in Bruges tonight, possibly not until the end of August," warned the friendly lady clerk at the Hotel Sint Jurishof (Saint Georges) after we pulled over and popped inside to casually inquire if there might be a reasonable twin available. She explained that Bruges was simply too postcard cute for its own good, overrun with wealthy German tourists who occupied every nook and cranny there until September. "Fifty years ago they came with tanks. Now they come with American Express cards," she said and cackled gently, checking her availability.

Luckily, she had a room for us and exchanged a skeleton key for our passports, noting that Ghent was the best kept secret in all of Belgium and the Sint Jurishof was the oldest functioning hotel in all of Europe. This unexpected tidbit, plus an excellent room rate, seemed a perfect reason to put down our rucksacks and go exploring.

After we tossed our bags into the room and hurried out beneath golf caps and parkas into the narrow rain-swept streets of the Korenmarkt around austere St. Baaf's Cathedral to investigate her claim, and see if we could discover what the heck would bring out so many folks in an unrelenting downpour, Jack had wanted to know what the woman had meant by "all that stuff about the Germans."

Ducking down a charming cobbled alley where there appeared to be one fabulous shop window after another, arrayed with spectacular *gateau des roi*, ranks of sculpted marzipan fruits, handmade toys, and richly draped tapestries which must have cost a small fortune, I explained to him that most of Belgium had been occupied by the German forces during the closing days of World War Two. The Belgians were devastated first by the invaders themselves, who—according to the historians I'd read (Keegan, Ambrose, Gilbert, and company)— massacred and terrorized civilian populations and leveled historic towns in order to subdue a population that had always been something of a Ping-Pong ball in European history, due to its strategic location. The country had been fought over, partitioned, and claimed at various intervals in the past five hundred years by Spanish, French, German, and Dutch powers, consumed by periods of bloody internal religious strife between Catholics and Protestants, and, finally, very nearly reduced to face powder by two world wars less than a generation apart.

Whatever the Nazis failed to destroy upon overrunning and occupying Belgium in 1940, America and her allies pretty well finished off when they pushed east after the Normandy invasion to liberate the country and drive the German occupiers back over the Rhine. Most Belgians, I pointed out to Jack—though I really didn't personally *know* any Belgians—were only a generation or so away from that terrible time, and it must add insult to injury, I speculated, to have the well-heeled children and grandchildren of Nazi soldiers who may have slaughtered your grandparents and burned their farms show up waving credit cards and asking which way, if you please, to the beer festival. It suddenly occurred to me why lovely Medieval Bruges was so popular with these kinder and gentler German invaders; it was one of the few places they hadn't destroyed.

Jack seemed to ponder this irony of history as the rain pelted on our golf caps and we skipped larkishly from bookshops to map sellers, took in a hand-puppet theater, downed hot tea and warm scones in a bustling patisserie with steamed-up windows, attempted without luck to calculate the rough exchange rate between Belgian francs and Dutch gilders, watched a magic show in a crowded square, got lost in a maze of extremely tidy stone streets and canal-framed plazas, where vendors were selling flowers and farm cheese the size of radial tires and couldn't have been nicer to shoot the breeze with, happy to elucidate Belgium's somewhat psychotic social history.

A ruddy-faced farmer selling cheese (who sold us a wedge large enough to stop a cathedral door from closing) explained, for example, that the country had *three* official languages and Belgium's Flemish north and Walloon south lay at the heart of much of the historic tension, because the Flemings were more Dutch in disposition and orientation (plainer in taste, lovers of art and architecture, city folk hoarding most of their wealth), whereas the Walloons to the south took their cultural cues from France (pretty villages, finer gastronomy, fewer stoplights, country bumpkins who made a mean foie gras and knew living well was the best revenge)—all in a country about the size of, say, Arkansas, if you can believe it. About the only thing your average Fleming and Walloon could really agree on, he added somewhat cagily, was that both sides made damn good beer and the Dutch and French were essentially arrogant imbeciles who wouldn't know when to come in out of the rain if their hats filled up with water.

Farther down the block, a tapestry seller named Hilda added another layer to the social intrigue by explaining that stately Ghent had once been one of the civilized world's first great industrial cities and the principal home of the European cloth trade and that serious shooting wars had erupted from time to time over, of all things, lace patents, tapestry designs, and discounted cloth, which may or may not have been a factor in the decision to sign the treaty ending America's War of 1812 there, so the visiting wives of the principal parties could do a little outlet shopping afterward. Given all the crap Belgians had survived, all I could think was how either perfectly reasonable or completely insane it was to have *these* people in charge of managing the European Union and phasing in use the much-maligned Euro, which was scheduled to replace EU member currencies at the stroke of midnight 2002 and was already in use on the streets of handsome Ghent, confusing visitors like us all the more.

Somewhat exhausted by this unexpected fund of knowledge, we pushed on with our cheese wedge through the maze of ancient rainy streets, only to discover, charmingly, as the rain suddenly ceased, that we'd somehow bumbled back to where we'd started from, Saint Baaf's looming over us, the sun's rays bobbing wetly out from behind rag-wool clouds, the air sweetened by the passing deluge, and large crowds filtering into the tented square where the band was cranking out Bob Dylan's "One Way Trip to the Promised Land." Soaked to the bone but much wiser about tiny Belgium, we joined the migration and snagged a small round table where someone had thoughtfully left a cigarette burning and a dry copy of the *Herald-Tribune.*

Hence, while Jack disposed of the ashtray and smoldering butt, I caught up on the news of the world, first noting the intriguing item about the chicken poop in the Trappist beer then learning that back on the home front singer Mariah Carey had suffered a mental break-down, the Dow and Nasdaq had collectively plunged another thou-sand points, the miserable Bosox had started their annual late-summer collapse a few weeks earlier than normal, and MTV was celebrating its twentieth anniversary. I pictured Middle Eastern terrorists everywhere glued to their TV sets, inhaling Domino's pizza by the boxload.

What a genuine pleasure it was, I suddenly and completely realized, to be traveling in a place where you didn't speak even one of the three official languages and couldn't fathom what sort of things you were *not* missing until you picked up an English newspaper and saw what truly mindless things folks were up to back home. For some reason there was no mention in the *Herald-Tribune* whatsoever about rainfall levels in Maine, so I assumed my garden at least was growing okay without me. No news is good news in gardening, as far as I'm concerned.

Anyway, that's more or less about the spot in this narrative where I made the crack about my beer being older than the United States, prompting Nibsy to look at me as if I'd been watching way too much late night television without proper adult supervision.

"I don't mean this *exact* beer is older than the United States," I am-plified, but merely that this *type* of beer had been around longer than our people had been a functioning republic. I pointed out to him that Belgians weren't just famous for making wheel cheese and lace and allowing Germanic hordes to occupy their beautiful country; they were also famous for the high quality of their beers and ales, which were produced in *hundreds* of hues, textures, and varieties and sometimes sold like expensive wine or champagne. I knew a Belgian tavern in lower Manhattan that sold something like 250 different varieties of Belgian beer and ale, for example, where I promised to take Jack someday when he was about to graduate college and had a nice six-figure job offer on the table, in which case he could buy the beer. In the meantime, I wondered if he wished to sample a small taste of my intriguing Belgian brew.

Jack glanced speculatively at the beer, which I guess was technically an ale. Then he glanced worriedly at me. Then at the beer again.

"I kind of would," he admitted. "But I'd better not."

"Why's that?"

He said he was afraid that Trooper Buchanan might find out he'd been in Belgium drinking beer. Trooper Buchanan was the female Maine State Patrol officer who taught the Drug Alcohol Resistance Education program at Woodside Elementary, of which Jack and his buddy Andy Tufts were recent honor graduates, a very nice lady in a somewhat unflattering wool uniform to whom you probably wouldn't wish to give any unnecessary lip if she pulled you over for doing forty through a school zone. She struck me as Maine's version of a Walloon policeman.

"I'm not suggesting you *drink* beer, Boss. I was merely offering you a small taste of something that's pretty unique."

I pointed out that there was some historical value to sampling my Trappist brew. After all, ale was by far the most popular drink of the Middle Ages, consumed by grown-ups and children alike, according to every credible source on domestic Medieval life, because it was much safer to drink beer than water in those faraway days, as the boiling and brewing process killed dangerous microbes and any unpleasant things left by thoughtless teens who washed out their delicates in the family water bucket. I'd recently read somewhere that one of the most common and treasured artifacts discovered in the ancient graves of highborn Anglo-Saxon women was, of all things, kitchen sieves—valued for their use in removing unsavory "things" from family beverages, usually their homemade beer.

"Okay," he relented and quickly picked up my glass and swallowed a sip of beer that a good-sized chickadee would have been proud of taking, narrowly glancing around to see if anybody was on an international cell phone direct to Trooper Buchanan's cruiser.

"So. What do you think?"

"Not bad. Tastes a little like chicken poop, though."

Actually, Jack didn't say this. I just made that part up. What he actually said was "Awesome. It's . . . really good. Well, sort of okay. I mean, to be honest, I don't really get why people *like* beer all that much. Even Belgian beer. I mean, do *you?*"

I smiled and explained that beer was definitely an acquired taste, best taken in thoughtful moderation, like German opera and French politics, something he should keep in mind when some popular ace with his papa's Buick offered him a Pabst tall boy to prove he was really a guy among guys.

Jack's sweetly unlined brow wrinkled ever so slightly. He asked what I meant by this.

"I mean, Boss, the day isn't far off when some kid who has more horsepower than brains will offer you beer or something stronger to see if you're cool enough to hang around with."

"Oh, you mean *peer* pressure," he replied in the language of DARE, nodding and washing away the taste of the beer with a slug of his Coke, a credit to the moral instructions of Chairwoman Buchanan. "Well, we learned all about that in DARE. I'll just say no."

He sounded so utterly certain about this it was possible to believe for a fleeting moment or two that he might really do it when the moment of truth arrived. In some ways, Jack was the most stubborn and iconoclastic kid I'd ever seen. He enjoyed (or at least didn't appear to mind) being a square peg in a round-holed world, a bit of an oddball, a different drummer. He didn't follow the pack or behave in a way calculated to earn him points with the in crowd, and he seemed, on the whole, oblivious to how or why anybody felt the need to trade friendship for popularity. I cherished this quality in him, for it would take him far and teach him much and probably earn him many heartbreaks and enduring friendships and more than a few laurel wreaths in life, unless I missed my guess entirely.

A good example of this was pretty Bethany Bellnap, the adorable little scamp who desperately hoped to trade up to a more popular kid and didn't hesitate to give dreamy old Jack the boot when the chance presented itself. The good news on that front was he seemed to be rapidly getting over his first real heartache, or at least putting it in safe perspective. I wished I could have said the same for me.

"Glad to hear it," I said, toasting such clearheaded thinking with a lofted pint of excellent beer. Since nobody was driving, I planned to have another.

"What I don't get," Jack said with distaste, glancing around at the happy festival crowd, "is why everybody in Europe smokes! Don't they know it's really bad for you?"

"Of course. They just don't care what you and Trooper Buchanan think."

I explained how people in Europe, as a rule, think Americans are ridiculously Puritan about little things like public cigarette smoking, strategic missile defense, and having clean public rest rooms. That's why they live in Europe and we live in America.

"Did you ever smoke?"

I admitted that I did—for two weeks back in college. My singular objective was to look like Jean-Paul Sartre to a certain shapely coed in the English department at East Carolina University. Instead, I looked like Timmy from the TV show *Lassie* sneaking a Pall Mall behind the barn. I didn't get the girl but I got a wicked sore throat. Then, luckily, I read that Arturo Toscanini smoked his first cigarette and kissed his first beautiful woman on the same night and promptly gave up smoking for life, hoping to get the girl. He did all right, going on to become one of Europe's most celebrated Lotharios.

"Did you get the girl?"

"Nope. She acted like I didn't even exist. That's as close as I ever got to being Jean-Paul Sartre."

A man seated at a table close by and obviously eavesdropping on us leaned forward and inquired, with touching formality and a briskly clipped accent, "Forgive me. You are Americans?"

He had bright round eyes and large gingery whiskers exploding like sofa springs from the side of his ruddy face, and happened to be sucking on a smoldering Meerschaum pipe, a sight you almost never see anymore in America thanks to clean-living tobacco Nazis like my son and Trooper Buchanan.

"Yes, sir," Jack dutifully answered.

"I thought so." He smiled. "You can always tell the Americans. They're the ones feeding beer to their children in Europe."

I realized he was German, perhaps one of those overbearing German tourists the clerk at the Sint Jurishof had warned about. I was tempted to say, *Oh,really, Adolph? Geez. You must be German. You can always tell the Germans because they're the ones visiting countries they formerly occupied with a crushing iron fist.*

But I didn't say this, of course. Being my polite son's father, I simply smiled back and said, "We were just thinking of firing up Cuban cigars. Care for one?"

"Really?" The man gazed at us with new respect.

"No, sir. He's always joking around," Jack felt compelled to reveal, blushing to prove it.

"You are touring Belgium then?" the man demanded, making it sound more like a direct command from Berlin than an innocent travel question.

I didn't try and deny it, adding that our delightful Belgian interlude would be sadly brief, however, because we hoped to push on and explore the Normandy coast before attacking Paris on Bastille Day, to tour the sewers and catch the fireworks along the Seine and whatnot. In retrospect, I guess *attacking Paris* wasn't the smartest thing to say to a German who probably thought Americans were a bunch of anti-smoking, missile-loving, clean-toilet weenies who ruined the Germans' shot at world domination back in 1944.

"I hope you already have a booking," he warned, making his pipe gurgle disgustingly. "I visited Paris once on Bastille Day. Complete madness."

The woman beside him suddenly spoke up. "Have you seen the Van Eyck altarpiece yet?" She wasn't smoking a pipe but owned the same gingery hair as he did, minus the sidewhiskers, plus a square, handsome, and ruddy face that resembled his. I wondered if they might be brother and sister or just a married couple who'd grotesquely grown to resemble each other the way pets and their owners or convicts sharing a prison cell for decades sometimes do.

I admitted that we hadn't seen the Van Eyck altarpiece yet, that we'd only been in town long enough to drop our bags at the Sint Jurishof and go hunting for beer and cheese. To be honest, I wasn't aware there was a Van Eyck altarpiece worth seeing anywhere around. For that matter, I wasn't sure what a Van Eyck altarpiece *was*.

"The Jurishof," the man said, "is the oldest hotel in Europe. Did you know? It once housed the Flanders Crossbow Maker's Guild."

"Cool," said Jack, briefly putting aside his concern about Germans— or so I thought.

"You should go see the Van Eyck," the woman persisted. "Thousands come great distances to see it. Some even have mystical experiences."

I said we would try and check it out before leaving Ghent. Then I asked them where they hailed from. I was fairly sure it wasn't Arkansas.

"My sister and I reside in Bonn," the man explained almost primly, offering me an American-style handshake. His name was Jurgen Koop and this was his sister Marta. She taught art history at an American extension university in Bonn and he ran a small custom printing shop in that city's suburbs.

"On your way to holiday in Bruges?" I guessed.

"Oh no. We are here to bury our mother, who passed away this week."

"I'm sorry," I said, feeling like a dolt who had just put his elbow in his beer, if not his shoe in his mouth.

"Not a problem," he said gravely. "She had been ailing for many years. It was for the best. It was her wish to be brought back to Ghent, where she met our father in late 1945. He was a prisoner of war of the Americans, you see, not far from here."

I saw Jack's eyes widen with sudden interest. My own may have widened, too, because this wasn't the kind of thing you ordinarily expected to hear out of the blue from strangers in a sunny café in the New Millennium.

"Where was that?" I asked. For a time around the Battle of the

Bulge, it just so happened, my father ran a small prison camp at Compiègne in northeast France. What a truly small world it was, I guess, even in the midst of a world war.

Jurgen removed his pipe, thoughtfully poked at the dying bowl as if trying to decide whether or not to go into the further details, then told us how his father came to Ghent and met his mother.

Herr Koop was a decorated tank captain in the 5th Panzer Corp, which saw action in Normandy and later in the Ardennes during the counteroffensive that attempted in late 1944 to break through the Allied lines, what Americans took to calling the Battle of the Bulge. After throwing a tread that probably saved his life, his father was attempting to catch up with his retreating division (which was heading for the port near Antwerp) when he ran out of petrol and simply walked into a village near Ghent with his hands raised, expecting to either be shot or taken prisoner. The Allies had overrun and liberated most of Belgium by then, and Belgian partisans were shooting retreating German soldiers on sight. His tank driver opted to try and make it safely back to the German lines on foot and was never heard from again.

Marta gently interrupted her brother's narrative at this point, first murmuring something in German and then looking at me and switching to nearly accentless English, offering a wintery little smile to boot. "You probably don't wish to hear about such private family matters."

"On the contrary," I assured her. "The beer's great, the band's bad, the sun is shining, and we have nowhere to go until tomorrow. Besides, we're Americans. We love other people's private matters."

"O.J. Simpson," Jurgen said, grinning. "Monica's dress."

"Precisely."

"It *is* rather a charming story, I have always believed," Jurgen allowed with a sigh, more perhaps to his sister than us; she stared at her brother as if she'd been gently slapped. But he resumed the tale anyway. Jack, I noticed, was transfixed, but frankly no more than I was.

"There was a farmer raking out his winter garden, trying to see if there were any turnips left from the autumn. Food was extremely scarce, of course, and suddenly there was a Panzer Corp captain standing by his garden wall. Unarmed. Tunic open. Weary and dirty. A bit confused, I think. He offered my father a bucket of water to wash, something to eat. He directed the soldier to the village policeman and went back to his work, but my father refused to leave. He picked up a hoe and began helping the farmer search for turnips."

The captain wound up sleeping in the farmer's shed for several days, refusing to go any farther, unearthing potatoes and turnips in his filthy SS uniform. Eventually, a girl arrived on a bicycle, the farmer's niece. She was fifteen and horrified that her uncle was keeping a German officer in his garden tool shed. That evening a priest and several men were summoned from the village to see the German officer for themselves and discuss what should be done with him. Some of them wanted to chase him away at gunpoint, but the farmer wouldn't agree. There was an Allied prison camp nearby. The farmer decided to drive the German officer there on his tractor and turn him over.

"My father was treated very well by the Americans," Jurgen concluded, glancing at his sister, who seemed to have relaxed a bit. "He was a prisoner of war only a few months, of course, because the war soon ended. A year or so later, I believe, he returned to thank the farmer, only to discover that the man had died. Someone else had already bought his farm and planted wheat. My father went into the village to see if he could find the priest, and discovered the girl on the bike working in a records office. She must have been sixteen or seventeen by then. That is our family story. She became our mother." Jurgen smiled wistfully, tapping his tobacco-stained stem with his blunt brown teeth.

"Awesome," Jack said, clearly as taken by the story's unexpected O'Henry twist of wartime romance as I'd been. The lemon was sitting all alone at the bottom of his empty Coke glass.

"That *is* a charming story," I agreed and remarked what a small world it was because my father, Jack's grandfather, had briefly run a German POW camp near Compiègne in late 1944 and early 1945, probably less than two hundred miles from where we were sitting. I explained to Jurgen how my father had come to have great affection for the fifty or so regular German army soldiers he was responsible for taking care of at the small detention camp that was used by the Eighth Army Air Corps as a processing center for collecting abandoned

weapons, clothing, and other material scattered in the wake of the retreating German Army.

"And now we are friends and allies," Jurgen remarked, looking at
Jack and smiling a little sadly. "Proving time really does heal wounds,
or simply makes embarrassed fools of us in the end."

There was a brief lull in the conversation. So I asked Marta Koop
what she taught back home in Bonn. Jurgen had already told me, but
due to his father's dramatic story, her discipline had slipped clean out
of my brain.

"Art History," she replied, adding that that was why she thought we
might wish to view the Van Eyck altarpiece while visiting Ghent. Not
many people realized that Jan Van Eyck possibly invented the process
of oil painting and was northern Europe's first great landscape painter.
The altarpiece in Saint Baafs was his masterpiece, she assured us, and
one of the great art treasures of the civilized world. Not to be missed,
if at all possible.

I smiled at Marta, the graying daughter of an SS captain who
changed his life by picking turnips. She'd said almost nothing during
these friendly exchanges about her father and my father—former com-
batants dueling over France and Belgium, a couple foreign warriors
who in other circumstances probably would have savored a fine Belgian beer and friendly chat together in an outdoor beer garden like this
one.

For all that, I got the feeling she disapproved of her brother's intimacy with strangers and couldn't wait until we pushed along. Something told me her life had been far more difficult than her brother's.
But I might have been wrong about this. Maybe she just missed her
mom. I certainly missed mine. Not to mention my dad, too.

"Well," I said, finishing off the last bit of my Al Gore beer and setting down my empty glass, "I guess it's time to go dry ourselves off and
hunt for some dinner. We're on the American plan, you see. That
means we have to go find something interesting to eat every three
hours or risk passing out from food deprivation."

"In that case I might recommend the Amadeus over in the Pater-
shol. That's just across the river," said Jurgen, standing up to shake our
hands and pointing to the rooftops behind the square. "You should try

the Gentse waterzooi, the local speciality. It is like a thick soup or maybe a stew to you. The Jurishof also has a fine restaurant, very French, though somewhat expensive."

I thanked him for this useful information. Then we shook hands and said good-bye. I could hear Marta speaking quietly in German to her brother as we ambled away. My guess is that it wasn't about the soup.

"Dad," Jack said, a couple hours later, after we'd hiked back to the Jurishof, showered, dressed, and taken our baseball gloves out onto the wide plaza in front of the town hall to get in a little evening practice before chowing down on waterzooi or whatever other Belgian delicacies we could get our greedy hands on. "Do you *like* Germans?"

What a funny question. But then, as you know by now, what a funny kid.

Actually, Nibs asked this after we'd been throwing for a while and had then stepped into Saint Baafs, twenty minutes before the doors were scheduled to shut for the evening. I was standing just over the threshold staring up at the cathedral's spectacular nave, which was highlighted by slender stone columns arching upward, giving the vast interior a rather light and even cheerful look for a building that was so dreary and unwelcoming on the outside—a little like Ghent itself, come to think of it.

"Depends on the Germans, I suppose. Jurgen and Marta seemed pretty nice. I liked their papa's story. The soldier and the farmer's niece, finding true love among the turnips. If this was America, somebody would make a movie of the week about it."

He admitted that he liked them, too. It was good to see not all Germans were like the Germans he'd seen at the Holocaust Museum in Washington or in *Saving Private Ryan*.

"So that guy wasn't, like, a Nazi or something."

"Oh no," I assured him somewhat distractedly as I angled him over toward a glassed-in side chapel where a man was still selling admission tickets and renting headphones for the Van Eyck altarpiece, which was housed in a soundproof glass room off to the side.

The room was crowded with folks reverently holding phones to

their ears and reminded me of LaGuardia Airport on a Friday afternoon just before the market closes. I realized Jack probably needed a
bit of clarification on the difference between modern Germans and
Hitler's Nazis before we went in.

"Officially, Boss, the Nazi Party ceased to exist in 1945. That
doesn't excuse the unforgivable things the German Army and government did to people—particularly the Jews—but it also doesn't mean
everybody in Germany approved of it, either."

Great, I thought. *Now you're an apologist for the Third Reich.*

"What I mean is," I continued, somewhat lamely, as we took our
tickets and headphones and started toward the side chapel doors, "wars
make people do awful things. Things they might otherwise have never
considered doing. The fact is, a lot of people opposed Hitler and his
thugs and paid for it with their lives. Even a lot of decent Germans."

Wunderbar. Dig yourself in really deep, mein Lieber.

A thought came to me, a possible way out of my quandary. I
stopped Jack outside the glass doors and asked if he remembered my
stories about growing up in the deep South during the 1950s and '60s.

"Right," he said, nodding. "You saw Martin Luther King or something."

"I didn't see Martin Luther King," I clarified, "but I did see the first
peaceful sit-down civil rights demonstration, thanks to your grandfather."

In those days, which must have seemed like ancient history to him,
I said, there were a lot of decent people around—some of our neighbors, folks at church, even a few of my parents' friends—who didn't
like the way black people were generally treated by the white major-
ity, but basically didn't have the nerve to do anything about it.

People in the American South, like people in Germany, allowed old
racisms to flourish and things to drift along until life literally blew up in
their faces and a war had to be fought to put things right. The Germans
had to lose the war in order to get rid of the terrible Nazis, while in the
South it took the courageous battles of the Civil Rights Movement to
finally get rid of the kind of apathy and ignorance that created wackos
like the Ku Klux Klan—our homemade version of the Nazis. One day
when I was in the second grade, I explained, my father showed up and

took my brother and me out of classes two hours early. He drove us downtown to see the first nonviolent mass sit-down demonstration in American history. He predicted it would *make* history and change the South in a good way. He'd been right about that, too.

"Oh," said Jack, "I get it. Not everybody in Germany liked Nazis and not everybody in the South liked—what were they called?"

"The Klan. Right." It wasn't a perfect analogy but it would have to do for the moment.

"Besides," I ribbed him playfully as I opened the glass door to the glory of Jan Van Eyck, "we're German, too—at least partly."

I reminded him that my mother, his paternal grandmother, was the youngest of eleven brothers and sisters whose grandparents immigrated to the hills of West Virginia from southern Germany around the turn of the twentieth century, producing a big-boned, jolly race of dumpling-making aunts and beer-drinking uncles who made family re-unions feel like summer beer festivals and were some of the most generous souls I'd ever met.

"So *I'm* German?"

"A little bit, I'm afraid. Part redneck, too. Heil hominy grits."

Someone shushed us as we stepped inside the chapel.

We quickly took the only available seats—on the floor directly below the altarpiece—and gazed up at the dramatically lighted *Adoration of the Lamb*, as the painting is formally named. Jack, sitting Indian style on the hard stone floor, had his earphone working in no time flat and was quickly absorbed in the narrative of the painting's creation.

I, on the other hand, sitting painfully cross-legged on the same hard stone floor, switched on my earphone only to discover someone speaking either in Swedish or Swahili. I pushed several buttons at random and, to my delight, a plumy-voiced English lady began explaining how the archangel Gabriel's wings delicately touched the timbered rafters of a classical Flemish house, a brilliant example of Van Eyck's revolutionary use of light and shadow—more chiaroscuro!—only a dazzling hint of the extraordinary treasury of "light and faith" that awaited viewers on the opposite side of the altarpiece.

For a moment, I was stymied, artistically speaking, wondering where the heck Gabriel and the Flemish house were on the painting.

I mean, on the left side of the panel I saw knights parading on ponies, on the left a deputation of gray-bearded monks and a barefoot guy wrapped in a scruffy red robe, possibly John the Baptist. Between these panels lay a truly impressive assemblage of monks and holy men in ecclesiastical attire kneeling around a fountain, which sat just below a gentle rise of green turf where angels knelt around a lamb standing dramatically on a sunlit box, obviously the Lamb of God and, I guessed, the Ark of the Covenant. Above that, arranged across three large overhead panels, sat a woman who was possibly Mary (reading a book) and a man in a green robe (no idea) and an Oriental-looking guy (your guess now) wearing a magnificent red robe and gold crown. It was tough to know who these dudes were supposed to be. On the upper panels both left and right, on the other hand, framed by darkened arches and standing naked and placidly covering themselves, stood the most dramatic renderings I'd ever seen of Adam and Eve. Eve's belly was swollen with pregnancy, her face full of regret, holding what looked to be a walnut or maybe a small black golf ball. Adam held a fig leaf over his privates, his face looking as if he'd just seen a holy ghost.

I pushed some more buttons on my ear machine and inadvertently brought back the Swahili-Swedish interpreter. Finally, I just shut the stupid thing off and sat there searching for the missing Flemish house and the archangel Gabriel. Whatever else was true, the painting was one of the most amazing things I'd ever seen.

I felt a nudge from Jack and leaned over.

"Dad, what's a mystical experience?" he whispered.

I whispered back, "Reaching a par-five hole in two or a lifetime batting average over three hundred. Yaz comes to mind."

"Do you *mind?*" An American voice rebuked us sharply from directly aft. Both of us turned our heads and saw an angry middle-aged woman actually baring her frontal canines at us.

"People are trying to *concentrate* here," she hissed.

"Oops. Sorry."

Just as things quieted down nicely again, wouldn't you know it, some nitwit's cell phone went off, tooting out "Moonlight on the River Schelde," or the Belgian national anthem. The nitwit turned out to be me, so I got up and hurried out of the crowded room as quickly as my gimpy ankle would take me.

"Hi, it's me!" chirped Wendy all the way from where she was busy loading the dishwasher with breakfast dishes. "So how's Jim and Jack's Big European Adventure going? What the heck are you guys up to?"

I told her we'd been drinking beer and were now making a paying nuisance of ourselves in a famous cathedral in Ghent, explaining my banishment from the aspiring mystics. I quickly filled her in on our splendid hike around the surprising ancient city, the good beer, the amazing conversation with the Koops, and the breathtaking *Adoration of the Lamb.*

"Sounds wonderful," she said. "Where exactly is Ghent? I can't remember exactly." She was tracking our movements with pushpins on a map in her office the way the FBI follows last known whereabouts of escaped convicts.

I told her Ghent was the ancient capital of Flanders, an accidental discovery but all around great place in my book even if the overpriced earphones in the Van Eyck room didn't work worth a damn.

She said she was calling to confirm our hotel for Paris on Bastille Day. The holiday fell over a weekend and we had been asked by management to confirm our arrival date and time. Would we make it there in five days?

"No problem," I assured her. And since I had her on the phone, I asked how her new married life was holding up.

"My husband disappeared the day after the ceremony," the funny girl replied, sighing heavily. "Haven't seen him since. Almost three weeks and counting. Word has it he's been spotted in Europe, though, bothering people in churches."

I tried to console her. "Look on the bright side. You've got all this free time to weed and water his flower beds. I understand he didn't even bother to buy you a decent wedding ring."

"Yeah," she said sweetly. "I may have to go hunt one down. Or better yet, him."

We probably would have kept up this light-hearted global love banter for hours, I suppose, if she hadn't reminded me this satellite call cost three bucks per minute, so I blew her a transoceanic kiss, hung up, and traipsed back inside Saint Baafs, where I found Jack chatting with a tiny old guy who had a face like a Dakota prairie dog. Nibs had apparently either been kicked out of the Van Eyck room, too, or else decided to leave on his own recognizance and follow me outside to see what was up.

"I was just telling this boy that I was about his age when I was taken from here," the man explained, patting Jack on the arm, with an accent so thick with Belgian lace it took me a moment to understand him.

"Really?" I said, a bit distractedly, noting that the large American lady trying to have a mystical experience in the Van Eyck room was bearing down upon us. She looked unhappy about her time with the altarpiece, or maybe she'd just heard the news about Mariah Carey.

Jack wondered, "Who took you where and why?"

"Here! Here! The *Germans*, of course!" the little man shouted at us, veins in his neck leaping, pointing excitedly at the cathedral floor. "One Saturday morning I am riding my bicycle on my way to see my grandmother in Ghent, the next I am a boy being sent to Germany on a labor train to a factory in Leipzig! They call Leipzig the city of light, you know! Ha! Listen to me! I am there for almost three *years* working as a slave in that dark factory thinking of only one thing—going home and seeing this!"

He paused, whipped his tiny bald head around and stared at the shimmering relic inside the glass room.

"They took that, *too*, you see? The Germans did! They put it in a cave in Austria. But the American soldiers found it and brought it back where it belongs!"

"No joke?" I said, open-mouthed.

"Wow," Jack echoed articulately.

"You two come with me," the man demanded almost irritably, shuffling off toward the nave, taking Jack's right elbow with him. "I show you something else . . ."

We permitted him to drag us back into the church, to a darker ambulatory where he stopped in front of a swirling, poorly lit landscape painting that looked like something Peter Paul Rubens might have slopped on canvas after a long night of singing old Dylan tunes and drinking with pals in the square, a muscular, bluish, muddy portrait showing obscure figures writhing toward heaven.

"That's Rubens," the little man said with a proud sniff, grinning at it fiercely.

"Cool," Jack said politely.

"Very nice," I agreed, realizing even artistic geniuses can have bad days.

The three of us stood admiring the painting, which I later learned is called *Saint Bavo's Entrance into the Monastery in Ghent*. It's considered a relatively minor work of Flanders's greatest painter.

The little man resumed his tale without prompting, eyes drifting adoringly over the canvas. "One day after the bombing stopped, I walked away from that terrible factory in the city of lights. I said *enough* of this. I will either go home or I will die. A door was open so I walked out it and all the way back to Ghent."

"You walked all the way from Germany to here?" I asked, not certain if I'd heard him correctly.

"Yes, yes."

He smiled slyly at me over a set of truly unfortunate teeth. "This painting and I . . . we came home two months apart. We *both* fooled the Nazis!"

Before I could congratulate him on this impressive feat, though, he was off and scampering like an agitated rooster, motioning us back to the cathedral's massive front doors. It was officially closing time and most of the tourists from the Van Eyck room had already left, and as he whipped out a circle of keys, I suddenly realized he must be a docent or some kind of church official, possibly even the Saint Baafs custodian general.

"I will show you one thing more before you go," he said to Jack, wiggling a come-here finger. He shuffled over to some worn nave steps and pointed to what looked like runic symbols or maybe a set of crude personal initials cut into the stone.

"Do you know what that is, boy?"

Jack dutifully shook his head. He didn't seem to have the foggiest idea, and neither did I, to no one's particular surprise.

"That is a mason's mark."

He explained that Medieval cathedrals across Europe were filled

with such arcane markings, crude telltale scratches in stone that indicated which illiterate stone mason had been there and done the work.

"That was their only way of being known," he said. "That is how
the phrase *a man making his mark in the world* got started."

"Cool," I heard myself say, borrowing a direct quote from Nibs the
Lost Boy. I was still processing what it must have been like to hike all
the way from Leipzig to Ghent, or for that matter to be a prisoner of
war who married a local girl. Whatever else was true, the smartest
thing we'd done that day was *not* proceed to Bruges.

Before he shooed us out into the night, the tiny man patted Jack affectionately on the shoulder. Then he reached up and ruffled his hair
the way he might have done his own grandson's.

"Someday you will make your mark, too. I believe this."

I thanked him and said I believed so, too.

As we stepped out into the balmy evening, I turned to thank the
little docent or janitor or whoever he was for showing us these amazing things, but at that instant he slammed and bolted the cathedral
door in our faces.

"Official time for waterzooi," I announced cheerfully.

"Great," Jack agreed. "What's that again?"

NINE

My Father's French

We slipped out of rainy Flanders before dawn that Sunday morning with our faithful ever-shrinking Belgian farm cheese wedge in tow and some orange juice and cold coffee purloined from the stately empty kitchen of the Sint Jurishof.

A Dark Age rain followed us all the way to Rouen, which was positively bleak in the gray morning light when we finally abandoned the motorway just before eight to snoop around the historic town where Joan of Arc was tried, convicted, and sent up in flames. A chilly Atlantic rain whipped across the garbage-strewn plaza of the famous cathedral where a couple bent-over stragglers hurried toward early mass. I pulled over to the curb in front of the cathedral to take a longer look at the famous west facade that Claude Monet, among others, studied for changing effects of light and placed on canvas more than thirty times. Now it was engulfed in an almost sooty darkness, its head tipped in low cloud, a somewhat forbidding gothic bulk animated by a lone civic lamppost on the boulevard, where a garish advertisement flapped in the wind; the poster featured a young blond woman perched astride a wooden chair in nothing but her Calvins, her thin teenage legs provocatively bracketing a telephone number. I asked Jack if he wanted to check out the service at the church that sent Saint Joan to meet her maker, but I got no reply. I glanced at my travel pal and discovered he was asleep again, still holding his souvenir cheese wedge.

Oh well. The hatchback was cozy and warm, Sibelius was playing on the radio, and the rain showed no indication of easing up. Just then a flickering blue light appeared at the end of the block in my rearview mirror and a small white police car glided slowly past, a fishy white face regarding me through the watery glass as if I might be waiting for a rendezvous with the lonely *mademoiselle* on the pole. I took this as a sign from somebody to keep moving, so we did.

We wandered up the Seine, past the ancient fortifications at Les Andelys to Giverny. The parking lot was empty and the curtain of rain, though I wouldn't have thought it possible, was even heavier. The Volvo's illuminated clock said it was ten past official opening hours, but no one had officially appeared to open up Giverny yet. We waited for another maddening half hour more, through several scenes of Shuman's childhood and a dull étude or two by Freddie Chopin. Then we gave up and abandoned the place, a major personal disappointment to me since Monet's home and gardens—said by some to be his *real* masterpiece—house none of his original paintings (most of which are at the Musée d'Orsay in Paris) but contain gardens the famous Impressionist spent almost forty years lavishly attempting to perfect. In my own modest way back home, I fancy myself on a similar botanical mission from the Muse Diana, to transform eleven hemlock-girdled acres into a civilized small garden in the wood, *Les petit jardins de la forêt.*

"*Comme ci, comme ça,*" I said to Jack, firing up the hatchback and aiming for the road back to Caen. My traveling partner was at least halfway awake by then, and, yawning, ingesting a pinch of Belgian cheese for sustenance, he wondered what the popular expression meant.

I explained it was my father's French, one of his favorite expressions picked up during the year he spent in France at the end of the war. It was his way of shrugging off disappointment and simply saying something wasn't meant to be. Obviously, Giverny wasn't meant to be.

"Did he speak French?"

"Not really. But he thought so. Unfortunately the French people didn't agree."

I explained to Jack how, touchingly, his *grand-père* fell deeply in love with France and French people but managed to grasp only a few rudimentary words of their romantic language, predicating nearly

every utterance of his with *"pardon moi"* and *"S'il vous plaît"* and/or
placing the helpful pronoun *"vous"* after any transitive verb or adverb,
speaking with moronic slowness for effect, loudly if necessary, usually
accompanied by a series of earnest if somewhat confusing hand ges-
tures, a pantomime meant to illustrate what he was attempting to ver-
bally communicate. Thus, in search of a decent café around the Paris
Opera, for example, he might stop a proper French matron on her way
to market and politely inquire, with a loopy American smile, while
simulating a steam shovel plate-to-mouth motion with arm and
cupped fingers, *"Pardon moi, madame. S'il vous plaît, would you happen
to know where a fella might find a swell café to eat-ee-vous?"*

Jack chuckled drowsily. "That's not French."

I smiled at the rainy road ahead. "True. But that never stopped
him." As I said this, I thought about my funny, funky, ever-
optimistic father and how I really missed him. In some ways, God
bless him, he stayed in touch with his inner eighth grader until he
was eighty years old.

I must have said this aloud because Jack agreed, "I miss him, too."

My own grasp of the French language, I'm afraid, was scarcely better than *mon père's*—a walking disgrace to the noble efforts of Miss
Myrtle Hines, who labored tirelessly for two long years of junior high
school to teach me something more than how to find my way through
a French-speaking world to the public library or the nearest men's
room. After six grueling semesters of French lessons, the best thing she
could say to my parents about my grasp of her favorite romance language was, "Well, Jacques certainly has nice manners. And he's *so*
clean!"

"Comme ci, comme ça," I believe my father replied with a Gallic
shrug.

For better or worse, I got stuck with my father's French, though curiously it had never been too much of a cultural hindrance to me. For
years, I explained to Nibsy, I'd wandered safely at large around this
magnificent country spouting bits of my father's colorful Franco lingo
and nobody but the odd snotty Left Bank waiter appeared to mind
overly much. The French, particularly outside Paris, it seems to me,
have great tolerance for earnest imbeciles and innocents abroad

because they simply reinforce the cultural view that France is the superior civilization after all. I fondly recall a time in Provence when I posed a simple directional question in my father's French at a patisserie and was instructed to wait while the baker went to speak to the unshaven guy sweeping the street, who nodded and tossed down his Gitane and went to summon the mayor, who abandoned his haircut and came back followed by his nagging wife and a small boy armed with a plastic fire truck. Everyone except the boy began to talk energetically at once and pretty soon arms were being waved, fingers pointed, and things being said that sounded rather body specific and highly personal in nature to my uneducated ears. After several minutes of this entertaining ruckus, the boy with the fire truck walked to the front door of the shop and pointed directly across the street to the ATM machine I'd been trying to find all along. I thanked everybody—*Merci beaucoup, y'all*—patted the kid on the head, walked across the street to get some money, and looked back to see them all laughing and slapping each other on the back. The unshaven guy went back to his sweeping, the mayor went back to his barber chair with his family in tow, and the baker waved affectionately before pulling down his awning for the day. I think that was the very moment I fell hopelessly in love with France, where every encounter has the possibility of turning into opéra bouffe by Georges Bizet.

"Maybe I could talk for us or something while we're here," Jack sleepily proposed, smiling at my story and rubbing his eyes.

I snorted and glanced at him. "Right. You speak French, do you?"

"Yes, sir. We just studied it this spring at school," he provided. "I don't think it's very hard."

I cast him a long look across the seat, very French, which means you allow the natural bags beneath your eyes to sag all the way to your lap.

"You *don't?*"

"No, sir." And with that, he spouted off an impressive stream of nimble French phrasing that clearly *wasn't* my father's french, or mine either for that matter.

"Fine, *cherie*," I said, a bit wounded I confess, sensing the end of a family tradition, and not certain if I'd called him a girl or a boy, "you can speak for us both unless we need to find either a bathroom or a public library in a hurry. In either of those situations, though, stand clear and watch a pro go to work."

Encouragingly, the sun swam out of the murk at Longues-sur-Mer, where we parked the hatchback and moseyed down a dune to a decaying German artillery battery and eavesdropped on a sandy-haired man's lecture to a group of English schoolchildren about a brave ten-year-old French boy who, on the eve of the D Day invasion, pedaled up on his bike and innocently asked the German officers quartered here if he could snoop around the nearby surrounding fields. The boy claimed to be visiting from Paris and that the fields had belonged to his *grand-père* before the war. The officers permitted him to wander at will, and later the boy passed the precise coordinates of the gun batteries on to the local resistance, which in turn radioed them to Allied gunships lying just offshore. The batteries at Longues-sur-Mer were among the first knocked out by Navy artillery.

"Do you think he was scared to do that?" Jack wondered as we hiked back to the hatchback a little while later. "I sure would be."

"Probably," I said. "But people do amazing things during wars. You'd do just fine."

The Sabbath solemnity of the place had its unmistakable effect on us, but it was frankly nothing compared to the overwhelming sadness that descended a little farther along the coastal road, at Coleville-St. Laurent, where we stopped and strolled for a long time in silence among nine thousand perfectly aligned stark white crosses spread over the wide lush lawn on the cliff heights above Omaha Beach, the slopes of which were still pitted with shell holes and German bunkers. Eventually we followed a signpost that warned of wild pigs, down a meandering path to the innocuous-looking beach itself, where five thousand Americans were killed or wounded in the first hour of Operation Overlord. Then we walked the entire length of the beach itself. Jack, I noticed, was picking up stones and looking at them. He was always bringing rocks made smooth by the sea home from the beach in Maine.

"Do you think they would mind if I took some of these home?"

"Probably not." I suspected the beach had been built and rebuilt many times since Bloody Omaha, but the rocks at least came from *somewhere* in the vicinity. If stones could speak, these would probably tell some kind of tale.

"Dad," he said, as we resumed walking, looking down the beach where a family and their dog were frolicking in the whispery surf. "Would you have wanted to fight at D Day?"

I thought for only a moment, stopping to pick up a flat stone of my own. I flung it at the sea, making it skip twice before it flipped and sunk.

"Yep. I would have." I admitted that I sometimes had a feeling I'd been born a generation too late. I'd probably read every book there was on World War Two, fancied the music of that era, liked the way people behaved and did their duty to God, country, and each other, loved the way women looked then, too. It was far too simplistic to say World War Two was the "Last Good War" America had fought in, but there was certainly a grain of truth in that perspective.

"Why?"

"I don't know. Bullies are the same everywhere and sometimes you just have to stand up to them, even if it costs you something dear. That's what Britain and America did, and France, too, by the way. Don't forget that brave boy back at Longues-sur-Mer . . ."

We strolled along Bloody Omaha in silence, great battleship clouds now floating inland off the tranquil Sabbath sea, casting mighty shadows on the sand and bluffs of Pointe du Hoc, where two thousand American Rangers perished in a matter of a few hours.

Jack said, "There's a boy at Woodside who picks on people."

"I think I know the guy you mean."

"You do?" He seemed surprised to learn this. But also maybe a bit comforted.

"Yep. Face only a blind mother could love. Mouth like an unflushed toilet."

Nibs smiled and nodded; I'd watched this kid try and operate on the nicer kids at Woodside Elementary for years, marveling that somebody his own size didn't just lower the hammer on his snout. Then he made the mistake of targeting Jack's older sister, Maggie, a pathetic attempt at bully courtship. She backed him into the cinder-block wall and offered to rearrange his overbite. Maggie, who was now five-six and captain of her junior high field hockey team, was our family Crusader; Jack was the born diplomat and peacemaker, just like both his world-traveling grandpapas.

"Does he worry you?"

"No, sir. It's just . . . that I'd really like to punch him in the mouth."

This was something new—a more assertive Nibs revealing himself. Frankly, politically incorrect as it might be, I wasn't sorry to see it, because part of the trick of growing from boy to man is learning when to sue for peace at all costs and when to dig in your heels and put up your dukes and make a stand for some sort of ball-yard justice.

"I know the feeling. I had it back in Amsterdam. But that guy was just your garden variety jerk, not your world-class bully. He wasn't worth it."

"Hitler was a bully, though."

"One of the biggest."

"Is that why granddad enlisted in the army?"

"Yep. Funny story about that, though."

As we strolled along, pausing to pick up rocks and examine them or fling them into the surf, I explained how his grandfather came out of Chanute Field outside Chicago in late 1942 as one of the Army Air Corps' top-rated glider pilots and an expert in parachute packing. Most of the early part of the war he spent on England's Lancashire Coast inspecting parachute packing operations—fully expecting to fly a troop glider into occupied France once the brass gave a green light for the air and sea invasion to liberate France that everybody including the Germans knew was coming.

"Unfortunately for him—but probably fortunately for *us*—he wrote a letter to your grandmother explaining how he'd just been assigned to the glider corps. She worked for an admiral at Annapolis. I guess this was a couple months or so before D Day. Anyway, the next thing your grandfather knew, he was called into a colonel's office and reassigned to a floater unit that was going into France after the third wave to repair bridges and restring telephone wires."

"I don't get it," Jack admitted. "Why didn't he fly a troop glider?"

"Your grandmother and her admiral. The casualty rate among glider pilots was extremely high. Never underestimate the power of a determined, worried woman, sonny."

"*Oh.*" He grinned and looked back at the long beach. "Did he land here?"

"Somewhere in the neighborhood," I said, not entirely certain where he came ashore. "But by then most of the shooting was over with."

The sun grew stronger at Bayeux, one of the few towns in the area spared the mass destruction resulting from the Allied invasion, the place we simply hoped to find a modest hotel room and an evening meal, and maybe snag a glimpse of the famous tapestry of William the Conquerer before tucking in for the night.

The first hotel we checked on the outskirts of town was booked solid, and the woman who managed the place advised us that the chances of us finding accommodations were not good because it was the final afternoon of the town's famous Festivale Medieval and the crowds were very large. She suggested that we wait, though, while she checked a couple other hotels in town.

She came back a few minutes later beaming.

"You are truly fortunate, *monsieur*," she declared. "I phone my little friend Babette at Lion d'Or and she will take you in! She has a room in the, um, ceiling?"

I thanked her and asked how to get to the Golden Lion, vaguely wondering why I knew that name. Then it came to me from all my D Day reading. That was where Hitler's favorite general, Fredrick van Paulis, bunked before the Allied assault sent him fleeing back to Paris.

A little while later, Nibs and I followed a young woman named Babette up several flights of stairs to a cozy room on the, um, ceiling floor of the famous old hotel. She opened the twin window shutters to a nice view of the cobbled courtyard below and wondered if we were there for the Fête Medieval? I explained that we'd mostly come to eyeball the nine-hundred-year-old Tapestry of Bayeux and then head for Mont-Saint-Michel and possibly Chartres in the morning, but that, speaking entirely for myself, I could go for a spot of Medieval festival-going this afternoon. Where, exactly, I wondered, was the fête?

She smiled, tossing my rolling duffel on the bedside luggage rack, and for a horrifying moment I thought she might actually open it and try and unpack my things, in which case the whole hotel would have to be evacuated and fumigated.

"*Bon.*" She gave a sharp single nod like a working girl who knew somebody had to take charge of our movements for the precious few hours we'd be in town. "In that case, if I may say, you should view the *tapisserie de la Reine Mathilde* another time. It is a lovely thing, true, very nice indeed, but it is not even a true *tapisserie*. It is technically a *embroidie*. Very interesting to see if you have the time to spend but a little like . . . what do you say? . . . a *strip de comic*. Also, there is too much to do, you see, even before you are permitted to view the *tapisserie* itself—functions, a movie, that sort for thing. Besides," she consulted the black-strapped watch on her thin freckled wrist, "there is less than one hour before the *tapisserie* closes. It would be a waste, you see? You should go straight to the fête. Nothing is like it, I tell you plainly. There will be a grand procession for the boy, many things to see and buy. Tell me, do you care for French food?"

Charmed by the force of her argument and cute little button nose, I was compelled to admit that I cared deeply for French food, probably more than I should have. When it came to traveling in France, I was something of a serial eater.

"*Bon.*" A small, triumphant smile played across her freckled face, and I vaguely wondered if she pushed all her Anglo guests around so pleasantly. "Then, with haste, you must go to the fête. There is a grand procession very soon."

And so, mere minutes later, town map in hand, we slipped out the old coaching inn's front doors, crossed the cobbled courtyard, and proceeded up Rue au Coos instead of taking the right on Rue St. Jean, as instructed, and strolling downhill to the fête.

Call me stubborn, but as we hoped to get an early start for Chartres in the morning, I was determined to at least take a passing glimpse at a true icon of Western art history before we left town, an objet d'art I'd wanted to see basically since I was knee-high to a French hotel clerk. Five minutes later, we were pleased to discover the tapestry museum utterly devoid of paying customers, a ticket seller drowsing over his garish crime paperback, and only an elderly English couple shuffling slowly up the marble steps to the tapestry salon ahead of us.

Not to boast or anything, but I'm something of a trained expert at flying through deadly dull museums and audiovisual preliminaries, which typically explain, in language cleverly designed to inflict as much mental anguish as possible on small children and the patience-impaired, the importance of what you're about to see. In this case, though, there was a helpful bilingual film followed by an informative and entertaining passage along a corridor of illuminated displays telling the fascinating history of how in 1065 Englishman Harold Godwineson (one of many potential heirs to the throne left by the sudden death of childless Edward the Confessor) fell into the hands of William of Normandy and was persuaded—or tricked—into swearing an oath of fealty to William, probably in exchange for the courtesy of keeping his head, then marrying (according to one account) William's own somewhat homely daughter and pledging to assist William's succession to the English throne. A year or so later, Harold returned to England, repudiated his oath to his new father-in-law, and claimed the English crown for himself at Westminster Abbey on January 6, 1066. Wicked boy.

Nobody seems to know what became of William's daughter, but later that same year, after endless delays, the Duke of Normandy slipped across the Channel under cover of darkness, on favorable winds, and landed a relatively small but well-armed force of armored cavalry, foot soldiers, and seasoned archers on English soil. After a few days of rest and cribbage, William's men advanced on Harold's battle-weary army, which was billeted on a hill at Hastings (having just beaten off a pack of smelly Vikings from the north). Using hatchets and swords, Harold's soldiers gallantly repelled three Norman assaults until a break in their siege lines late in the day allowed William's armored cavalry to penetrate the heart of the English defenses and his archers to decimate Harold's army. According to one legend, William had three horses killed beneath him, and Harold personally massacred scores of Normans before taking an arrow through the eye—fighting on until he was brought down by a flurry of broadswords. The battle lasted about ten hours, or roughly the equivalent of a modern Super Bowl telecast.

With time running out before the museum closed for the day, we absorbed as much of this fabulous bloody history as possible before we trooped hurriedly down another set of steps to the entrance to the tapestry itself. A young male attendant standing at parade rest there demanded to see our admission tickets, perhaps a bit suspicious because we were panting like a pair of Anglo-Saxon *chiens*.

At that point there were maybe only five minutes before the tapestry museum closed, but he agreed to let us proceed and spend the remaining time walking through a dramatically cooled and darkened corridor examining a work of art many historians feel is the most important relic to come down from early Medieval times, commissioned by William's half-brother Bishop Odo of Bayeux, a spectacularly detailed and beautifully stitched piece of frail-looking linen stretching impressively more than half the length of a standard football pitch, safely displayed behind airtight glass, depicting the fifty-eight separate scenes of William's life in Normandy, his meeting with and betrayal by Harold, the assembly of his fleet, the months of plotting and waiting, and finally the landing and the bloody assault on Hastings—most of which we got to see, until the same young guard appeared at our elbows and informed us, none too friendly like, that it was time to clear out.

I didn't notice until we were stepping out of the tapestry corridor that the ceiling above us was made from the hull of an upturned ancient ship. I pointed it out to Jack and we both decided this crowning architectural touch was, like, truly and totally *awesome*.

I could see Jack's disappointment, though, at being abruptly booted from the tapestry and let him talk me into buying a staggeringly expensive pewter action figure on the way out through the empty gift shop. As usual it took Jack several minutes to decide which figure he wanted while the *madame* in charge of the shop kept glancing at us with undisguised impatience, tartly tapping her shoe, picturing her Sunday evening pot roast burning to a crisp.

Personally, I'd have selected William, with his noble visage, elegant mail shirt, and vision of civilized governance that would bring artistic and spiritual renewal to all of Angle-land, not to mention his really swell conical Norman helmet with nifty Chicago Bears nose guard—just like the one we'd been tempted to buy back in Amsterdam.

Jack, wouldn't you know it, picked the doomed King Harold instead, and as we went up the steps back to the village's main drag, I casually asked why he picked Harold the Defender.

"I don't know," he said, looking at the splendid spear-chucking action figure in his hand. "I kind of felt sorry for him. He was the underdog. I'll bet not many people buy Harold."

I couldn't stop myself from reaching a paw over and mussing up his combed sandy hair. He owned such a nice heart.

To be honest, though, as we emerged topside, I calculated that due to the hour or so we'd spent snooping around the museum, the fête would probably either be over or very nearly so. But luckily I was wrong again. We marched down the street, turned the corner, and ran smack dab into the glories of William's merry Middle Ages. The narrow cobbled streets around the gorgeous stone cathedral were teeming with costumed vendors and siege tents filled with artisans selling everything from goat cheese to hand-forged Medieval weaponry, weavers at the loom, minstrels at the lyre, jugglers juggling their brains out, even a parade of mythical giants—guys on stilts—making their way through the crowds toward a festival stage where a Medieval consort was sawing out real foot-tapping Medieval oldies on period instruments. The procession's lead giant was a laughing green man covered in a chain mail of vines and bay leaves; he was followed by a somewhat spooky fertility goddess with flashing dark eyes, wildly flowing tresses, and violently hirsute underarms; she in turn by a lurching man in wolf skins and a fierce black-winged creature with a red beak. We briefly stopped at an artisan's tent, where I purchased a wedding gift for my new wife, a beautifully carved wooden apple and a woman who looked like Eve made of stone, and then we tagged along behind the mythical grand procession to a festival stage where spectators were being summoned to join in a traditional Medieval circle dance and Jack suddenly looked at me.

"What?" I said. "You want to join in or something?"

"Do you?" he wondered.

"Not on your life, Slick."

I explained that my ankle still hurt from Glastonbury and that white men my age don't (or shouldn't) dance in public. Besides, somebody had to hold our booty, so I volunteered.

"Okay," he said with a slightly disappointed shrug, deposited Harold and his ball glove on me, then slipped through the crowd to link hands with a pretty brown-haired girl and her mother and a guy dressed like the village buffoon. Round and round they went, as the music reeled, pausing to skip and clap hands and have a high old time. I climbed up on a low stone wall and watched the frolic through the lens of our new digital camera, faintly wishing I hadn't been such a stuffed shirt.

After that, we found an archery booth where folks were lined up several bodies deep to try and hit a painted bull's-eye on a bail of hay. There were two lines—one for kids, one for adults. Interestingly, Jack stepped into the grown-up line which for twelve francs required shooters to use a large ash strongbow and send six arrows flying toward a target hung more than thirty paces away. The kiddie target was maybe ten feet away and the bow, accordingly, half the size.

We watched several young bucks notch their arrows, take beads, and let fly. None came close to the mark. The bow master—an unshaven guy in mended green leggings and crested felt cap, smoking your basic Medieval Marlboro Light—seemed to take proprietary pleasure in the fact that nobody could hit his target.

Finally, it was Jack's turn. The bow master glanced at him with Gallic indifference, murmured something in French, put his cigarette back in his mouth, and presented the bow and a first arrow to Jack.

Jack calmly notched an arrow, drew back the bow with little or no fanfare, and let it go. The arrow struck the lower third of the target and someone behind us whistled admiringly. The bow master looked mildly surprised. He presented Nibs a second arrow; this time, though, before Jack could notch the arrow, cigarette still dangling, Master took firm hold of Jack's fingers and moved them to a more proper attitude on the bow.

We all waited a small eternity for Jack to release that arrow. When he finally did, it thudded the heart of the target and the surrounding rabble gave a lusty little cheer.

Jack blushed, glanced at me, then beamed. Someone patted him sharply on the back. *"Magnifique, monsieur!"*

The bow master looked at me and said something in French that sounded a little like "Look, pal. If your kid hits that damned bull's-eye again, you can just put on this silly felt cap and stupid tights and run this booth till we close. I'll go have a nice Pastis with the boys."

"I'm sorry," I said to him, "I don't speak much French."

An elegant woman with gray-streaked black hair who was standing behind me leaned close enough for me to see the nubs on her beautiful linen jacket and catch a whiff of her lemony perfume. She helpfully translated, "He says the boy has a fine skill. He wonders how long he has, um, schooled at archery?"

"About five minutes, I think."

She smiled at me. "Those are lovely," she said, looking at the carved apple and chisled Eve I was holding in my hands.

"Wedding gifts for my wife," I explained, with only the teensiest pang of nostalgia for my bachelor years.

"She will love them."

"Hope so."

Jack's final two efforts struck the hay bale, just wide of the target. But by this point in the unexpected exhibition even the doubtful bow master had been won over by Nibsy's plucky bowmanship. The man actually smiled, and a made gracious little ceremony of presenting Jack with one of the arrows of his triumph and a scrolled paper certificate which looked like something you'd get from a cheesy chiropractic college or a Midwest diploma mill, ornately lettered gothic French proclaiming he was henceforth an official Bowman of Bayeux. I know this because the lady in the linen jacket translated this, too, moments before her husband and teenage daughter beckoned her from across the courtyard and she waved good-bye.

"Hey, Jack. Where'd you learn to *shoot* like that?" I wondered as we hoofed up the hill to the shadows of the cathedral, where stonemasons were cutting huge blocks of limestone and wood-carvers were busy chiseling seraphic figures and designs into a spectacular arched wooden door. The joy of this Fête Medieval was its wonderful authenticity, the numerous demonstrations of long-forgotten skills that would have been everyday labors six or seven hundred years ago. I was awful glad we'd seen the world famous Tapestry of Bayeux, but I sure would have hated to miss this.

*   *   *

"Bowdoin Day Camp."

"Really? You guys did archery?"

We were standing by one of the cathedral's flying buttresses, gazing down on the milling crowds and flying flags and the festival stage, where jugglers were now tossing flaming torches past the head of a small, terrified boy. If you forgot for the moment that we were living in a world where people blew up embassies just to keep kids like Jack from going to East Africa, you'd swear it was just another summer afternoon in the Middle Ages.

"Dad, are you looking for that lady?" the sly little devil wondered.

"No," I lied a little. "I was just thinking about how Dame Wendy would love all of this."

I really *was* thinking this, Dear Reader. Besides, my new wife didn't mind if I looked at other pretty women safely from afar. Looking simply meant I was still alive and kicking, as she herself had pointed out on more than one occasion when she caught me browsing her Victoria's Secret catalog or watching *Baywatch* without proper adult supervision. Like a small child in a large candy store, I just wasn't supposed to *touch* anything. If I did that, I probably wouldn't be alive and kicking for long.

"It's okay," he said. "I'm kind of looking for that girl, too."

"Oh well. Boys are us. Which girl would that be, Squire?"

"The girl in the dance."

"Oh, *that* girl."

"She was really pretty, Dad."

"I'll say."

I was pleased to think he was noticing pretty girls again. As I'd meant to say during our evening walk in Oxford, there were lots of pretty girls in this world besides Bethany Bellnap. But he would never find them unless he joined the dance—which of course he'd just done.

"I could eat a French farmer's ox," I proposed. "Are you by any chance hungry?"

"Oh yeah," he said, sweet Medieval music to my ears.

The old fella and his wife were having port in the hotel drawing room when we came in from dinner. I recognized them instantly, the elderly Brits we'd whizzed past on the stairs at the tapestry museum. A nightcap seemed in order, so I ordered Jack his usual Coke with lemon and asked for a tawny port of my own. We took possession of two stuffed chairs by the window. Lovely Bayeux lay in full summer darkness with a hint on the air of wood smoke from the fête's extinguished fires.

The wife, who had a rosy-complexioned round face that made her appear as if she'd been hiking all day up Ben Nevis, glanced over at us and smiled pleasantly. The husband seemed to be in a dead sleep in his boxy tweed sports coat.

"Good evening," she said with a soft midland English accent. "Have you had an enjoyable day?"

"Very nice," I replied, thinking fondly of the asperges blanc and filet de boeuf à l'humange rouge I'd choked down with the help of two glasses of a very distinguished breed of Cabernet Sauvignon. Jack, for his part, had discovered an unexpected fancy for foie gras and canard de l'orange, and we'd capped off a day of splendid serendipities with strong café au laits and one fine crème brulée burned elegantly on top.

"And yourself?" I asked this as if we were all sitting in a proper English drawing room instead of an even more proper French one.

"Very restful indeed. But then," she remarked dryly, eyeing her drowsing husband, "it's been that way for almost fifty years. Perhaps a wee bit *too* restful, eh, Tatty?" I suddenly thought I heard a trace of the Borders in the accent now, which made me think of the Queen Mum, who should be finishing up her inspection tour of Scotland about now and heading home to take my daughter on a girls' weekend to PEI. I also realized we'd been having so much fun I'd lost track of the actual date. All I knew for sure was that we had to make Paris for a birthday party in two more days.

The old gent abruptly snuffled awake and cranked forward, cupping his good ear. "Say that *again*?" I had to smile at the sight of this, picturing myself and Dame Wendy in a couple years, when it would probably take more than the passing scent of a pretty French woman to keep me from falling asleep over my nightcap.

They were Major Harold Huff and wife Sarah from Shropshire, England, and after we made polite chitchat for several minutes we learned they were making their annual July visit to the Lion d'Or.

"The same hotel," Lady Huff gave a little sigh, "and even the same room for forty-nine straight summers."

The major snorted amicably, "You might think they would give us the frequent visitor's discount, eh? But no go. That's the French for you. They loved Eisenhower, of course. He stayed here, too, you see. Don't know why we even bother."

Leaning forward myself, I wondered if I'd actually heard her correctly. Had she really said *forty-nine* summers straight?

"That's right, dear. Harold came ashore here with the lads on Gold Beach."

"A picnic at Battersea compared to what the others had all around us," Harold remembered, clearing his throat and gripping his untouched port.

"You were in the D Day landings?" I asked him, purely for Jack's benefit and my own, hoping I might coax a story or two out of the old fella before he fell back asleep and I had to drink his tipple for him.

"Came ashore in the first wave with the Fiftieth Division, East Yorkshire regiments, along with the flail tanks and Hobart's Funnies. Absolutely filthy weather. Three-meter waves at high tide. Awful glad to get clear of those damned LCTs. Many of the chaps brought their bicycles along, you see. The few Jerries we saw in our sector were holed up in the seaside cottages the Navy guns set on fire. There were snipers aplenty, though. I lost seventeen lads before we got off the beach. Three damned fine officers."

He took a sip of his port and fell silent, to let that sink in. Then he cleared his throat again and explained how after spending their first night on Gold Beach, his platoon followed a path cleared by the royal engineers through the antitank coastal defenses, and the going got easier through open hay fields and over stone walls, with little or no enemy resistance encountered. His objective was to reach the main road between Bayeux and Caen, the very road to Paris itself.

"We could hear the great bloody pounding going on around us, but beyond the occasional sniper it was a fairly easy assault. I remember one sniper kept us pinned up several hours," he said, pausing to study Jack, then blink at him as if he'd forgotten the rest of the story—or maybe didn't think it was appropriate. Then he resumed.

"When we found him he was folded up peaceful as a cat in a barn, a lad not much older than you, my boy. One of Hitler's supposedly invincible Jugend. Fifteen or sixteen by the look of him. Disgraceful."

The major took another nip of port and disappeared into his own thoughts.

"Like that boy who told the Americans about the gun." Jack put in his six francs' worth, looking solemnly at me. "Only he was French."

I nodded and explained to the Huffs how we'd eavesdropped on a school group's lecture early in the day and learned how a brave ten-year-old helped take out the coastal battery at Longues-sur-Mer.

"Tell them, Tatty, about the man in Bayeux," prompted Sarah Huff. "It's rather dear."

"Oh all right," grumped the major, hesitating again. He took another slug of his port and swirled his glass.

"We heard there was a German hospital and perhaps half a garrison of troops in Bayeux. We were expecting, I can tell you, far more trouble than we got. By the time we reached the village here, my count was up to twenty-three men down, including nine officers."

He turned stiffly in his seat and pointed a stubby finger over his left shoulder, indicating the northern edge of the town. "Everything was a bloody ruin around this place when we came down that road out there. On the edge of the village, the shutters flew back and an old farmer came running out of his house waving a dusty bottle of something at us and carrying a Union Jack. Not a tooth in his head, as I remember. It was he who informed us that Jerry had fled entirely—cleared out of the hospital straightaway, the hotel, the whole sorry lot of them gone. He offered us a drink of something to celebrate Bayeux's liberation, so we just bloody well stood there in the road and passed around the bottle. Highly undignified, I suppose, for officers."

"A decent vintage?" I asked Tatty.

The major smiled ruefully. "It was Calvados. Bloody awful stuff. Put me straight off it forever, I'm afraid."

We all smiled (even Jack) and I delicately inquired why they insisted on returning year after year to the same town, same hotel room,

probably the same bed for all I knew. I only hoped they weren't the
same bed sheets. Whatever else was true, theirs was a touching tribute to something private and perhaps largely forgotten; a fidelity
forged in war.

"To be honest, I really can't say," Sarah Huff replied as if no one had
ever bothered to ask such a thing before. She glanced almost tenderly
at her husband, who looked as ready for bed as I was. "Can you, dear?"

He cleared his throat again, swirling the last bit of his port. It
hadn't gone to waste, after all. He cleared his throat for the third or
fourth time and I realized it was from unbidden emotions this time. He
gazed at Jack and then at me, though I don't think he really saw either
one of us.

"I was a young lieutenant at Dunkirk and later I chased old Rom-
mel around North Africa a bit. Lost a lot of chaps along the way, you
see. Fine men all. Coming here put things straight for me, for the lot
of us." He thought a moment more and added, "There's a moment in
every chap's life he's born for, to do what he's meant to do best. For me,
good or ill, Bayeux was it."

A little while later, after saying good night to the Huffs, Jack and I
were mounting the long steps to bed when he remarked, "Hey, Dad, do
you know what was really cool about today?"

I had my own A list of unexpected pleasures—the moving walk at
Omaha Beach, the amazing *tapisserie*, the even more amazing fête and
Jack's unexpected legerdemain with a Bayeux longbow, topped off by a
dinner that was darn near something to phone home to Dame Wendy
about. Tomorrow we might have Mont-Saint-Michel and the mystery
of Europe's most famous labyrinth at Chartes to talk about, but for the
moment I was content and highly interested to know what my son
found really cool about today.

"What's that?"

"We met one Harold who lost France and then another one who
helped win it back."

"You're right," I agreed, the point having entirely escaped me as
usual. I placed my hand on Jack's head and pondered this private irony
of history as the stairs creaked beneath our ascent. For a moment, as
we climbed, I tried to come up with something snappy or at least amus-

ing to say in my father's French—a plucky latter-day jester's rejoinder to frame the whole wonderful day in perspective.

But all I could manage, quite honestly, was a very sleepy nod, a drowsy smile, and a happy yawn that was, under the circumstances, most authentic.

TEN

L' Eminence Gris

On the road to Chartes, wandering into an older world, I told Jack the modified Cliff Notes version of the Second Crusade, which some historians feel kicked into overdrive when Saint Bernard of Clairvaux, acting on behalf of King Louis VII, showed up one evening in 1146 at the mighty cathedral at Chartres to rally popular support for a second Crusade to "liberate" the Holy Land from the Muslims. Fifty years before that, just thirty-three years after William's conquest of Britain, Norman holy warriors had besieged the Holy City and the Temple Mount and massacred virtually every resident of Jerusalem— by one Muslim account more than seventy thousand men, women, and children—stripping every mosque and home of its silver and gold, stealing anything of perceived value and sending it home to fatten the coffers of Pope Innocent II.

A successful holy Islamic counteroffensive, or jihad, was finally mounted when the Arab tribes allied themselves behind an unlikely champion called Imad ed-Den Zengi—an austere, self-styled cleric who slept on straw mats in caves and imposed the strictest regimens on his followers—and overran the Christian city of Edessa, slaying the Frankish soldiers and selling their women into slavery but, by several accounts, protecting the lives of the remaining native Christians. The fall of Edessa galvanized the Muslim world, and after Zengi's death his son Nur ed-Din rose to even greater heights of power, sending panic through Western Christendom.

Thus, mere weeks after working the crowds to such a frenzy at Vezelay they nearly tore off his robes, the charismatic Saint Bernard came to the steps at Chartres to promise that any man who joined the Second Crusade to kill Muslims would be guaranteed full remission of his earthly sins, all the worldly treasure he could carry home, and a nifty speed pass into the arms of the queen of heaven if he somehow got killed in the process of serving God and France. *I opened my mouth,* Bernard later wrote to his pope, *I spoke; and at once the Crusaders multiplied to infinity. Villages and towns are now deserted.*

Mothers and wives, the story went, soon hid their sons and encouraged their husbands to get drunk whenever Saint Bernard came to town. For the record, I pointed out to Jack, the so-called Second Holy Crusade wound up a dismal failure when another charismatic Muslim named Saladin, the sultan of Egypt, surpassed Nur ed-Din's feats and recaptured Jerusalem for Islam, setting the stage for a Third Crusade and an epic confrontation between Saladin and none other than Richard the Lionheart, the two heavyweights of their respective faiths.

"Is that the knight on my wall?"

"I believe it is."

The Maine artist who painted my court jester had also done a magnificent oil of a Crusader knight sitting on his horse, reminiscent of N. C. Wyeth's rendering of a battle-weary Richard Coeur de Lion. The painting hung on the wall above Jack's bed, and when he was smaller and more gullible, I used to tell him the knight was keeping watch over the night—and him. One of the seemingly minor details Chet from the embassy let on in our brief travel consultations was that a guy named Osama bin Laden was suspected of being the mastermind behind the devastating Nairobi bombing that was keeping us out of Africa—an elusive self-styled charismatic cleric who reportedly lived in caves, probably slept on straw mats for all anybody knew about him, and had called for a jihad against the Christian West. Funny how history, given the chance, not only repeated itself with a similar cast of characters, but did so with a holy vengeance.

Fortunately the sudden appearance of Chartres cathedral interrupted these sobering thoughts, a visual cliché of postcard France, looking amazingly like the famous photographs you see of it floating on a sea of wheat from a Millet painting. To be honest, Chartres looked even more magical sitting off in the noontime distance than Mont-Saint-Michel had when we motored past that famous coastal landmark for a fleeting peek earlier that morning. I explained to Jack that Chartres cathedral was believed by many to be the best preserved example of Gothic art on earth, built by a series of unknown masons with little more than the rudimentary tools of straightedge, compass, and string, a structure so blessedly spectacular in ambition and execution it had been compared to Pericles' Acropolis in terms of revolutionary impact on Western architecture. It was home, among other things, to the world's greatest floor labyrinth and a piece of venerated cloth believed to have been worn by the Virgin Mary at the baby Jesus' birth.

"Cool. Could we see them?" Jack wondered.

"If we ask nicely, I bet they'll show us anything we'd like to see there."

Rupert Rivers was a living legend, but he didn't seem like a particularly happy man. A tall, rangy Englishman with a wavy scallop of graying hair, Rivers was the acknowledged authority on Chartres cathedral's stained glass windows and extraordinary statuary, a famous tour guide who only performed two lecture sorties through the cathedral per day. We happened to bumble through the church's massive portals just as he was counting heads and taking tickets, and we quickly paid up and joined the cluster of fifty or so camera-toting pilgrims clustered around him in sturdy wooden chairs for the afternoon lecture.

On the way in, I'd just been telling Jack about the somewhat grisly mythological tale supposedly conveyed on the original brass disk at the heart of the Cathedral's famous floor labyrinth, the Greek legend of brave and headstrong young Theseus, who slew the fearsome man-bull Minotaur in the darkened labyrinth built by the famed architect Daedalus beneath the Palace at Knossos, sailed home to Athens in triumph but neglected to put up the white sails as he approached home to reveal to his worried father, King Aegis, that he'd survived his ordeal. Seeing black sails, overcome by grief, assuming his beloved son had perished at the hands of the Cretan monster, good King Aegis leapt from the cliffs into the sea—a sea forever called the Aegean in memory of a father's needlessly broken heart.

"Oh wow," Jack breathed respectfully as our eyes adjusted from bright noon light to the cathedral's vast waxy-smelling murkiness. Hundreds of votive candles were flickering around us like Medieval campfires in a Crusader's dream. "Do you think we could go there?"

"Where?"

"Wherever that palace was with the monster beneath it. I'd like to see that labyrinth, too."

Steering him toward the gathering spot of the lecture tour, I said sure. It was somewhere on Crete. I would love to see Knossos myself because that was also where the poignant tale of Daedalus and Icarus took place, a papa's cautionary story as old as the Greek hills.

"I know that story!" Jack piped up happily, causing several elderly tour bus ramblers waiting quietly in the cathedral seats to turn and stare at us. Rupert Rivers was about to begin his lecture. "That's the one about the boy flying out of his prison on waxed wings made by his father!"

"Right," I whispered, mashing Nibs down into a chair. "He ignored his father's advice and flew too close to the sun and perished in the sea. Please remember that when you get to Mount Ararat Middle School this autumn."

Rupert Rivers himself was staring at us none too happily, too, I regret to say, and it took me only a moment to realize that the chairs where we'd deposited ourselves at the back of the lecture group were arranged in rows directly on *top* of the famous floor labyrinth, basically dashing any hopes we'd had of strolling the thing the way it was meant to be walked, as countless thousands of ancient and modern pilgrims had done before us. In recent years, ancient labyrinths have grown immensely popular again in Western spiritual worship, used as meditative devices for prayer, spiritual healing, and finding the little bald monk within. Dame Wendy, among others, had recently walked a portable labyrinth at her former Episcopal church in upstate New York that was copied from Chartres's famous labyrinth. She summed up the experience as "Really nice. Very relaxing. But I can't see *you* doing it without trying to hop it on one leg or something."

"Are the two of you possibly prepared to begin?" Rivers asked me pointedly over the snowy heads of the ramblers.

"Yes, sir." I was anxious to inquire if we might have the opportunity to shove back the chairs and walk the labyrinth afterward, but this didn't seem like a good moment to make that request.

"Very well."

He nodded, smiled mirthlessly, then launched into a pedagogic spiel about the cathedral's early construction and devastating fire and miraculous discovery of its unburned relic, the Virgin Mary's birth tunic, it was believed to be, a gift from Irene of Byzantium to Charlemagne which prompted a frenzy of popular support and a massive rebuilding scheme unlike any the world has seen before or since, resulting in the virtually total reconstruction of the "marvel of the Gothic age" in less than thirty years' time.

As he conveyed this impressive information, I saw Jack staring at the stones of the labyrinth underfoot and could pretty well read his thoughts. Having come this far and heard the tales of high church intrigue and ancient mystery, he was as anxious as I was to walk his dogs on that arcane path of stone.

As Rivers droned on about how the four thousand or so sacred and secular stories contained in the cathedral's vast array of windows—the greatest stained glass collection to be found anywhere in the world—amounting to nothing less than a "complete Medieval library" for the Christian pilgrim, Jack began shifting his feet along the labyrinth's mystical pathway. The next thing I knew, before I could stop him, he was standing up, moving silently among the empty chairs, gingerly stepping between their backs, working his way ever so quietly but diligently toward the heart of one of Christendom's most enduring mysteries.

"*Ex-cuse* me, young man." Rivers froze him mid-step, halfway over a chair. "This is *not* a frolicking ground! If you cannot contain yourself physically, I shall have to ask that you leave this group and possibly the cathedral itself."

I felt badly for my page. He'd just wanted to find his own little bald Medieval monk within. Now he had Rupert Rivers and fifty snowy-haired bus ramblers all glaring like constipated eagles at him.

"Sorry." I spoke up in Jack's behalf, somewhat ineffectually, tugging Nibs back into his seat before he got us both thrown out on our ears.

"I just spent the morning telling my son about the Second Crusade and the Cretan labyrinth and the Minotaur and how this labyrinth came from that one, as things tend to do in human history, and so forth. He'd love to know a little bit about it. For that matter, so would I and—"

"Well, in that case I suggest you go elsewhere. The labyrinth is *not* part of this lecture," Rivers said, briskly cutting me off before I could ask him about the possibility of moving back the chairs. "If you would care to sit there quietly and pay attention to my lecture, you are free to stay and just might actually learn something about Chartres. If not, I suggest that you go outside and run wild in the streets with the rest of the rabble."

The ramblers tittered and he promptly resumed his narration about the atheistic zealots of the French Revolution who closed Chartres cathedral and first made actual plans to demolish it but then changed their minds and turned it into a municipal office building where Dark Age locals, I gathered, came to pay overdue parking tickets on their donkey carts and delinquent property taxes on pig farms and such.

First it was Shakespeare with machine guns, I thought. Then it was rude Dutch guys on bikes. Now it was a condescending tour guide who thought he owned the world's greatest Gothic cathedral. I guess I was expecting (or hoping for) something more like the delightful, fact-filled toothless man from Ghent who'd hiked all the way home from a war just to see a silly painting and couldn't wait to point out the hidden treasures of the church he clearly adored. But Rivers obviously didn't have that common touch, or half as much class in my book. But at least he brought out the inner eighth grader in me.

"Rupert Rivers has nothing on Saint Bernard of Clairvaux," I whispered consolingly to my red-faced son, probably not as quietly as I could have. "Both are genuine Medieval blowhards."

Nibs grinned but Rivers fell silent again. *Uh oh,* I thought.

"I'm sorry. Is there something *else* you require?"

Yeah, Bozo. Can I get my ninety francs back? We'll just purchase a nice guidebook and go hang with the street rabble. Maybe start a revolution for kicks.

"No, sir," I lied, pie-eyed, like a choirboy caught writing blue words in the hymnal, wondering what he might do if I just started mindlessly humming, say, the theme music from *Hawaii Five-0*. The truth was, I shared my son's big disappointment at being denied the chance to walk the labyrinth like a million other Chartres pilgrims before us had, dismissed as mere intrusive ruffians, and found everything about this supposedly learned man a bummer to the spirit of pilgrimage.

"Good," Rivers snapped then switched on a wintery smile to the rest of his audience, most of whom appeared to be fighting to stay awake anyway. "In that case, if you all would please care to follow me . . ."

He trooped them off to a huge strained glass window showing Charlemagne defeating the Moors or Roland massacring the Infidels or some other proud moment of compassionate Medieval Christendom, and Jack slid me a look that asked what the heck we were going to do next. It was clear we weren't particularly wanted by Rupert and the ramblers. It was clear Nibs didn't care for Lord Rupert Rivers any more than I did.

"Let's follow them and try and get our ninety francs' worth of fun," I suggested optimistically. "That way we can either learn something interesting or at least bother him some more."

My page smiled slyly. Sir Rupert clearly brought out the best, or worst, in him, too.

When he visited Chartres almost seventy years before us, our fellow well-behaved New Englander Henry James found the cathedral and its famous windows an unforgettable retreat from the grind of the outside world. *More eloquent than the prayer book, and more beautiful than the autumn sunlight,* he wrote, adding that anyone who gave the place half a chance could *feel its glory like a child.*

The inner eighth grader in me didn't feel a whole lot of glory here, frankly speaking. The windows were admittedly stunning, true works of art—alone worth the price of the tour. But the church itself felt gloomy, vast, smug beyond belief, clammy, and thoroughly unwelcoming—the first time I think I've ever felt genuine discomfort in a self-proclaimed house of God. Maybe Chartres cathedral should have been a town hall after all, I decided, as we stumped along beneath the extraordinary windows and Lord Rupert went on like a John Houseman wanna-be, where you could ogle the pretty windows or kill time following the neat labyrinth while you waited in line to renew your goat-tending license or brought summer squash to the king.

Honestly, I tuned out much of Lord Rupert's monologue until we all traipsed out the giant front doors and around to the outside of the building to the spectacular north portal, to gape at various worried-looking saints arranged in a distinctly Medieval hierarchical fan over the cathedral's side doors.

At that point, a finger politely tapped me on the shoulder, disrupting my disruptive thoughts, and I turned around to see a shyly smiling middle-aged blond woman wearing a bright blue Denver Broncos sweatshirt. There was a big lug wearing a matching Broncos ball cap standing beside her on the sidewalk aiming a Minolta camera at the hierarchical fan who reminded me of . . . well, *me*. Just another New World hayseed poking around the glories of the Old World. I immediately guessed they went together the way Cheez Whiz goes with a Ritz.

"Hi," the Bronco wife chirped. "We joined the tour group kind of late. Can you tell me if he's talked about the floor labyrinth yet?"

"Not yet," I replied, wondering if she had any inkling that she was supposed to pay good French folding money for Rupert Rivers's rambling expertise. He wouldn't be one bit happy to discover a couple of American cultural deadbeats had slipped into the congregation. "But why don't you ask him if we can move the chairs and walk it or at least climb over the chairs?"

"Pardon me. Am I interrupting something again?"

It was You Know Who talking to You Know Who.

"Hi! We're from Denver," the lady fessed up cheerfully to the indignant tour guide. "Have you talked about the floor labyrinth yet? We're Mormon, you see."

"How nice for you." Chartres cathedral's distinguished *l'eminence gris* was unimpressed, to say the least. He added coldly, "As I told your friend earlier, the labyrinth is not part of this tour. This tour is concerned only with the cathedral's stained glass windows and statuary."

The woman glanced at me, perhaps wondering if I was really her friend after all.

"Don't give up," I quietly encouraged her. "He just *seems* like a guy who brushes his teeth with embalming fluid."

"Well, sir, we're really here for only today," the Mormon lady bravely persisted. "Is there at least any chance we could maybe *walk* the labyrinth? I mean, that's really why we came. A ladies group I belong to back in Denver is thinking of making a portable labyrinth, you see . . ."

Lord Rupert sighed heavily.

"Madam, have you been with this lecture group since the beginning?"

"Uh, well, no . . ."

"So I gather you have not properly paid?"

"Oh. I thought maybe it was free or something . . ."

"Well, it isn't. This tour is ending but there is another one scheduled for tomorrow morning at ten o'clock sharp. You are encouraged to properly pay and join us at that time."

With that condescending kiss-off, Rupert Rivers began to pleasantly converse with some ramblers about how they could sign up for a Friends of the Cathedral organization, become official patrons of Chartres, make donations toward the church's much-needed renovation, and receive regular email updates on the status of the work. If they gave enough loot, I could swear I heard him say, they would be eligible to receive really nice sponsorship gifts—a life-sized replica of the Virgin Mary's famous silk birthing cloak and a suitably framed copy of Saint Bernard of Clairvaux's fiery Second Crusade recruiting speech, *All's Forgiven, Boys. Now Let's Go Get Abdullah*. But maybe I was just hearing things.

The Mormon lady, at any rate, peered sheepishly at me, blushing in her big Bronco sweatshirt.

"Wow. Sweet guy, huh?"

"What a fart head," the Mormon husband summed up over our shoulders, more or less taking the words out of my mouth. This surprised me, I must say, because I didn't think Mormons were allowed to use words like "fart."

"This concludes our tour of Chartres cathedral," Rupert Rivers announced in a prissy fare-thee-well voice to his followers. "If you would care to follow me into the cathedral book shop, however, there will be several of my books on the stained glass windows and other aspects of the church available for purchase. I'd be happy to sign them, as well."

With that, he turned and marched away.

I was tempted to send Jack tagging after him to inquire if there was a guidebook on how to have a meaningful spiritual experience while climbing over the chairs of Chartres cathedral. But you can't send a boy to do a man's job so I gave the pious bugger chase myself.

"Excuse me?" I called after him.

Lord Rivers paused, pivoted gravely on a heel, and stared at me as if he felt a sudden gas pain.

"*Yes?*"

"Hi," I said as I caught up to him. "Remember me?"

"How could I possibly forget you? You belong to the boy who can't sit still."

"That's him. A regular Theseus in Jungle Mocs."

I smiled and spouted my bit about us aiming to wander the world like a couple New Age Medieval pilgrims, noting how we'd already lost the black rhino and Great Wall but still hoped to visit Crete, check out the ruins at Knossos, see the labyrinth that inspired Chartres, explore the taproots of Western Civ, maybe play Marco Polo in the Aegean and see how far we've come as a so-called race.

"I'm sorry." Rivers cut me off for a second time in an hour. "I do have a pressing engagement. And your point would *be* . . ."

I hesitated, wondering if I was simply wasting my breath on this strolling cadaver.

"No point. Just wanted to say I was sorry if we caused you any difficulties inside. We meant no harm. On the contrary, we're very interested in this place and I was hoping I might convince you to tell my son and those nice folks from Denver a little bit about the labyrinth. I'd even be glad to make a donation to the Friends of Chartres Cathedral—as long as I get one of the swell premiums or at least a souvenir T-shirt."

Rivers faintly smiled, and for a moment or two, I swear, he seemed about to apologize for being such a jerk and actually walk back down the cobblestones with me to convey a few endearing tidbits about the mysteries of the great floor labyrinth to Nibs and the waiting Mormons. If he did this, I'd march straight inside and purchase *all* of his guidebooks and ask him to sign them. We could start fresh, pop across the square afterward for a nice double latte mocha and some friendly conversation.

He hesitated only a moment more, giving me that eerie wintry smile.

"I suggest," he said pleasantly, "that you consider purchasing one of my books on the cathedral. They're highly informative. Good-bye to you now."

And with that, *l'eminence gris* of the greatest Gothic church on earth turned and briskly strode away.

ELEVEN

Madame Defarge

I woke to a dreadful smell and the sound of running water, wondering how on earth we could have wound up sleeping in Paris's famous sewers.

Rain hammered mutely somewhere and then I suddenly remembered Nibs and *père* were at the cute Hotel Lido just off the Place de Madeleine. My partner in myth-chief was still an unconscious lump beneath his duvet, in a matching twin bed to starboard, and a wall of water appeared to be running down the window through a slit in the heavy velvet draperies. After a few moments of gathering my scattered wits, I recalled a couple other facts relevant to the dawning day at hand.

Today was my new wife's fortieth birthday and France's celebrated Bastille Day. *Happy Birthday, France! Vive la Wife!* And I made a mental note to remind Jack to remind me to phone Dame Wendy at some point during our day's peregrinations to wish her a proper birthday salutation across oceans and inform her she'd have to come all the way to Italy if she intended to pick up her birthday presents, only two of which I'd actually acquired yet—the stone Eve and the wormy wooden apple from the Medieval fête at Bayeux.

With these objectives now summoning, I hopped up and peeked through the draperies at a biblical-sized rain falling on Place de Madeleine. *Mon Dieu*. Talk about raining on an entire nation's parade! I mentally reviewed the basic plan of attack I'd worked out for Bastille Day: to do the major museums we'd missed yesterday; scale the Eiffel

Tower; eat French food whenever possible; hike the Left Bank and see Luxembourg Gardens, where Tommy Paine was kept prisoner and Isadora Duncan once danced topless; buy some naughty French undies and perfume for new ladywife; eat more French food; watch patriotic parades; salute the tricolors and the president of France if we saw him; and finish up with a thrilling boat ride along the Seine as the holiday fireworks exploded overhead.

Then I glanced over at Jack, who was dead to the world. Poor tyke. I'd apparently tuckered him with our forced march around the city of lights yesterday. Then I spotted his Jungle Mocs sitting beside the door and realized *they* were the source of the disgusting smell that might soon have the gendarmes pounding down the door to find the decomposing body. I made a mental note to toss them into the next municipal trash barrel we passed.

Jack's beloved Mocs had basically disintegrated the preceding day when I marched him through three or four of Paris's better known *arrondissements*, all the way up to the Sacre-Coeur (for best view of the city) and back downhill through funky Montmartre, past the Bibliothèque Nationale to a back door of the Musée du Louvre where, on a tip from Madame Defarge in the Lido's basement breakfast cave, we found an alternative entrance (rarely used except for national holidays, she insisted) and only a two-hour wait into the world's most famous museum.

After a stroll along Rue de Rivoli, we hiked through the Tuileries to the Place de la Concorde, where once upon a time Louis XVI had lost his head and it's still possible on an average Parisian day to get flattened by a speeding tradesman while waiting to cross. On this day, however—which was really *yesterday*—due to the Bastille holiday, traffic had been reduced to a welcome level of mayhem because police were setting up all sorts of barricades and putting mobile swat units in position for a visit tomorrow—which was actually *today*—by the president of France.

The Jungle Mocs, at any rate, officially expired somewhere around the Arc de Triomphe, amid the surging crowds of holiday shoppers, about the time we innocently stopped off for a quick café noir and Coke with lemon at a café draped with the tricolors and accidentally offended several patrons who appeared to be under the general impression one of us had thoughtlessly tracked poodle poop into the restaurant, prompting us to make an emergency beeline straight across the busy boulevard into a hip shoe shop, where the teenage clerks were all wearing electronic headsets and vacant stares and the only designer sneakers that actually fit Jack's growing feet were bright puce and cost three thousand francs. We passed on them and wound up a couple doors away at an "outdoors" shop where the male clerks were all unshaven and wearing lumberjack shirts and the female clerks were dressed like Daisy Maes. We bought the first footwear that fit Jack's feet and didn't cost the price of a plane ticket home—a pair of nice Danish sandals. Perfect for the warmer world we were aiming for!

After a failed attempt to reach the observation deck of the Arc de Triomphe, which was mobbed with patriotic peckerwoods just like us, to finish the tale of two new sandals, we broke in Jack's shoes by hiking all the way to the famed Trocadero, crossing the muddy River Seine only to discover an annoying two-hour wait just to get to the steps of the Eiffel Tower. We pushed on and ultimately wound up at the Museum of the Grand Army of the Republic, looking at old war pictures with our tongues hanging out from sheer physical exhaustion, at which point I flagged down a taxi on Quai Voltaire and a Moroccan guy wearing a Mick Jagger earring drove us home to the Lido.

"How do you like Paris?" our friendly taxi guy inquired, simultaneously dodging police barricades and displaying a gold tooth in the rearview mirror. I felt myself doing a Queen Mum lurch for a brake pedal that wasn't there and vaguely wondered if Mick might have *stolen* this taxicab from somebody.

"Great," Jack replied, oblivious to the police whistles and wild gesticulations of an angry traffic gendarme as we whizzed through a prohibited area across Le Pont-Neuf toward the Place de la Concorde. "People here are so nice."

"True. But that wasn't always the case, monsieur."

The Moroccan Mick Jagger explained, with a chuckle, taking a corner on two wheels past the United States Embassy, how Paris used to be celebrated for its rudeness to foreign visitors, snobby and downright condescending toward provincials and immigrants alike, especially

toward visiting Brits and Americans. But all of that had changed in recent years and Parisians these days actually liked American tourists
and the good life they brought.

"Do you have a theory why?" I wondered conversationally, gripping
the door handle and feeling faintly nostalgic for the haughtiness of old
Paris that made a provincial visitor instantly know his or her place and
appreciate his or her cultural inferiority, not to mention the slower
taxicabs. Recently I'd read somewhere that some dedicated Fran-
cophiles view this warming of relations as an irrefutable sign of de-
clining French culture. Unlike the Dutch, if one may stoop to crass
generalities, Parisians have never made any bones about being naturally superior to the rest of the world, which explains their foreign policy and splendid cooking.

"Oh yes. Very simple, *mon ami,*" Mick said, glancing at me in his
rearview, just missing a woman and her little dog by inches as we skidded around the corner past Hediard and stopped directly in front of the
Hotel Lido. He held up a thumb and forefinger and massaged them together like a Chicago bookie, indicating the true source of this new-
found friendliness.

"That is the new Paris, monsieur. We love what Americans bring
here—money, Gap jeans, movie stars. Did you know Britney Spears's
mother was in this very taxi? She tipped me two hundred francs."

"No kidding?" I said, carefully shoving Nibs out the door into the
quaint cobbled street and recalling that in the Paris of old no self-
respecting taxi driver or arrogant waiter would think of asking for a tip,
much less one like that.

"That may be," I said, fumbling for my pocket change, "but I can't
help missing the Paris of old." And to prove it, I tossed him twelve
extra Francs for his trouble.

Madame Defarge was at her post in the basement breakfast room of
the Lido when Jack and I came down for Bastille Day.

She welcomed us with a no-nonsense grunt of vanishing Paris and
directed us to a small round café table in the corner, where she
slammed down a small china pot of tea for Nibs and poured me out a
brisk cup of black French roast and then spread her large hands on her

much larger hips and demanded to know if we'd been able to get into the Louvre the way she'd instructed us to yesterday.

"*Oui, madame.*" I dazzled her with some of my father's French and went on to explain that we only had to cool our heels for two hours in order to get inside the famous museum due to the holiday throngs. Jack had loved *Mona Lisa* and I had this continuing thing for *Winged Victory*.

"*C'est dommage!* You obviously went to the wrong door," she declared in disbelief, shaking her large gray head and marching off to make sure the meek English couple weren't taking any unauthorized extra Gentilly cream with their tea or shedding toast crumbs at the tiny but gorgeously arranged breakfast buffet table set by the cave-like wall.

Despite the biblical deluge outside, I felt my spirits lift immeasurably. Whatever else was true about the changing social weather of Paris and the worrying new niceness of its citizenry, Madame Defarge was clearly a guardian of the old ways.

Defarge wasn't her name, of course. I have no idea, in fact, what her name was. But she struck me as a woman not to be trifled with, like the watchful midwife of the French Revolution who chillingly knits to the scrape of the falling guillotine in Charles Dickens's *A Tale of Two Cities*, the kind of yeoman ladywife who would happily have charged the Bastille wearing a bloody apron and wielding a major league meat cleaver at any cake-eating aristocrat who foolishly got in her path.

Jack seemed to be quietly terrified of her, to be honest, politely refusing to go anywhere near the buffet spread of goat cheeses, crusty breads, boiled *heufs*, and plain white yogurt. When I suggested he put something in his pocket for our day of French follies ahead, he leaned forward and whispered back in so many words that the Lido's breakfast offerings were so bleak he would rather eat his cloth napkin. I suspected his plumbing was plugged up again. Breakfast in France, he admitted when I pressed him on the subject, struck him as even worse than breakfast in Holland.

Tilting discreetly forward so Madame couldn't hear me, I explained to my son that the French really don't care much for the kind of breakfast we favor, which is why they disdainfully refer to it as *petit déjeuner*.

Generally speaking, they regard breakfast as a mild gastronomic intrusion that occurs daily, somewhere between scratching their underarms while having the morning pee and sitting down to a six-course lunch with a nice Cabernet at the Closerie des Lilas.

Jack openly giggled at this, fiddling with his teacup, then fell deathly quiet because Madame cast him a quick reproving look across the room from where she was busy straightening up the silver yogurt spoon some slob had fractionally disturbed.

"Can we go down to the corner and get some of that duck stuff on raisin toasts or a croissant?" he whispered, meaning he wished to pay a visit to the famous striped red awnings of Hediard, the gourmet charcuterie we'd immediately set upon after hitting town. It was there that Nibs discovered his heretofore unknown passion for *pain au raisins* and goose liver *foie gras*.

"Excellent suggestion," I agreed clandestinely, no particular fan of goat cheese, boiled eggs, and the standard French hotel breakfast fare myself. But at exactly that moment, wouldn't you know it, Madame swooped back down on us, wiping her hands on a white bistro towel in a manner that would have done the flying knitting needles of Madame Defarge no insult whatsoever.

"So," she declared, "which *musée* today, *monsieur?*"

"The Musée d'Orsay." I smiled cheerfully up at her. "Then we're planning to do the Left Bank and watch the fireworks."

"Ah. *C'est bon*," she concurred grimly. "But this is a great deal for the boy in only one day. I fear too much—especially today of all days."

I explained that we only had, regrettably, a single day left in Paris. So we planned to try to cram in a lot of sight-seeing. Tomorrow night we hoped to be in Carcassonne.

She frowned—or maybe this was simply an old-fashioned Parisian way of smiling.

"You have been to Paris for Bastille Day before?"

"Never had the pleasure. Is it lively?" I pictured pie-faced Collettes doing the cancan in tricolored bloomers, French Barneys saluting on every corner of the Republic, Delacroix nudes reclining on the Champs de Mars, Chirac performing a sporty send-up of Maurice Chevalier, one big happy Visa commercial reminiscent of the city's jubilant liberation celebration of summer 1945. My father had been there for that one; we were here for this one. Life's little coincidences never failed to astound me.

She shrugged indifferently, snatched up Jack's half-finished teacup, then paused and sighed. For a moment I thought she was going to plant a parsnippy finger in my face.

"Who can say in such weather? But usually people go a little mad at Bastille Day. There will be trouble, *monsieur*. Count on that. Fools drinking. A night of true lawlessness. Much public indecency, I am afraid to have to say. No place for a boy."

Sounds really fun, I almost said but, fortunately, didn't. I have no doubt in my mind she would have smacked my insolent face with her bistro towel.

"A responsible father, *monsieur*, will have his child off the street by ten," she advised primly, solemnly dipping her good eye to make sure I got her point.

Our morning at the Musée d'Orsay was truly exhilarating. For two solid hours we walked leisurely up and down the magnificent suspended floors of Victor Laloux's vertigo-inspiring renovated train station, staring at an almost unbelievable array of famous Impressionist paintings, Degas's fragile ballerinas and Manet's bare naked ladies, classically writhing nudes, Rodin's *Gates of Hell* and Carpeaux's frolicking *maenads* which caused such a memorable civic uproar when the statue was publicly unveiled in 1869.

"Dad," Jack wondered as we moseyed from stately Renoir and Millet to risqué Delacroix and Manet, "why are there so many pictures here of, you know, of *naked* people?"

Being no expert on art or really anything else, for that matter, except possibly how to kill expensive lawn shrubbery, I attempted to explain to *mon fils* that from the beginning of time the classical artist revered the nude human form because it beautifully embodied man's eternal quest to achieve both union and liberation of the spirit and flesh, and that during the particular period of French art housed at the magnificent d'Orsay, covering roughly the years from the mid-nineteenth century through the Great War, coinciding with the world's first great industrial revolution, when machines replaced work-ers at an unprecedented rate in Western society, the artwork could be viewed as a kind of reactionary statement about the inherent dangers of a modern world racing pell-mell toward its own self-destruction by forgetting the lessons of its mythical past, focusing more on the indus-try and machines than the spirit of the men and women who made them.

Or, on the other hand, maybe they just liked painting naked people.

Thus, in any case, Édouard Manet's famous bathing scene with two formally dressed Edwardian gents sprawling on the ground with a beau-tiful woman who has casually disrobed and appears to think nothing of it, as I explained to Nibs, was probably destined to create quite a stir of indignation when it first appeared at exhibition in 1863. Symboli-cally, I suppose, someone could argue, the lady in her birthday suit (*Vive Dame Wendy!* I naughtily thought) was a symbolic messenger muse sent from the ancients to warn modern men of commerce and ambition not to forget the lessons of Eden. Or maybe she just didn't want tan lines.

"The nude body," I pointed out to my son, nudging him along on his new Danish sandals, "is nothing to be ashamed of, Nibs. Unless of course it's mine."

"Oh," he said, and wandered ahead into the next salon to see what interesting things were hanging there while I paused to see if I could make out the nipples on Édouard Manet's astutely named *Blond Woman with Bare Breasts*. Almost instantly, Jack was back, blushing to the soles of his new footware.

"I think *that* room is for adults only," he stammered.

I smiled at his backwoods innocence and stepped into the salon to see what got him so hot and bothered. It turned out to be a huge oil on canvas called *Origin of the World* by Gustave Courbet which boldly depicts, ahem, a young woman reposing on her back amid rumpled bed linens, visible only from upper torso to calves, dimpled knees casually parted and—how shall I put this, *amis*—her dark fundament spectac-ularly exposed to all of France.

"Wow," I think I said, pretty amazed myself, to be perfectly truthful, wondering if Madame Defarge had any idea this sort of bohemian thing was hanging in Paris's second most visited public museum. Pushing my heir along to the exit, I suggested that we go downstairs and look at Eugene Atget's famous black-and-white photographs of Old Paris which had in turn inspired my favorite French photographer, Robert Doisneau.

At Notre Dame, we were forced to join a long queue outside in the heavy rain that had crept back up the Seine by the time we reached the church, making the city's eternal interplay of the monumental and personal all the more vivid. I purchased a cheap umbrella from a cart vendor and held it over Jack's head as he disappeared for a little bit into Middle Earth, thinking as I did how the new city still appeared to match Robert Doisneau's sympathetic eye.

For fifty years between German occupation and the early 1980s, Doisneau, a Renault factory photographer, wandered the streets and suburbs of Paris capturing thousands of unforgettable images of life with his simple black-and-white camera, an amazing record of the city's evolution through the changing landscapes and faces of its people. Many of Doisneau's most unforgettable pictures feature children about Jack's age cavorting in streets of postwar rubble, schoolboys with leather satchels, couples getting married in dim bistros, old men and women dancing in empty cafés, lovers passionately kissing at Saint Michel, dogs doing goofy stunts, jumbled shop windows and rainy passageways, and a thousand ordinary moments animated by a childlike sense of wonder and human optimism you can almost feel radiating from the page.

One of my favorite Doisneau photos—we keep a thick water-stained museum edition of his work in the loo at our house, which is fun to browse while soaking in *le tub*—shows an old dog standing on a vegetable crate peering into a bar window in the Twelfth Arrondissement and a pair of surprised, round-eyed children peering back at him through the thick watery glass. Another unforgettable one features a beautiful old man standing beside the hanging head of a freshly slaughtered cow in a market stall at Les Halles, a dismembered head so classically serene it appears almost sculpted. Doisneau called that photograph *L'Innocent*.

Mon Dieu, I thought, as we shuffled closer to the great cathedral doors, *there's a photo for Doisneau right there.*

He was filthy, soaked to the bone by the drubbing rain, maybe more like a man from Victor Hugo come to think of it, a blind beggar with darkened craters for eyes, holding a deeply creased hand out silently from his spot on the cathedral's lowest step, basically invisible to the tourists shuffling past him into mighty Notre Dame.

Jack glanced up and followed my gaze to the wretched man.

"What's he doing, Dad?"

"Asking for money."

Jack looked at the man for a long moment and then observed that the Queen Mum or maybe his stepfather had recently said no one should ever give money to homeless people because they would only go and purchase alcohol or cigarettes with it. I told him I'd heard this theory and understood its well-intentioned logic but I respectfully rejected it. In my book, I expounded as we inched closer and closer to the sad human wraith, if someone had the courage or sheer desperation to stand on a crowded street and beg for help . . . then I wasn't above offering whatever I could spare. I tried to think of a famous line from Blake about a dog starving at his master's gate being a sure sign of a state's spiritual decline, but I couldn't come up with the actual quote, so I simply explained to my son that, personally speaking, I never passed a homeless man or woman without trying to remember to leave something in his or her hand.

"Who knows?" I said quietly, studying the man, hoping to inject a ray of lightness into the unexpected gloominess. "They might be angels or something, come down to see who is being nice to whom."

I told Jack about a good friend of mine from high school who'd somehow fallen between the cracks and was now reportedly living in a public park. It happened every day, to good people and bad. In Paris. New York. Even small towns in Maine.

"Can we give him something?"

"You bet. When we come out."

We followed a pair of bearded Greek Orthodox priests up the steps into the crowded cathedral, which seemed to be illuminated by ten thousand votaries, and wandered down a side aisle to the sacristy chapel, where we paid admission to see the church's more prized sacred relics.

As we entered, Jack asked me what a relic was and I explained to him that since the early Middle Ages Catholic churches everywhere promoted ownership of venerated objects believed to have some direct association with Jesus and his followers. The word came from the Latin *relinquere* or "remains" and could be anything from wooden splinters supposedly taken from the cross at Christ's crucifixion to pieces of the vinegar-soaked sponge Christ put to his lips near death. Bits of apostles' clothing and even body parts of saints were believed to hold magical healing power and had been used for centuries to attract the visiting faithful. During the Middle Ages, I added, droning on a little bit more like Rupert Rivers than I intended, ordinary people undertook long and dangerous pilgrimages just to touch or catch sight of these holy relics, often claiming they were healed of the worst infirmities as a result of their encounters. Chartres cathedral, I reminded him, supposedly kept the Virgin Mary's birth tunic and Paris's Notre Dame—maybe even this room we were slowly shuffling toward—supposedly contained several of the very carpenter nails used to hang Jesus on the cross. According to one legend I'd read somewhere, during one of the Seine's periodic massive floods, a French cardinal held aloft one of these surviving nails and commanded the river to recede, which it supposedly did. If I recalled correctly, too, Notre Dame also claimed to own Christ's original crown of thorns—missing one thorn, I guess, which Joseph of Arimathea smuggled off to Glastonbury to grow the thorn tree from.

"Wow," Jack murmured respectfully, as we reached the admission booth, where a baby-faced young man was dispensing sacristy tickets.

I handed him a fifty-franc note and inquired if it might be possible to see Christ's crown of thorns or maybe the Calvary nail that pushed back the flooding Seine. The way it was raining outside, I joshed with him in the spirit of the *new* Paris, somebody might need to run and fetch those suckers any minute.

"You wish to view *what*?"

"The nails that hung Jesus on the cross."

He looked at me as if I'd lost my mind.

"*C'est impossible.*"

"Do you mean it's not possible to see them or it's not possible they are here?"

"*C'est impossible, monsieur. S'il vous plaît!*"

Inside the crowded sacristy, we snooped around a bit looking at various artifacts and doodads belonging to lots of dead French popes and greedy Crusader kings, including the somewhat girly bedclothes of Saint Louis himself, half a dozen gold crowns crusted with knockout jewels, ornate Liberace-style rings, breastplates of gilded armor, and other Holy Roman hardware that would have sold out in no time flat on QVC and made the good old Queen Mum's Scottish Red Tide blood positively boil with contempt for such wretched material excess.

Then something really scary happened.

I lost Jack.

It happened in a New York instant. One moment he was loyally by my side peering through security glass at a bejeweled sword that probably once separated an infidel's head from his shoulders in the name of a New Jerusalem. The next moment I was jostled by someone in the crowd and I realized Nibs the Lost Boy really was nowhere to be seen!

"Jack," I called out above the many shuffling feet and murmuring voices. In the background, I could hear organ music being played in the cathedral proper and the cash registers merrily ringing up a brisk descant of sales of holy Notre Dame souvenirs.

There was no answer and no sight of the boy—and my heart, I must tell you, plunged. After a moment of reeling personal panic, I did what any reasonable American parent imagining the worst things happening to their lost child in a foreign place would have done under similar circumstances.

I got on my tiptoes and shouted his bloody name.

"*Jack Braxton Dodson! Where* are *you?*" I yelled, probably a little louder than I needed to, in retrospect. I mean, I didn't intend to wake the dead or anything.

Someone instantly seized my elbow. But unfortunately it wasn't J. B. Dodson.

"*Monsieur!* Silence! *S'il vous plaît.* Ziss is a *hole-ee* place!" It turned out to be our young *frère* from the admission desk.

"Right," I said, prying loose my arm. "And so's my son, pal."

"Dad!"

The muffled but familiar voice was true angel music to my ears. Heart racing like a Moroccan cab driver, I glanced over to see one of the Greek Orthodox priests smiling sweetly at me. He pointed to the back of the sacristy where, a dozen yards along, give or take a Holy Roman relic display case, I saw my only son on the planet hopping up and down like Toulouse-Lautrec on a crowded train platform, waving his arms at me over the heads of the baffled crowd.

"You must be quiet or you must leave *zee* church," the clerk informed me in no uncertain fashion, obviously a son of *Old* Paree.

"No problem, Ace. We're going to lunch in the Latin Quarter."

I politely pushed my way back to the alcove where Jack had been eyeballing Saint Louie's war armor and sword and hugged the little dude like there was no tomorrow.

"Let's get out of here," I proposed, "before they send for Rupert Rivers to give us the bum's rush." I angled him for the exit, where the older of the Greek priests was waiting for his friend.

"What's a bum's rush?"

"Basically what I'm doing to you."

As we passed, the priest reached out and patted Jack's shoulder reassuringly, then smiled at me inside his solemn gray beard. He seemed to feel my joy.

"Thanks for the help," I said to him, not certain if he understood me.

The priest merely bowed his head elegantly, eyes twinkling. Finding a lost sheep, I guess, is basically the same in every language.

The blind man was exactly where we'd left him on the lowest step of the church, as we hurried past the front of the cathedral toward the Petit Pont, only now the Bastille Day rain was coming down at a much heavier clip. His creased hand was still patiently extended, glistening wet. Jack paused, glanced back at him, and reminded me of my promise never to pass a needy palm. I gave him the first bill I pulled from my pocket, another fifty-franc note.

"Wait," I said, as he loped off. "Give him this, too."

I handed him our cheap umbrella. It wasn't really doing us much good—one more thing to cart along to Crete, if things went that far.

"Cool. Thanks."

Nibs jogged over and placed the franc note gently in the man's palm and handed him the umbrella. The man's fingers closed over the money, and he fumbled for a moment before realizing what else this young stranger had given him. He smiled, popped up the umbrella, said something beyond my earshot, and then reached out a hand and found Jack's shoulder, his thick furry fingers groping their way to the top of Jack's head.

It was a perfect Doisneau moment.

Jack ran back, grinning like one of the photographer's street urchins playing in a burned-out car on Liberation Day, and together we sprinted across the Petit Pont into the narrow alleyways of the Latin Quarter.

The wind picked up, the rain blew harder. A postcard kiosk blew over in Place Michel, scattering glossy postcards of Paris across the wet pavement, and an awning canvas untied itself, wildly flapping. On Rue St. Andres des Arts, we ducked into the narrow shop to wait out the violent burst of weather. Some birthday party Paris was having.

"Oh, man, Dad, *look*."

We were surrounded by chess sets, dozens and dozens of gorgeous chess sets.

For the next half hour or so, we shamelessly fingered half the sets in the shop. Naturally, Jack wanted to purchase a travel set for the road, prompting me to remind my son that I didn't have a clue how to play chess.

"That's okay. I'll teach you," Nibs volunteered brightly, needlessly reminding me that he was the reigning ten-and-under chess champ of Bowdoin College's Summer Day Camp. The little scamp had already settled on the set he wanted, too, a small but exquisite set featuring hand-painted Crusader knights and Moorish warriors. The knights were on horseback, the Moors on camels. The pieces were made of hand-carved wood and beautifully detailed with ceramic paint. The travel box they came in was handsomely upholstered and folded out to make a beautiful, tidy playing board. I asked the clerk how much for the set, bracing for his reply.

"Five hundred francs," the man said. He was perched on a narrow stool reading *Paris Match*. He peered at me neutrally over half-moon lenses.

"But since the boy is a chess champion and this is Bastille Day . . ." He shrugged. "I will let it go for four hundred fifty. Perhaps you will learn something new, eh, *monsieur*?"

"Would you take four hundred?"

"*Dad* . . ." Jack seemed worried I would blow the deal, but as I later took pains to explain to him, all seasoned world travelers must learn to cagily barter with the locals, if they don't intend to be robbed blind. A lesson Britney Spears's mom would do well to learn before returning to the City of Light.

"*Non, monsieur*. That is the last one I have of this type. Very good craftsmanship. Made in Morocco."

"Right," I commented, picturing identical sets stacked all the way to the ceiling in back. "By any chance do you know a taxi driver called Mick?"

The clerk blinked at me uncomprehendingly and went back to his newspaper, and Jack's worried expression grew visibly more worried as I picked up a Crusader on a horse and a warrior on a camel.

"Would I get to be a Crusader knight or a Moorish warrior?"

"Whichever you want," he graciously offered, "although I'd kind of like to be the knight."

"Did you know," the clerk chipped in from somewhere behind his newspaper, "that chess originated in the Middle East? It was actually brought to the West by the Templar Knights."

"Really? How about three hundred?" I suavely countered—just to show *Monsieur* was no hillbilly from a dirt road in Maine.

"*Non*. Four hundred, *monsieur*."

"Okay," I said. "We'll take it."

The windows of Café Flore were nicely steamed over, but the snotty doorman—another guardian of *old* Paris!—refused us entry because we were wearing safari shorts for an African safari we were no longer planning to take. The story was disappointingly the same a dozen meters along Saint Germain at Deux Magots, where holiday diners and aspiring surrealists were crammed to the bistro's famous rafters.

A bit farther down the wind-lashed boulevard, though, we happened upon a cozy nook with checker-clothed tables sitting beneath a shuddering awning, a scattering of patrons farther inside who looked reasonably happy with their food, a promising air of warmth and dining hospitality that summarized the new Parisian attitude, plus a burly waiter who sympathetically said to me as we ambled past, "You should get out of the rain, *monsieur*. Eat here and you will smile again. I promise."

I hadn't realized I was frowning. But we promptly took a table near the front of the Grille Saint Germain and eyeballed the menu, which the waiter brought along with a lovely basket of warm bread and *beurre* and a thoughtful bottle of *l'eau minérale*.

Jack set up our new chessboard and more or less outlined the objective of the ancient Templar game, explaining how each piece was permitted to move this way or that. Either chess turned out to be much easier to grasp than I'd expected it to be or Jack simply explained the game in a very nice, sensible way. In any case, he offered me my choice of armies and I selected the Moors because (a) I knew he wanted the knights and (b) I really liked the nifty blue Moor robes and golden swords and had always wanted to ride a camel.

Nibsy ordered foie gras and toast, grilled gigot with rosemary, braised carrots and parsnips, plus a basil tomato salad and a tarte pommes, eating like a Templar heading to the Holy Land. I considered ordering the grille lapin but settled finally on the *plait du jour*, which happened to be steak tartare. Paris, I happen to know from hearing some really French-sounding guy wearing a chef's hat say so on the Food Channel, is really the *only* place in the world where you can eat steak tartare and be reasonably assured you won't have to throw up afterward in the municipal begonias.

"What exactly *is* steak tartare?" Jack wanted to know, after I'd placed my order with our burly *garçon*.

"A famous French dish. Basically raw beef ground up with anything interesting the cook can find lying about in the kitchen—onions, cheap sherry, various rotting vegetables, yesterday's early edition of *Le Monde*, maybe a few soggy tube socks from the French national rugby team. That sort of thing."

Jack smiled, deftly flicking one of my Moorish pawns off the board. You had to watch this kid, I realized. He *was* very good at chess. I was already missing four or five guys and their camels.

"Can I try it?"

"Sure. Live dangerously. But only if you give me some of your foie gras."

As we each pondered further moves, I sipped a glass of lightly chilled Sancerre and fondly remembered a wonderful night Wendy and I had had not too long ago in Chantilly, the night before I marched her to the second platform of the Eiffel Tower and proposed that she abandon all common sense and marry me. We never managed to reach the top of the Eiffel Tower, but we did reach the altar and now she was sitting home on her birthday while Jack and I were living it up along the Saint Germain. Didn't seem one bit fair, to be honest, and I remembered I needed to buy her some authentic oo-la-la Parisian underwear and perfume before we set off to ancient Carcassonne.

"I've got a great idea," I said to my budding chess master. "After we buy some nice unmentionables for Wendy, let's climb all the way to the top of the Eiffel Tower and phone her to wish both her and France a happy birthday!"

"Great," he said, executing another quick move. The little creep glanced up and, smiling, announced, "Sorry, Dad. Checkmate."

I was shocked, to say the least, admitting that I thought the average chess match took *hours* rather than minutes to complete, wondering also what was keeping my steak tartare. They'd probably had to send out for fresh dirty tube socks or something.

"It does. But you're a beginner, Dad. Don't feel bad or anything. You'll probably get better."

Lunch arrived and I lost another game even before Jack's *gigot* was fully dispatched down the little red lane. We played a third game over dessert and coffee, with the same depressing result. By the time *l'addition* arrived, Nibs was up three-zip and all I got for my efforts was the bill.

Many hours later, somewhere around midnight in the city of lights, footsore and sleepy, with my pockets stuffed with Dior perfume and lacy sweet nothings that had set me back another four hundred francs, we finally reached Dame Wendy to bid good night and a proper happy birthday. But it wasn't from the top of the Eiffel Tower.

We reached her from somewhere along darkened Quai Branly, where we were being swept along by a street mob of late night partying Parisians in the general direction of Place de la Concorde after the fireworks display and a fairly tranquil boat ride along the Seine. There were no taxicabs anywhere to be seen, and most of the Métro stations had apparently been bolted shut for the night, which meant it was either hike all the way back to Hotel Lido or find a cozy un-peed-upon spot in the civic shrubbery to curl up and sleep—which probably would have been nigh impossible given all the random gunshots, bleating police sirens, exploding cherry bombs, illegal crackling bonfires, whooping packs of roving skinheads, blaring car horns, and solid French citizens making love everywhere you stepped. Madame Defarge had sure been right about Paris after dark!

"Happy birthday!" I yelled to my wife over the din and the darkened Atlantic. "Wish you were here instead of there. I've got something really great for you in my pocket!"

"Thanks," she replied. "But don't be crude. Tender ears might be listening. By the way, where exactly *are* you two?"

"I don't know. Somewhere along the Seine. How about you?"

"I'm outside watering your new bushes. It's been kind of dry. How's the weather in Paris?"

I said it wasn't the least bit dry but that didn't stop people from watering the bushes here, too. I was half-tempted to unzip and join them. Too much Belgian lager on the *Baton Mouche*.

"Well, goodness. It sounds like quite a party," she hollered pleasantly back—her voice fading in and out, possibly due to flaring sunspots or a widening hole in the Ozone.

I thought I heard her ask how things had gone that day, so I quickly filled her in on our adventures—the d'Orsay's timeless tributes to the feminine form, the strangely wonderful Doisneau-ean events at Notre Dame, the blind man, the Medieval chessboard, our nice post-lunch amble through *Jardins du Luxembourg* and stopping into a fancy lingerie shop where the clerks all looked like Catherine

Deneuve and handed out fresh-baked cookies as you walked through the door.

My new spouse laughed robustly somewhere across a darkened ocean.

"You bought me French underwear?"

"This is Paris, madam, where except for tonight people are extremely discreet. Let us just say they were the most expensive free cookies I ever ate."

By the time we reached the foot of the Eiffel Tower, I amplified, the Paris Police were shutting down the place due to unspecified "security" reasons, so we ate dinner at a crowded bistro on Avenue de Suffren and then went for a long ride on a *Baton Mouche* along the Seine. With no taxis or trains available to take us home, we'd joined up with an unruly mob of teenage punks that was reenacting the storming of the Bastille and promised to drop us off at the Hotel Lido on their way.

"Nice folks. Parisians have turned very friendly, by the way. Especially the ones with pink hair and safety pins through their cheeks."

Just then, someone fired a revolver—or maybe it was a police cruiser backfiring as it rushed past us with its blue light flashing.

"What was *that?*"

"Not sure. We're not sticking around to find out."

She said she had some good news. She'd found a great little hotel for us down in Carcassonne. Problem was, because the famous Medieval fortress city had its own summer festival going on, we had to get there by four the next afternoon. To do that, she said—actually, hollered—we'd either have to take a high speed train or an hour commuter flight to Toulouse. Orly had a flight at seven-forty. Surprisingly reasonable, too.

"Do you think Jack could handle flying again this soon?"

I glanced over at my late night sidekick. He was wide awake and merrily booting empty wine bottles along Quai Branly and humming "Le Marseillaise" and didn't appear even the slightest bit perturbed by the random acts of violence going on all around us.

"Go ahead and book it. Maybe we can get there early enough to see a prehistoric cave painting or two."

"Great," she said, and then added with concern, "Are you guys *really* okay out there? It sounds kind of . . ." Her voice began to break up and vanish before I had the opportunity to tell her how excited I was about seeing her in eight days' time in Milan. I tried to redial but the phone was dead, probably because I'd forgotten to charge it up that morning at the Lido.

The front door of the hotel was locked and I saw only a single table lamp burning in the cozy lobby. I tried my room key in the lock but the door wouldn't budge.

"Uh-oh," I said to Jack, rattling the door. "I think we might have to sleep on the stoop tonight, Boss. Madame Defarge was right. It is the best of times, the worst of times. The age of wisdom, the age of foolishness. But that's actually Dickens. Anyway, sorry I kept you out so late."

"That's okay," he said, as if he could easily kick wine bottles till dawn. He sat down on the Lido's front step and placed his new chess set on the pavement, glancing up at me. "We could play another match."

"Okay," I agreed, sitting down beside him. "Maybe soon I'll be just average."

At that instant, though, a large figure loomed from the shadows within. Someone had been dozing in a lobby chair and I recognized the unsympathetic figure of Madame Defarge advancing upon us. She clacked opened the door, frowned, and pushed a rebellious stand of gray hair behind an ear, motioning us rapidly inside.

"*Bon*. You have finally returned."

She gave a snort, locking the Lido's door behind us with a violent twist that sounded like a jail cell being locked on poor Sidney Carton. "It is not wise, *monsieur*, to expose a child to such *debaucherie*."

"I know. You're right. But he begged to see it."

She fixed me with a hard stare. I guess she didn't find this sort of *nouvelle* thinking very amusing.

"You will be two for breakfast?"

I hated to tell her no, that we would be clearing out for the airport long before she began harassing untidy tourists in the breakfast cave. So I simply nodded and thanked her and said good night. She mumbled something unintelligible and shuffled back to her wing chair.

"*Bonsoir, madame,*" Jack said sweetly to her as we climbed the steps to our room.

"*Oui, monsieur. Bonsoir,*" she snapped irritably, settling down into her lobby chair again.

"Kind of warms your heart that she missed us so much, doesn't it?" I reflected to Jack as we hurriedly undressed for bed and placed his new sandals by the door.

"But, Dad," he pointed out, slipping between the sheets, "she was really mean and bossy."

"True. But all that means, son, is that French civilization isn't really in decline, after all."

TWELVE

Bean with a Past

That evening, between the walls at Carcassonne, Jack really had his stuff.

He threw the baseball with impressive velocity, spotting it possibly as well as he ever had, perhaps because we hadn't thrown in several days or maybe simply because he seemed so at ease with the world around him. We were throwing near sunset, in either case, between the high stone walls of Europe's first and finest Medieval fortress *cite*, in an area called "the lists," a strategically brilliant double-walled area where in ancient times invaders who'd breached the outer defenses paid a dear price for their valor because all sorts of unspeakable things rained on their heads from the besieged defenders within—arrows and spears, chucked stones, cascades of molten lead or scalding water, the contents of last night's chamber pot, old Charles Aznavour eight tracks—whatever was handy.

During an informative guided tour of the fortress and walls earlier that afternoon, Nibs and I had heard an engaging tale about a beautiful Saracen princess who ruled the fortified city during the Arab occupation of the region over a thousand years ago, Lady Carcas, who was surrounded and laid siege to for almost five years by Pepin the Short's ambitious boy, Charlemagne, who was also known as the king of the Franks and the emperor of the West. He was fresh from taking Spain from the Moors and also being named king of the Lombards by the Italian pope. With supplies running low and her troops starving, Lady Carcas cleverly ordered her soldiers to gather up every bit of grain and feed it to a large pig. (Being good Muslims they didn't eat pork.) The pig was then flung from the fortress walls to the feet of the future emperor of the West, whereupon it burst open and scattered grain and innards all over the place. According to the tale, Charlemagne decided on the spot that if the Arabs were so well stocked they could afford to waste perfectly good grain on a pig, further siege was pointless. An army marched on its stomach. So he called off the hostilities and packed up for a return to Paris. Watching him go, though, the princess was seized by melancholy at the thought she might never see the dashing title-mad monarch again, so she beckoned him back by ringing (*sonne*) every bell at her disposal as she surrendered the city and her heart. The legend holds that the king of the Franks was so moved by this gesture he gave the hand of Lady Carcas to his right-hand man, one Roger Trevencal, thus creating the family dynasty that faithfully ruled the city until the terrible Albigensian Crusade against the Cathar heretics devastated Carcassonne and murdered most of its peaceful residents in 1209, permanently annexing the city and its environs to the Crown of France.

By my crude estimations we were throwing the baseball somewhere about the actual spot of the famous pig throwing incident and I couldn't help thinking the Carcassonne Chambre du Commerce was missing a bet not to install a commemorative plaque of some sort marking the fateful place: *Pig Exploded Here. Mind How You Step.*

"Dad," Jack called, interrupting these random thoughts about flying pigs and the romantic violence of history, while pretending to look back at an imaginary Yankee runner at first, "would you ever want to coach again?"

"Sorry. What's that?" I wasn't certain I'd heard him correctly. For a silly moment I could have sworn he asked me if I would ever wish to be named king of France or maybe emperor of the West. For what it's worth, if that happened, I would immediately ban all left turns in traffic, banish pesky telemarketers who phone during dinner hours, and forbid the playing of personal radios in public spaces by all of my loyal subjects under seventy years of age. People who use nouns as verbs and merchants who use those infuriating price tag stickers you can never quite get off stuff would be greatly concerned about keeping their heads, I can tell you flat out, and so would the UPS guy who repeatedly drives over my lawn. While we're at it, I'd send *both* Trent Lott and Tom Daschle home for unacceptable partisan bickering, outlaw valet parking, cancel the TV show *Friends*, and place anyone who had more than fourteen items in the express checkout line in protective leg irons. Call me Jim Bob the Cranky or maybe King of the Old Farts.

"I *said* . . . would you ever like to coach baseball again?"

"Oh. I don't know," I admitted truthfully. I was having sufficient difficulty just seeing a ball whizzing at my head at fifty or sixty miles per hour. I wasn't sure managing the hardball dreams of fifteen eleven- and twelve-year-olds and their parents was really my cup of tea anymore. "I got lucky once. Don't know if I'd want to push my luck."

Once upon a time in Atlanta, I'd been sent out by the editor of the magazine where I worked to write a ditty about a bunch of inner city kids trying out for a down-at-the-heels Little League that didn't even have enough coaches to go around. The next thing I knew, I'd "volunteered" to coach the rambunctious Virginia-Highland Orioles, who, over the next two seasons, mysteriously went thirty-four and two, collecting two league championships and demolishing the upholstery of my aging Volvo in the process. As I'd already explained to Jack on several occasions, the team's unexpected success had far more to do with their Oriole exuberance than my baseball expertise.

"I might consider it," I surprised myself by saying, rather nonchalantly, tossing the ball back to him, realizing as I did that, like millions of American home teams, our extended family's typical weekly work/school/activity schedules already resembled the flow chart of a small but energetic Utopian commune. Realistically, between the ruthless demands of work, my lawn, cranky house pets, field hockey practice, chapel choir rehearsal, ushering at church, searching for my misplaced car keys and wallet, being a newlywed for the second time around, debating foreign policy with the Queen Mum, and catching up on my thirteen-year-old daughter's ever-expanding social life, the last thing I probably had any business promising at this point in time was to coach a youth baseball team with or without my son on it. On the other hand, as the experience both in Atlanta and on this trip had proven beyond a shadow of a doubt, hanging out with a kid sure made you feel like one again. Maybe I could find a way, and the time, after all, as I had for this trip.

"It isn't easy being the coach's son," I felt it was only fair to inform him, though. I explained that I ran a tight ship and didn't play favorites or permit complaining of any sort, no badgering for positions, no unsightly Gummy Bear spitting in the dugout, no use of the word "suck," and no unflattering remarks about the team's skipper.

"Great. Can I pitch?" he asked, blithely ignoring one of my first cardinal rules of command.

"If you're good enough. I'm not promising anything, Pedro."

I hated to sound like Earl Weaver, but the truth was there were several boys Jack's age in our village who already had much better-developed pitching arms. He'd come to the game fairly late, from ice hockey, but struck me as a promising middle relief guy, and maybe a natural shortstop or third baseman. On the other hand, as every Little League coach worth his Charleston Chew understands, you can't teach heart and desire, and these intangibles Nibsy possessed in spades. "We'll keep throwing and see what develops," I said, sounding as if I'd already accepted the position without first notifying either my wife or my big time sports agent.

I realized, as I said this, that we were being closely watched by a group of French boys about Jack's age who'd been kicking around a soccer ball farther along the lists when we came out of the Narbonnaise Gate on foot (a really cool double drawbridge) to fetch our rental car and somehow maneuver it through the maze of brutally narrow streets to our hotel in the heart of Carcassonne.

"Give me one more good one," I said, adjusting my catcher's crouch. "Nice and smooth. See the target. Nothing too fast now."

He reared back and nearly knocked me over. The ball popped out of my mitt and rolled a few yards away. A small soccer boy bolted after it and brought the ball back to me, holding it out at arm's length as if it might be radioactive.

"Would you like to try?" I said to him.

He was a wiry, dark-complected mite with a dusty pugnacious face and intensely curly hair. I wasn't sure if he spoke any English, but he gave a quick nod and came forward like a shot.

"What's your name?" I said, handing him the old mitt—whose laces, I noticed, were beginning to fray and break. But then again, so was its owner.

"Philippe," he replied, jamming a small fist into the large glove. I helped him place his tiny fingers in the proper slots and showed him the basic action of the mitt. After a moment he grinned at his soccer mates as if to say, *See? Not much to this stupid game.*

"Jack," I said, "Toss Philippe an easy one."

Jack nodded, wound up easily, and looped a pitch into the gravel, bouncing the ball between Philippe's sandaled feet. It rolled away and the boy scampered after it like a mongoose.

"Sorry," Jack called out.

"Hit the mitt," I barked like Earl Weaver. "Not the ground, if you please."

His next pitch was a decent toss, softly thumping Philippe's extended mitt and dropping to the ground at his feet. Philippe scooped up the ball, examined it for a moment, reared back, and flung it crazily in the air, a comic wild throw that sent the ball ricocheting off the fortress's outer wall and bouncing off down the gravel slope.

Jack jogged after it, and I suggested to him that he come much closer and start with underhand pitches to help "our little French friend" get the hang of it.

Philippe glanced at me as if he resented being called that, and then smiled hugely.

Jack returned with the ball, and within minutes the two boys were underhanding the baseball back and forth like hopefuls at the same league tryout, exchanging words, grinning at each other, having a high old time.

It seemed an opportune moment for me to retreat and ponder my options in life and baseball, so I mounted a set of steep stone steps and took a seat up on the top of the ancient citadel's outer wall. The last rays of the sun were spilling over the serrated peaks of the Spanish Pyrenees into the vast Aude River Valley, tinting the storybook fortress's towers and stone ramparts pink in the tranquil evening light.

Some book I'd recently read noted that seeing Carcassonne for the first time was like dreaming with your eyes open, and that's exactly

what kind of day it had thus far been for us, beginning with a remarkably easy flight from the dawn drizzle of Paris to the morning sun of
Toulouse, no trace whatsoever of flight jitters in Jack, and the unexpected bonus of an upgrade at no additional cost to a sleek and sporty
Audi 6 because the Hertz clerk at the airport found our reservation but
not, alas, the economy compact Wendy had paid for in advance.

We spent the early part of the afternoon roaming back roads of the
Dordogne, talking a mile a minute about this and that—cars, girls,
baseball, the usual guy stuff—encountering charming little villages and
trying, without much success I'm afraid, to locate one of the two or
three Paleolithic cave painting sites in the immediate region I'd been
assured by knowledgeable friends hadn't yet been shut off to tourists by
the French government. A ten-year-old farm boy and his dog had found
those caves and managed to keep them secret from an army of Nazis.
But we couldn't find them with a Kummerly and Frey road map.

But as we batted along through sun-splashed vineyards and staggeringly pretty fields abloom with sunflowers south of Toulouse, any
disappointment we felt at failing to see prehistoric cave paintings was
mitigated by the first glimpse of mighty Carcassonne sitting on a distant hill, its ancient battlements rising in the afternoon sun.

The Cité is enclosed by just three kilometers of Medieval stone. No
auto traffic is permitted into it before six each evening, and all visiting autos must exit before eight the next morning, amounting to an
automotive version of the Bay of Fundy tides. I learned this from the
desk clerk at the cute Hotel Donjon, who presented me with a room
key and a printed diagram of the Cité helpfully outlined in pink
marker, explaining how after six Monsieur would be permitted to drive
his automobile across the Narbonnaise Gate and follow the pink line
through a maze of frighteningly narrow streets until he passed the
abandoned cathedral and outdoor ampitheater and spotted a double
wooden door with the number 77 on it, at which point he would tap
a special four-digit code into an electronic pad and the doors would
open, *voilà!* Monsieur was to park and lock up the car there for the
night and, if need be, follow the pink marker back to the Hotel Donjon. "The city is small," the clerk politely warned me. "But some of our
visitors find it, shall we say, a *mystère* to know where they are going."

Sounded fairly simple to me. Also a bit cloak and daggery, which I liked. But then again, I rarely worry about where I'm going until I realize I have no idea how to get there or how to get back to where I started. This predisposition alone qualifies me to be a youth baseball coach, because I'm always open to the element of surprise.

"Jack," I called down to the shapes in the darkness. "Let's go get dinner." My stomach was complaining again about being neglected.

"Okay. In a minute." His voice happily floated back. Translation: *Just one more half hour, Pops. Honest.* Jack hated leaving any kind of game, especially on account of a silly thing like impending darkness. But then again, to be fair, you should see me when I'm told I have to quit hitting golf balls into other people's fairways and go home from the course. I suppose the apple didn't fall far from the tree, as they like to say back in Maine, but this aging apple tree not only had to pee but had to somehow negotiate a large sporty rental through an ancient narrow gate and find the proper place to put it for the night.

I picked my way gingerly down the stone wall. My ankle was hurting less but my knees were hurting more. The human body, I sometimes think, is like an old inner tube on the road of life. You patch one hole only to spring a leak somewhere else.

Anyway, I asked our new local connection, Philippe, for a café recommendation between the walls of Europe's oldest fortress.

"Oh, that is easy. Emile's," he declared, adding, "Come. I will show you," and before I could issue a protest both Philippe and his new best friend were trotting up the gravel road of the lists together waving exuberantly for me to follow them, the boys of summer. The other soccer waifs, I noticed, had already melted away, off to pick some pockets or check out unlocked tourist vehicles. I fired up the Audi and gave pursuit at the speed of a donkey cart, actually holding my breath as I eased the big sedan onto the brutally narrow Narbonnaise drawbridge and through an even smaller stone aperture into a busy cobbled street about the width of your average American driveway.

Though it was just past twilight, the narrow ascending street was teeming with open shops and tourists. Just up ahead, as I slowly goosed the throbbing Audi to avoid knocking anybody over, I saw Jack waving a Crusader broadsword at me from the threshold of yet another cute shop peddling replicas of Medieval murdering implements. He waited until I was approximately parallel with the shop, then stuck the blade in through the passenger side window. I saw his best friend Philippe grinning in the background, egging him on. Maybe he got a commission or something from the shopkeeper.

"Hey, Dad. Can I get this?"

I could proceed no further along the crowded *rue* because two of the largest people I'd ever seen, male and female, were blocking the way, standing smack in the middle of the street trying to read a street map. At that moment a small car appeared behind me, and I could see the driver was anxious for me to move along, because he was already making universally understood hand motions. Any second now he was going to blow his horn.

Children—at least mine—are hardwired to know when they've got you over a barrel or, as in this instance, between a rock wall and a plump tourist. Given the proper circumstances, the nicest kid can work a ruthless bribe as swiftly as you can say, *Well, all right. But only this once. And don't tell your mother.* And that's more or less what happened here. I promised Jack I would "consider buying" the Crusader sword if he would kindly go ask the people blocking the street to move so I could proceed up the hill.

"Yes, sir," he replied briskly, and dutifully went to convey the message with his sword in hand.

The woman turned and blinked at me while the man, presumably her husband, continued studying his map. He seemed in no hurry to move. I smiled at her and attempted to look deeply apologetic and the woman said something to the man but, mystifyingly, neither of them budged an inch.

The guy behind me tooted his tiny horn. After a moment or two more, he blew it again, prompting me to gently toot my large one at the fat couple. The woman jumped a foot and the fat man turned around to glare at me and then waddled slowly around to my side of the car. He was wearing a T-shirt that said *I'm a Natural Lover.*

He looked more like, I dunno, a natural bowler or maybe a natural bingo player from Wisconsin, red-faced and rawly barbered, a guy who really enjoyed his dairy products, a ticked-off dairy farmer on vacation at that.

"Hey, fella," he said in his flat, unhurried Midwestern way. "What's your problem? I understand this is a pedestrian way. You're not even supposed to be in here with this big rig."

I tried my best to look apologetic and explained about the tidal flow of the Cité's streets.

"Well, that may be. But you scared the jeepers out of my sister, mister. That was totally uncalled for."

"Sorry. But the air conditioner is broken and the ice is melting in the cooler and if I don't get this vital organ up the hill in the next five minutes somebody's probably not going to make it."

I don't know why I said this, to be honest. Actually, yes I do. He looked fully prepared to beat me to a pulp. The organ in question was my bladder, of course, which was dangerously full of French lemonade and making trouble again. Can I help it if he thought I meant somebody was waiting up the hill for, golly, a heart or liver transplant?

"No problem. Let me help you out!"

What a peach of a guy he turned out to be! He not only went around and thoughtfully pushed his sister out of the Audi's path but also nudged several other startled tourists onto the curb so I could ease past. He was a natural *people mover*! A minute or so later I was idling in front of the hotel, looking at the pink squiggles, wondering which way to go from here, when Jack and friend loped up, panting.

"Philippe's uncle owns a restaurant, Dad," Jack explained between gulps for air, pointing toward an adjacent alley. "Its down there in a square or something. Hey, can I get that sword you promised?"

"I didn't promise," I reminded him, studying my own map now, realizing I had nowhere to go but forward into the municipal maze. "I only agreed to consider being bribed by you." I looked up and added, "Where's his uncle's café?"

"Right down there. In the square."

I didn't see any square. All I saw was a darkened alley.

"You're *sure* it's that way?" I asked Philippe.

"*Oui, monsieur.*" Another impish nod.

I made a snap decision I sincerely hoped I wouldn't regret. But the annoying little guy with the wavy hand and tiny horn was behind me again, which meant the big dairy farmer couldn't be far behind, wondering if the heart got delivered on time.

"Tell you what, boys," I said. "I'll go park the car and meet you at Philippe's uncle's café. Go *nowhere* else, Jack. I mean that. Straight to Emile's, order something to drink, and park yourself at a table. I'll be right there. Is that *understood?*"

He nodded. Philippe nodded, too. My bladder and the little guy behind me announced it was time to get moving again.

I put the Audi in gear and eased off, watching them scamper down the darkened alley—vaguely wondering, as I did, if I would ever see Nibs the Lost Boy again.

For the most part, I'm blessed with an excellent sense of direction and I can follow a street map as well as the next fully grown American male who pathologically detests following a map of any kind. But *this* map was absurd. First I turned left, then left again, followed by three more hard lefts and a sharp right. By my rough estimation I should have been more or less back where I started from, by the Narbonnaise Gate, but then I saw the vacant cathedral and the Rue Saint Louie and knew I must be going the right way after all. At least, in the process, I'd managed to lose both the tiny car *and* the large farmer. I went around a couple more dark stone blocks, turning left each time, and suddenly came to a set of wooden doors marked 77. I got out, tapped in the magic digits, and watched the doors slide open to reveal a small courtyard packed with sedans and hatchbacks. I drove in and found a nice parking place by the courtyard wall. The doors behind me automatically slid shut.

What happened next was very embarrassing. I suddenly realized I had no clue how to get *out* of the courtyard so I could follow the pink squiggles in reverse to find my son, who was possibly off learning the art of picking pockets or stealing food for a band of street urchins who lived in the abandoned cathedral. I mean, was there *really* an Uncle Emile? And where the *hell* was the parking lot door?

After several minutes of wandering idiotically around among the darkened sedans and hatchbacks, not seeing anything resembling an actual exit door for human beings, telling myself Jack would be just fine, I decided to try and reactivate and open the main doors, but, alas, I couldn't locate a button or pad to do that, either.

Then, I heard voices conversing pleasantly. They came from the opposite side of a (reasonably) short wall where bougainvillea was wildly in bloom. So I crunched that way on the gravel and paused to listen, wondering if I could possibly use the bumper of this cute little Renault to haul myself up and over the wall. It seemed a simple solution, and I managed to get up on the bumper of the car without any problem, then wedged a foot into a helpful chink in the stone, placed my hands on the top of the wall, and hauled myself up.

For a moment or two, straining at the top, I hovered there, gripping the stone and vaguely wondering when I'd last climbed over a wall like this one, decided I couldn't remember ever climbing a wall like this one, then threw a desperate leg over the top to prevent myself from falling backward onto the hood of the Renault. I paused to catch my breath, listening to the voices conversing in the darkness below. I saw lots of foliage and what appeared to be an illuminated park lamp shining through the bushes—obviously, some kind of park or civic garden. Rolling onto my stomach, I brought my other leg over the wall and attempted to ease myself down the other side, hoping it wasn't far to the ground.

My polo shirt snagged on a jagged piece of rock and after hanging pathetically on the wall for a few moments I simply let go and dropped. Gravity being what it is, there was nothing else to do. I landed on something prickly but fragrant, which turned out to be several rose bushes. After flailing around in them for a bit, cursing in a manner that would have made Earl Weaver blush, I staggered through several larger shrubs and stepped out upon a pair of Queen Mum sorts sitting on a park bench having a street-lamp chat. They were gently mortified—as if I were some crazed Crusader who'd come over the walls looking for a date with Lady Carcas.

"I'm sorry," I said to them, rubbing my chin where it had scraped painfully on top of the wall, "I couldn't find the damned exit door."

"But, *monsieur*. It is *there*," one of them said calmly, pointing to the exploding bougainvillea. I turned and saw a tiny wooden door covered charmingly with blooms. Apparently it had been there all along, hidden from view on the opposite side or possibly blocked by the Renault. In any case, I bid them a nice evening and hurried off before they could summon the *gendarmes*.

Half an hour or so later, after wandering around like a bleeding amnesiac through the dark streets of old Carcassonne, I turned a corner and came out by, of all things, the Narbonnaise Gate and the very tourist shop where Jack had begged for the Crusader sword. The guy was still open so I went in to ask directions to Emile's, if there was such a place, to get some toilet paper for my chin, and to inquire about using a toilet. After the man kindly allowed me to use his plumbing, the least I could do was purchase the Crusader broadsword. Then I walked up the narrow street swinging the sword, hung a left down the designated alley, surmounted a small set of worn stone steps, turned another abrupt dark corner, and came upon a sight to gladden any foolish wall climber's heart—dozens of happy people sitting in a crowded café where a band was playing Van Morrison tunes. Nibs and his new friend were seated at a table beneath a yellow striped awning eating bread and guzzling Cokes. I made a line straight for them.

"Oh, wow! You *got* it! Thanks, Dad!" Jack gushed when he saw the broadsword in my hand. Then he saw my face and shirt. "What happened to *you?*"

"Tough parking lot to find. Even tougher to get out of. No problem."

I took a seat. The band, at least, was excellent and a thick-set man suddenly appeared, smiling beneath a handlebar mustache. He looked about my age and girth.

"I'm Philippe's uncle, Emile," he said, offering a friendly glass of something dark that turned out to be an excellent sangria, though don't take it from me because I'm no expert on sangria, or the lost art of Medieval wall scaling, obviously.

I asked him was what was good to eat in Carcassonne besides the bread and wine.

"There is only one thing to eat in Carcassonne, *monsieur*." The house cassoulet was superb, he said, the native dish of Languedoc in fact, and nowhere better than Emile's because it featured the oldest family recipe in town. Every town in Languedoc, he expanded, had its own version of cassoulet, and his family's came from Toulouse, where they went back several hundred years to one of the original Cathar families protected by the Viscount of Toulouse.

"Very well," I said, wiping the wine and blood off my chin. "I think we'll both try the cassoulet. By the way, what *is* cassoulet?"

He smiled beneath his hairy lip.

"A bean with a past, *monsieur*. Would you care to see?" He motioned for me to follow, so I did.

I followed him to a cramped, overheated kitchen where three people—two younger men and one older woman—were ruthlessly chopping up stuff, broiling meats, sautéing things in large iron skillets that smelled absolutely divine. They didn't even seem to notice there was a stranger in their midst, and Emile led me past them to a large zinc-topped table in the rear where several crocks or earthenware bowls were being kept warm after emerging from a large steel broiler oven. He removed the lid of a small crock and presented it to my nose for inspection. The dish appeared to be some kind of bean concoction with a crusty top and bits of sausage or maybe chicken or duck baked in it. Whatever it was, cassoulet smelled unbelievably good.

"Nice, eh? This is cassoulet. Very old and very dear to the people of Languedoc."

Emile explained that recipes for cassoulet varied from village to town, but primarily it was composed of *haricot* beans (they resemble Navy beans) cooked slowly with pork rinds and garlic and other herb seasonings in an earthen stew pot properly called a *cassoule*, hence the dish's name. Sometimes the chef substituted a garnish of mutton or duck or pheasant when it was in season and available. But hailing from Toulouse, Emile preferred to use goose liver and sausage. The crowning touch, he explained, was the *gratin* crust made from bread crumbs and butter which was repeatedly "broken" and allowed to "heal" back during the slow baking process, giving the final dish a satisfying crustiness and an incredible texture. Some food purists believed cassoulet was the oldest original cuisine in France, he said, truly a meal for peasants and kings.

"You speak English very nicely," I complimented my unexpected host as we vacated the kitchen and went back to check up on the boys, who'd abandoned their seats and were now lounging around over by the band.

"That is because I worked at Disney World in Orlando for five years," Emile explained. "A most interesting experience but not, I fear to say, terribly fulfilling. Cooking at Epcot made me dream of coming back to Languedoc to cook cassoulet as soon as possible." He gave a little laugh. "I hope that doesn't offend you."

I said I wasn't offended in the least. Disney World has a few modest virtues but one of them isn't the home cooking. I'd have come back here, too, I agreed.

The history buff in me couldn't resist asking him if there were still any Cathars around Carcassonne. I remembered that the girl on the walking tour of the walls had said something about them mostly being exterminated before the fifteenth century. And my ignorance, I admitted, was even more complete than this, because I wasn't entirely sure what a Cathar was—some kind of Catholic dissident, apparently.

Emile poured himself a glass of sangria and sat with me for a moment; the café was full and his kitchen seemed to be momentarily chugging along at a productive level of controlled mayhem without him.

"To some extent, we are all Cathars here in Carcassonne. The memory you see is very long in Languedoc." The word *Cathari*, he said, was Latin for "pure ones," describing a charismatic group of Christian followers heavily influenced by the lifestyle of the earliest Christian followers, who believed Jesus set the best example of how to live. Accordingly, Cathars believed that the poor and pure of heart were the *true* followers of Christ, not the wealthy emperors of Paris or indecently corrupt popes of Rome.

In the Cathar worldview, he elaborated, the material world was considered irredeemably corrupt, the handiwork of Satan himself. Thus, wealth was considered the root of all evil and the pope and the Roman Church regarded as profane distortions of the true faith, rife with greed, avarice, and other unpleasant things.

"No wonder they put up such a fight," I said.

"Not really, *monsieur*. True Cathars were dedicated pacifists. They believed God would protect them against the evildoers. Cathar priests toured the countryside living as beggars, preaching the virtues of chastity and poverty and kindness to all, obedient only to God above—not Rome below."

I sipped his delicious sangria, rubbed my sore chin, and chipped in my philosophical two cents' worth, noting that Montaigne referred to the Holy Crusades as a lust for pepper and pearls. Who could have imagined that falling off a wall into the civic rosebushes would lead to an unexpected history lecture by a real-life latter-day Cathar?

Nodding and massaging the end of his mustache, Emile explained that by the start of the twelfth century, Catharism was spreading so rapidly through the Midi region of France and Spain that Pope Innocent III anxiously dispatched a sect of preaching friars disguised in rags to the Midi hoping to convert followers of Catharism back to the "one true faith." They later called themselves the Dominican Friars.

When this strategy failed—and here I'm paraphrasing Emile—the pope called upon the northern armies of Christendom to take arms against the plague of southern "heretics," providing all knights who came forth to serve an even larger compensation package than he'd offered against the Muslims, including total annulment of sins—for just forty days of service to pope and king—a free Vatican health club membership, convenient family flex time, fully vested retirement plan, and other goodies.

The first attack came at Breziers, fifty miles to the south on the coast, where an estimated twenty thousand residents of that city were hacked to pieces in a matter of hours, reminiscent of the bloody sack of Constantinople. Days later, Carcassonne was besieged and ultimately overrun, its lord protector, Roger Trevencal, hauled away in chains and its cosmopolitan citizenry, once the height of European culture and political prestige—Christians, Jews, Muslims, Cathars— ordered to vacate the *cite* with only whatever was on their backs. Anyone who refused was slaughtered on the spot.

Every house, every business, every Cathar-tainted church was stripped and plundered bare. The wealth was sent directly to Rome and the city was given to one Simon de Montfort, a veteran Crusader who pledged oaths of fealty to Rome and Paris and eventually got himself immortalized in the stained glass windows at none other than Chartes cathedral. For the next two decades, tens of thousands of Cathars were systematically hunted down and slaughtered throughout Languedoc, laying down a working blueprint for the Spanish Church's Inquisition one hundred years later.

"So you see," Emile summed up, sounding a bit resentful and looking around the busy square where much of this human misery had been perpetrated, "some of us simply cannot forget what was done, even that long ago. Blood is blood. Beans and citizen both have a past in these parts." He tossed down his last bit of sangria and excused himself to go fetch our cassoulet suppers from the kitchen.

I walked across the square and whistled for Jack, who'd left the band stage and was presently kicking the soccer ball around with the same soccer boys from the lists. Eventually Jack heard my whistle, looked up, and reluctantly jogged over, sweating profusely.

"Can't I play with the guys for a while?" he pleaded in an unbecoming way I hoped he wouldn't try on the baseball diamond. If he did, Earl Weaver would quickly morph into Simon de Montfort.

"Eat first, play later. Remember that I'm armed with a sword."

Our bowls of cassoulet were waiting for us at the table.

"This is so *awesome*," he said after a bite of the steaming historic bean stew, still a little out of breath. He washed it down with a large swallow of Coke, shoveled four or five more bites into his mouth, and said, "Dad, can I go back and play now?"

I gave in and let him go, probably more Roger Trevencal than Simon de Montfort or even Earl Weaver after all was said and done.

What an unexpectedly nice evening it had turned into, even if I'd ruined my favorite golf shirt in the process. I studied the replica sword and suddenly felt a little guilty about purchasing it, a souvenir reminder of the unspeakable things that took place in these same stone alleyways, possibly right where I was sitting.

After a little while my personal bean tutor, Emile, reappeared bearing a couple steaming cups of cappuccino and his usual hairy smile. He sat down and wondered where Jack and I might be headed to next, explaining that most people who stopped off to see Carcassonne were invariably heading somewhere else.

I explained about having to pick up my new wife at Milan Airport in six or seven days and how the three of us hoped to wander through Italy and Greece and maybe catch Crete near the end of our travels. "We're kind of making things up as we go along," I explained to him, and decided to leave it at that. I'd been spouting my piece about going around the world for months. It was time to stop saying that, I guess.

Emile nodded. "Is your wife the boy's mother?"

As a matter of fact, I replied, she wasn't. I explained about the divorce and our somewhat unusual extended family, which upon further reflection, I added, probably wasn't so unusual these days.

"Certainly not in France. Philippe is my younger sister's boy. A nice boy who drives my wife a bit mad at times. His mother works as a translator for NATO in Geneva. His father lives in Marseilles." Emile shook his head a little, sipping his cappuccino. "It is probably even more complicated than your story."

He smiled at me. I smiled at him. We were a couple simple men in a complicated age.

"Perhaps your son would enjoy a swim in the Mediterranean," he said.

"Yes," I agreed, remembering that the sea of Homer and Herodotus really wasn't all that far away.

I'd been toying with the idea of nipping across the Spanish border to try and see a bullfight, but the only bullfight I'd ever witnessed was a pretty appalling spectacle at the gorgeous ornate bull ring in Seville. Maybe, I thought upon deeper reflection, we'd just skip bull killing and keep the good vibes coming with a dip in the sea.

"A swim would be nice," I said to Emile, finishing his delightful cappuccino and reaching for Jack's leftover cassoulet because it was a sin to leave something that tasty lying behind.

"Very good," Emile replied. "I'll draw you a little map to a beach we love."

Three women came down the beach toward us carrying straw bags. This was mid-morning the next day and we'd just come out of the gorgeous blue Mediterranean near a rock jetty on one of Cap d'Adge's spectacular white sand beaches.

The women were different ages but had more or less the same handsome facial features, I noticed, admiring them discreetly—perhaps a mother, daughter, and *grand-mère* out for a day at the beach. They paused maybe twenty paces from where we lay drying in the sun and spread out various things on the sand—cane mats, towels, books, a sealed carafe of something—and then, one by one, they casually peeled off sweaters and cover-ups.

Jack was deep into *The Hobbit*. I rolled over facing the women and shut my eyes to enjoy the warm sun on my cool skin. A day at the beach was just what we needed, too.

"Dad," Jack suddenly whispered, "look at those ladies . . ."

I cracked open an eye. All three ladies had taken off their tops. Mother, daughter, and granny were sitting bare breasted on the beach.

"Are they, like, *nudists* or something?"

I shut my eyes again, remembering that I'd forgotten to tell Nibs about the quaint bathing traditions of French beaches. I rolled discreetly back the other way and attempted to explain a social custom I had absolutely no historical grasp of. "Remember the d'Orsay? Think of it this way—France is one big Delacroix painting. Try not to stare, though."

At that very moment, from somewhere beneath our own towels and folded-up clothes, our international cell phone rang.

It was, of all people, the good old Queen Mum phoning from the departures lounge at Heathrow. Her annual inspection tour of Scotland was complete and she was now headed home to take Maggie to Prince Edward Island.

She demanded to know where we'd gotten ourselves off to in her absence and who she needed to contact in order to properly sort out bail.

I rebuked her sharply. "Funny girl. As a matter of fact, if you must know, we're sitting on a nude beach in France. Your grandson is being exposed to France in all her glory. Three generations of French womanhood just sat down on the beach very close to us. You should see 'em."

"Cheeky boy. You're telling me *you're* nude?" She sounded fully prepared to fall over laughing hysterically.

"Absolutely. At least from the waist up. Just like them."

I put Jack on. He blushed and said, "Hi, Grandma! No, we're both wearing bathing suits. Dad was just goofing around . . ." and then proceeded to give her a running summary of the past two weeks—the rude Dutch, the friendly Germans, the fête at Bayeux, Harold the Defender, buying the Medieval chess set, the fireworks of Paris, and hiking along with skinheads after dark. I rolled back over and pretended to sleep, admiring the French muses through narrowly shut lids, wondering why we didn't have this highly civilized social custom back home in Maine.

"Okay, good-bye, Grandma. Have a safe flight!" I heard him fondly bid her adieu, casually dropping the news that I'd agreed to stop at a go-cart track we passed on the road to the beach so he could drive one of the mini Formula One race cars there before we headed off to Nîmes.

I felt a nudge on the shoulder.

"She wants to speak to you again, Dad." I sat up, trying not to stare at the muses. Unfortunately, at that very moment, a blond family of four plopped their stuff down in the sand between us and the water's edge. They seemed to be carrying the entire contents of a vacation minivan—coolers, umbrellas, folding chairs, and hibachi grill. They were all blond and far too physically fit to suit my tastes, probably German or Scandinavian. The father immediately set about wrestling with the umbrella, the mother unpacking the cooler, the sandy-haired boy foozling around in the sand. The daughter, who looked like a young Joey Heatherton, stood up, stretched lazily, and removed all her clothing.

"You're not really going to let him operate a *go-cart*, are you?" Mum wanted to know, nervously, half a Continent away.

"Oh no," I replied, somewhat distractedly. "He's probably too young for that sort of thing anyway. We'll probably just look," I said, adding, "It never hurts to look, does it?"

The girl picked up a beach ball and began bouncing it mindlessly up in the air, along with certain parts of herself that probably would have greatly interested the Impressionist Eugène Delacroix.

A couple hours later, we vacated the beach, where lots of additional topless sunbathers (and a few entirely nude ones) had by then come out to frolic and sun themselves, and Jack, I sincerely believe, was a little more comfortable with France's quaint bathing customs, although he did wonder as we went over the high dunes to the car if I thought the blond girl playing beach ball solitaire beside us had known we were, like, both watching her.

"You were *watching* her? Jeez, Jack."

He blushed. "Well, kind of. I mean, weren't you?"

I smiled, punched his arm playfully, and admitted that I was. But then again, I was only human, pushing fifty, and hadn't seen a teenage girl who looked remarkably like Joey Heatherton in a very long time. I said there was no doubt in my mind that she knew we were watching her, a tale as old as the pages of Homer's *Odyssey*. Some themes are eternal, and the only unanswered question in this instance, I assayed, was whether this teenage Nordic Calliope was trying to inflict more pain on Odysseus the father or Telemachus the son.

"I really like France," Jack admitted, pausing in the warm sand to take one long last look at the beach before we headed over the dunes to the Audi.

"I do, too," I agreed, looking back as well.

As a parting tribute to the clever Gallic mind, we stopped off to take an innocent peek at the Formula One racetrack—a very impressive pretzel twist of asphalt that featured breathtaking hairpin turns, protective walls buffered by stacks of old racing tires, and beautiful Formula One replicas that zoomed past much faster than they had appeared to from a safe distance.

Naturally Jack shamelessly begged me to let him drive one and naturally I firmly said absolutely not, and then relented because boys were us and the Queen Mum wasn't anywhere in sight.

He just satisfied the minimum height requirement, and next thing I knew Nibsy was standing in the queue for the next race with a bunch of much older French teenagers, strapping on a cherry red helmet and getting ready to take command of a bright yellow Formula car.

I called out to him to be careful, but he already had one leg in his car checking out the brakes. He seemed to be more excited about driving this dangerous little race car than about seeing two hundred bare-breasted strangers on a public beach. But that's naked youth for you, I guess.

"Jack," I called again, using the voice from Notre Dame Cathedral.

Fortunately, he heard me and glanced over to where I was leaning anxiously against the racetrack's security fence trying without much success to look worldly and confident he'd be all right. The hair was prickled on my neck, though, and my throat had actually gone bone dry.

"I think . . . you need to be *ve-ry* careful, sonny boy. Got that?"

"Yes, sir. No problem. I will."

He confidently hopped in, hooking up his safety harness as if he'd done this sort of thing a thousand times in his short life, and I retreated to the mini-grandstand bleachers to hide my face in my hands and sit near a group of sunburned and apparently *unworried* French parents who'd plopped down with beignets and movie magazines to watch this mini-spectacle of potential automotive death unfold.

A checkered flag dropped and there was a frightening roar of engines. Ten cars were off and I was surprised—and maybe even a little bit thrilled, though I hate to admit it—to see Jack's yellow Formula car zoom to the front of the pack and stay there heading into the first hair-pin curve.

The next five or ten minutes, suffice it to say, were alternately hellish and exhilarating. As they careened this way or that, I honestly didn't know whether to hide my eyes or stand up and cheer.

Tires squealed, hot metal flashed. Jack somehow held on to the lead, but a bright blue car driven by an older French boy who was obviously insane kept trying to overtake him. Every time the pair of them careened through a narrow turn, the blue car darted inside toward the rail and Jack cut him off. The blue car finally took the lead and held it until the final lap flag was waved, at which point Jack executed a nimble maneuver and retook the lead. The two of them were racing pell mell toward the finish line, taking the last turn wide through a small tunnel to the checkered flag, when Jack drifted a bit too wide and the French boy attempted to cut him off. Their cars bumped, my heart plummeted, and the yellow Formula One racer zoomed across the finish line in second place, only to plow headlong into a wall of painted tires.

By the time I reached him, two attendants were pulling tires off the cart and Jack was struggling to get out of his safety harness. I was nearly white with panic; he was nearly red with fury.

"Did you see what that creep *did*?" he fumed, yanking off his helmet and pointing at the bigger French kid in the winning blue racer. "That jerk ran me off the road!"

I tried my best to be the voice of reason, as I physically hauled him toward the track's exit. But he kept glaring at the smirking older French kid and pointing an accusatory finger at him and talking hotly about the injustice of it all. For a moment or two I feared we might have a mini international fistfight on our hands. I'd never seen Jack so angry about anything in his life.

"Let's go," I finally said sharply to him, "before we have to slug our way out of France."

One of the track attendants came trotting urgently after us as we approached the Audi, and I thought he was going to apologize for the older kid's reckless driving.

"Monsieur! Monsieur!" he called out. "You must to pay the tip!"

We paused and both stared uncomprehendingly at him. He pointed at Jack and then motioned to the collapsed tire wall which several other attendants were still busy picking up and rebuilding.

"The *paroi* is broken. You must to pay the tip . . ."

I finally realized what he was getting at. He wanted me to give him money for picking up the wall Nibs had knocked over, probably the wall that saved his life—and mine from being abruptly shortened by the Queen Mum. I was momentarily tempted to give the attendant a piece of my mind for allowing children to operate automobiles so fast and recklessly, but then I remembered how deeply relieved I was that Jack had survived my foolishness in permitting him to do it in the first place.

Instead, I took out a small wad of French bills and handed them to the man.

"Please don't ever let me let you do something crazy like that again until I'm way too old to know any better, okay?" I advised Jack as I gunned the Audi for Nîmes, where there was a nice extinct Roman coliseum I hoped we could safely snoop around in before supper.

Jack nodded but was still staring at the racetrack as if he had some serious unfinished business left in the South of France.

"Better yet," I proposed feeling as if we'd been up to something truly illicit that afternoon but had somehow survived to tell the tale, "let's just keep the topless women and crashing race cars between us guys for a while—at least until I can figure out how to tell your mother and grandmother about them."

"Right," he said, though I'm not certain he really heard me.

THIRTEEN

Almost Paradiso

At Villa Agape, a gorgeous Dominican convent set among flowering olive and myrtle trees in the hills south of Florence, a leathery little nun named Sister Patrice led us to a pair of minimally furnished un-air-conditioned rooms overlooking the gardens at the back of the convent and made Wendy deposit her things in one room, Jack and me in another.

Villa Agape seemed a perfect place to pause and catch our breath because we'd been going at breakneck speed for several days—first Nibs and I in Switzerland, followed by the three of us after picking up Dame Wendy in Milan. In Switzerland, we'd ridden a scary cable car to the top of the mighty Jungfrau and then idiotically hiked all the way down (slipping twice on cow poop), consumed our approximate metric body weights in fine chocolate, purchased a cheap Swiss Army watch for Nibsy, flooded a charming chalet's basement with soap suds while trying to wash clothes in a German washing machine, attended a terrific jazz festival at Montreaux, left Jack Pillow in a cute hotel by Lake Geneva, snooped around dreary Castle Chillon (where Lord Byron pretended to be a prisoner and peed moodily out a dungeon window into the lake), went back to the cute hotel by Lake Geneva to pick up Jack Pillow, briefly lost the cheap Swiss Army watch, and got stuck for two hours in a nasty traffic jam in a spooky tunnel that burrowed beneath the Alps to Italy. After Switzerland, I really could have used a nice relaxing vacation at home.

Italy was no Victorian picnic either, to begin with. First we got hopelessly lost in Milan rush hour traffic while trying to locate the old church housing Da Vinci's *Last Supper*. Then I cleverly checked us into a nice *pensione* conveniently located beside the airport where Dame Wendy was scheduled to arrive the next day at noon, only to discover she was arriving at Milan's *other aeropuerto*, the swank new international one sitting at the foot of the Alps damn near back in Switzerland. After picking up Wendy, we dashed for Camoli, a charming seaside village leaning over the Ligurian Sea, then pushed on, hoping to catch a glimpse of Chris Columbus's house—but, wouldn't you know, the city was under siege by violent anarchists protesting the annual meeting of the G-5 leaders. So we rambled to Pisa, elbowed our way through the madding crowds to see the Leaning Tower, then wound up wandering the handsome streets of ancient Lucca, visiting Giacomo Puccini's house, and checking into a beautiful hotel on the square where Neil Young had just stayed and the hot water was temporarily out of order. Among the more pleasant discoveries, I learned my new wife was a keen and discriminating Puccini buff and how to bathe entirely on a single bottle of fizzy mineral water. I guess Neil Young had used up all the hot water or something.

Now, mercifully, we'd come to beautiful, timeless Florence for a little bit of rest and relaxation in a famous convent that rented rooms even to dirt road transcendentalists and lapsed Catholics like me and my nearly new ladywife.

"No, no," I pointed the error out to Sister Patrice, indicating Dame Wendy. "You don't understand. She's my *wife*. We sleep together. It's part of the social contract we signed. Where she goes, I go."

My Italian is simply awful or, more accurately, nonexistent. Sister Patrice gave me an unfriendly stare and sharply thumped a small notice on the door with a bony no-nonsense finger, indicating that all convent guests were required to be safely in their rooms with the windows securely shut and locked by no later than nine at night, due to the convent burglar alarm system being armed.

"Why do they need a burglar alarm at a *convent*, for Pete's sake?" I wondered out loud, breaking into a small sweat due to the fact that the room we were in felt like a Swedish sauna. I glanced at Jack and asked if he would mind sleeping alone here. He had his mom's circulation and liked warm places.

"I don't know," he said warily, glancing at the giant wooden crucifix on the wall. "This place is kind of, I don't know . . . well, *freaky*. Would you mind staying in here with me?"

"Shh, guys, please . . ." Wendy blushed, smiling at the leathery little nun. "You don't wish to offend Sister Patrice."

Wendy, dear reader, grew up Catholic on the North Shore of Long Island, which partly accounted for her natural sympathy for the wiry little sister, I suppose. She also has an infallible sense of decorum, which makes our marriage both a lively trial of patience and a bit of a Puccini horse opera at times. For the record, Wendy was officially now a practicing Episcopalian—a fact I'll wager wouldn't have made Sister Patrice one bit happier to know.

"Poor thing," Wendy sympathized. "I don't think she understands English. They probably don't get many Americans here."

"So I guess there's really no way to find out if it's true that nuns are naked as jaybirds beneath their habits?"

It seemed an innocent enough question, something I'd kind of wondered about off and on since my own Lutheran confirmation thirty-five years ago. Jack, bless him, rewarded me with a loyal snicker. Wendy, on the other hand, blushed again. Sister Patrice simply sniffed and thumped the notice one last time and departed our cell—Oops, I mean nice convent room—dragging my new wife with her.

"Which bed do you want?" I asked Jack, pushing open the huge shutters and discovering that at least the room came with a great view of distant olive groves and a few tiled rooftops of suburban Florence. Down below, there was a snowy-haired gent pruning the roses. Somewhere I'd read that Villa Agape had been used as a setting for several big feature films, and it was certainly easy enough to understand why. The place was an absolute vision of the high Renaissance spiritual life, a gorgeous throwback to the salad days of young Dante Alighieri. Call me an uncultured boob, but I kind of wished we'd just found a nice Marriott instead.

"I don't know. This one, I guess . . . ," he replied, sitting down on one of the narrow bunks, the springs of which squeaked so outrageously the gardener actually glanced up.

I smiled and waved down at him, thinking how the place was cleverly booby-trapped to prevent any fun between consenting adults.

The gardener nodded at me and lifted a weary hand, but then got straight back to business pruning because Sister Patrice suddenly appeared, pausing to inform him that the Lord doesn't care for a dawdler, or possibly that there were potential troublemakers sleeping in the house.

That's how we wound up farther into the hills of Chianti a couple hours later, having found supper at a marvelous café in a small hill town of Greve. The ever-adventurous Jack, to establish the scene, was busy eating wild boar with truffles and I'd just topped up my wife's wineglass with a delicious local vintage and encouraged her to sample my zuppa lombarda, an unforgettable fagioli soup and companion wild mushroom risotto that was very possibly the finest meal I'd eaten since last night in Lucca.

"This is almost paradise," Dame Wendy cooed, eyeballing the picturesque roof line beneath the lapis lazuli evening sky. She sipped her wine and added playfully, "There's really only one problem I can think of."

"Really? What's that?"

As I asked this, I moseyed a discreet fork across the table and poked her delicious gnocchi, pine nuts, and pesto on the rough theory that what good is a second chance at marriage if you can't eat off each other's dinner plate without advance warning. Soul mates are dinner mates, in my humble opinion. But maybe I'm just old-fashioned that way.

"That poor ratty hat," she said with a little laugh. "I think it's seen its better days come and go. I kind of wish it had gone with them."

"My *hat?*"

I loved the hat I was wearing, a fancy Sea Island straw plantation fedora I'd had since my dashing cub reporter days in Atlanta. Admittedly, it was a little frayed at the edges, missing its former elegant silk band, and basically somewhat shapeless now due to time's merciless advance and a rather difficult passage to Europe at the bottom of my suitcase.

But other than that, it was a fine hat with an excellent history.

We'd been down many interesting *vias* together. And as I quickly explained to her, I'd brought it along just so I'd look like William Holden in the original *Sabrina*, or at least an Englishman on holiday in a Merchant Ivory film, while we were poking around the ancient ruins of Italy and Greece.

"I'm afraid you look more like Burl Ives in *Cat on a Hot Tin Roof*. Or maybe a New Orleans pimp. I'm sorry to have to break it to you."

"Anything else you need to get off your chest before we get on with this vacation and marriage?" I asked her a little woundedly because, let's face it, it's not every day you think of yourself as Bill Holden only to discover the world at large sees you as Burl Ives. And what exactly did she mean by the word "ratty"?

"Nope. Get rid of that silly hat and everything will be absolutely perfect. Tell you what, I'll even spring for a new one. Thanks for the stone mermaid and the wooden apple, by the way. I'll always treasure them."

One of Wendy's most endearing qualities, I sometimes think, is her polite directness. She's like a New York City beat cop with private school manners. Back in her own salad days at Bard College, when she was training to be a stage actress and holding down a full-time job at Bonwit Teller, for example, she was informed by a certain famous Broadway casting director that the sky could be the limit for her acting career if she would only agree to sleep with him. Her acting career soon ended and that guy had a funny limp for several days after that, apparently.

Anyway, I turned to Jack for a second opinion on the Burl Ives–Jeremy Irons hat thing.

"How about you, Nibs? Do *you* like my hat?"

"Sure," my son said loyally over his wild boar, adding with a tiny flush of embarrassment, "well, I mean, sort of . . . actually, not really. You maybe look a *little* funny in it, is all . . . No offense or anything."

"Right. None taken. Sort of."

I was fully prepared to mount a final holy crusade in defense of my Billy Holden headpiece when our cell phone suddenly played the opening aria from Puccini's *Turandot*. Wendy, the new official Keeper of the Contraption, switched it on and presented it to me. It was none other than good old Chet calling, our man from the embassy basement!

"Just wanted to catch you up and say that the official travel advisory for Kenya has just been unexpectedly lifted. Thought you'd like to be among the first to know." I detected an uncharacteristic lilt in Chet's voice and wondered if he might have been promoted to the embassy's first floor.

"Wonderful," I said, chewing a bit of distaff gnocchi, mentioning that unfortunately I'd officially just *canceled* our African dream safari from the hotel where we'd flooded the basement with soap suds back in Interlaken; the travel company back in Maine was in the process of graciously refunding our money and giving the valuable slot to somebody who wasn't being such a weenie about going to Africa.

Chet commiserated from faraway London. "Too bad. But it's probably better to have been smart about these things where small chaps are involved. Besides, you can always see Africa."

He made it sound like Africa was right next door to Maine, convenient as popping over to Vermont for a quick maple syrup breakfast. But even so, we chatted pleasantly for a few more moments about how the rest of the world was still acting up and probably no place you'd wish to take a child. Then Chet revealed that he wouldn't be able reach out and touch us for the next fortnight because he was going on holiday himself, this being early August and the height of the European vacation season. This news, I deduced, was the real source of Chet's unexpected cheerfulness, and I was curious to know where such a dreary bureaucrat like him would go on summer holiday—though, naturally, I didn't put it to him exactly this way.

I pictured him wandering off alone to some desolate Black Sea resort, putting on dark socks and sandals and sitting on a stone beach to read a moving transcript from the Salt II Treaty and admire the passing parade of wobbling Russian flesh. I was half-tempted to suggest a depressing hotel I knew in Amsterdam or maybe even the relaxing Hotel Edward Lear right there in Marble Arch.

"As a matter of fact," he answered with profuse happiness, "I'm bound for Switzerland, myself. For a spot of hiking and window shopping. Simply mad about the Swiss. They really know how to run a country. Know what I mean?"

I said I knew what he meant. We'd just spent two rather draining up and down days there. The *Suisse,* not to dwell on an unpleasant subject, struck me as a ruthlessly efficient if somewhat bloodless race of folks, to be honest, a bit fanatical about things like keeping track of time and making cheese with holes in it, avoiding actual shooting wars and managing the secret bank accounts of alleged South American war criminals. But aside from all that, they'd been kind of fun to torture with our natural slobbishness.

"Do you know why there are twice as many cows as people in Switzerland?" I used the opportunity to give him my best Swiss joke. (Actually, I believe it may be the *only* Swiss joke. The Swiss are big on properly making your bed and personal hygiene, not humor. To get jokes you have to go through a long scary tunnel to Italy.) "That's because only the cows are encouraged to breed."

"*Really?* Ha, ha. *Most* interesting . . ." Chet didn't sound particularly amused by my joke, though. In fact, he sounded a little offended by it. I sensed our relationship was drawing to its natural conclusion and used the moment to offer him a fond farewell.

"Travel well," I said. "Be sure to watch where you step."

"Please forgive the intrusion. But I overheard your wife say she doesn't particularly care for your hat. If it will make you feel any better, friend, my wife has been trying to throw away this very shirt I'm wearing for many summers now without success. Your hat probably has many good years yet. We are brothers on summer holiday, eh?"

The man who offered these humane and sensitive words was seated at the crowded dinner table next to us in Greve. He appeared to be the patriarch of maybe ten or twelve people young and old who were simultaneously talking to each other and stuffing their faces with indescribably good food, and he graciously lifted his goblet of Chianti as a sign of true sartorially challenged solidarity.

I smiled and returned his toast. In all fairness, I must say, his shirt really was one of the ugliest things this side of Bill Clinton in jogging shorts, a kind of hideous tangerine bowling shirt with large saggy white breast pockets, which made him look a total peckerwood from Pennsylvania. In other words, he was exactly my kind of guy!

His name was Robert, and half the chattering grown-ups and children seated at his table, it emerged, hailed from somewhere in New Jersey, while the other half came from a small village near Bethlehem—cousins who arranged to meet halfway across the world over a glass of tasty Chianti. Together, the fourteen of them were sharing a large villa with a pool just outside Siena.

For a moment, I'm a little embarrassed to say, I wasn't certain if they were Jewish or Palestinian tourists, until I saw a Star of David hanging on a chain around the neck of a pretty teenage girl who was approximately my daughter Maggie's age. By then, Robert and I were deep in conversation about various topics of mutual concern—how to keep beloved personal items from being tossed out by strong-willed wives, how to keep our pretty daughters from dating imbeciles on motorcycles, that sort of thing.

I happened to casually mention that we had originally hoped to visit the Holy Land, dip a toe in the River Jordan and visit Temple Rock, but that had all gone down the tubes thanks to the Palestinian intifada, and saw Robert's expression suddenly darken.

"That is too bad. Israel is such a beautiful and safe country. But I'm afraid we've just elected a man who intimately knows and loves war," he said with a little sigh, lowering the wine in his goblet. "Sharon is not insane. Actually, quite the opposite. He's bloody brilliant, a true military genius who knows exactly what he intends to do. Yassar Arafat, on the other hand, is quite insane, and a pathological liar. I believe his primary ambition is to become a martyr to his people. Neither one is good for business. God only knows where these two men will lead us—and the world—in the days ahead."

Wendy was finishing her wine and listening to this sobering verdict, as was Jack over his ginger ale—both visibly subdued by Robert's discouraging assessment of the situation in the Middle East. I asked Robert what kind of business he was in, and he explained that he owned a small electronics firm that manufactured wiring for light fixtures and security systems. Half of his employees were Palestinians who came from the West Bank. Since the new Palestinian uprising, Robert said, Prime Minister Sharon had severely limited access to the West Bank and Robert's electronics business was more or less going broke.

He shrugged philosophically. A sad little smile returned.

"So we did what any reasonably sane persons would do . . . ," he observed, glancing at his teenage daughter, who'd fallen silent and was also listening to her worried papa amid the din of her younger American cousins. "We took a nice extended family vacation to Italy while we still could afford to go."

He smiled at Wendy and Jack and added, "Perhaps someday you will come to Israel after all. These troubles will not last forever. They just seem worse than they really are."

"Kind of like my hat and your shirt," I added, bringing the conversation full circle, if I may say so, giving my wife my smoothest Billy Holden smile.

She reached over and patted my hand, it seemed to me, rather condescendingly—as if I were some color-blind hayseed she had to dress every morning.

"Don't worry. First thing tomorrow, sweetie, we'll look for a nice new hat for you in Florence."

"Don't forget the wedding rings," Jack injected from the other side of his ginger ale glass.

"Are you two getting *married?*" Robert's sunburned wife wondered from the end of their noisy table, where she couldn't quite hear what was being said at our end. I failed to catch her name, but she had intense green eyes, a tawny mane of hair, and a nice big loopy smile.

Dame Wendy leaned forward and explained, "We got married a few days before the boys here took off to try and go around the world this summer. Then they invited me join them for Italy and Greece, so I guess you could say we're having a little honeymoon in the middle of their vacation. Anyway, we'll probably have the wedding party when everybody gets back home in September. It sounds nutty, I know."

"It sounds like *us*," Robert's wife declared, and everyone laughed.

As she said this, I glanced at the pretty girl who was my daughter's age, thinking about how in a day or so she—Maggie, I mean—and the good old Queen Mum would be tooling off to Prince Edward Island with nary a passing thought in their heads about being blown to bits on a city bus by a child with a Pokémon knapsack full of dynamite. Maybe like Jack I'd simply been watching too much news and too many awful documentaries on Middle Eastern suicide camps. But I honestly couldn't imagine the world these people had left behind for a few weeks, and for all the tensions and dangers I couldn't help wishing we were still going there to visit.

Robert's wife asked where we were staying.

"A lovely Dominican convent in Florence," Wendy answered, proving you can take the girl out of the mother church but probably not the other way around.

"No TV. No air conditioning. But a great place to sweat off a few unsightly pounds," I put in a touch gloomily, wondering if I could possibly survive two nights in that celebrated nunnery.

"In that case, you should come to our villa for a swim tomorrow morning," Robert proposed, reaching for a paper napkin to sketch me a map to their place outside Siena.

I thanked him for the gracious offer but explained that we were supposed to take a walking tour of Dante's Florence in the morning with a friend of a dear friend from America. In the afternoon we were supposed to tour the Boboli Gardens and several museums. But maybe in the late afternoon we could find our way to Siena—and with luck, I'll admit thinking, Nibs and I could maybe even get us thrown out of Villa Agape so we could come *stay* with you nice folks!

As I considered this appealing scenario, I happened to glance at my watch and realized we were going to be well over an hour late for lockup at Villa Agape. Sister Patrice wouldn't be one bit pleased to hear us pounding on the convent's gate.

Oh well. Let her phone the pope.

Professor Benedetta Fantugini, who met us by the Ponte Vecchio promptly at eight the next morning, was thirty-three years old and newly married also, with long dark hair, classic Northern Italian features, a beautiful smile, and mirthful chestnut eyes. She was wearing a simple green linen frock with an elegant blue silk shoulder scarf draped around her bare shoulders.

A *real life Beatrice*, I thought, and then realized with mild embarrassment that I'd actually said this out loud.

"But Beatrice died in her twenties," Benedetta replied with a delightful laugh, presenting Wendy, Jack, and me each with a printed guide to our walking tour of some of Florence's most important historical and artistic spots. It was a stunning summer morning with golden rays of sunshine falling on the still-closed shops that frame the famous bridge (most of them were jewelry shops, I noticed) and there was no trace of the smog—or for that matter tourists—that supposedly plagues the city during the hot summer months.

"Who was Dante?" Jack wanted to know before we got underway.

Falling in step behind the two women, I explained that he was a dreamy Florence kid about Jack's age when he happened to see an eight-year-old version of Professor Fantugini walking on the streets of the city one summer morning in 1274, falling hopelessly in love and dedicating his life and writing career to her, though according to his pal Giovanni Boccaccio, the young poet never set eyes on his beloved again. He grew up and got married, had a family of his own, tried a disastrous hand at local politics, wrote the finest allegorical narrative poem ever conceived, got banished on trumped up charges of corruption, and died of a broken heart in Ravenna without ever seeing the girl of his dreams again.

"Keep that in mind before you lose any sleep over Bethany Bellnap," I advised Nibs, nudging him.

The art of Florence was Professor Fantugini's specialty, but Dante was at least marginally mine. The *Divine Comedy* was my favorite required reading back at East Carolina, I explained to Nibs and company as we set off toward the Palazzo Pitti and then angled off toward the Piazza San Spirito and the church of the same name. As a result of the poem's romantic allure, I continued, hearing myself run on a bit at the mouth, I'd very nearly foolishly switched my major from English Lit to Latin Studies, at which point I would have become so functionally unemployable I'd probably have been forced to decamp for Italy and mash grapes with my bare feet in order to survive.

"Would that truly have been so awful—a nice expatriate's life in Florence?" Professor Fantugini baited me wryly, looking at Wendy.

Benedetta specialized, if I understood her correctly, in teaching art history to visiting American scholars at a local university. Lucky kids, I thought. I'll bet half the class was madly in love with her, I sure would have been.

"No, ma'am. But that would have been a *really* divine comedy, I'm afraid."

Jack, scuffing along in the Arno sunlight, wondered right on cue what *The Divine Comedy* was about. Was it, like, really funny?

"About one hundred cantos or fourteen thousand lines long," I replied, trotting out an old joke that was nearly as tired as the cobblestones underfoot, and then explained that Dante's use of the word *Commedia* meant, in the classical sense, a theatrical play intended to amuse, entertain, and morally instruct. There wasn't much that was actually "funny" in the modern sense in Dante's famous epic, I further explained, adding that it was a story about a guy "midway through life's journey" who escapes a slobbering she-wolf and snarling leopard and takes off on an extended road trip with his long-dead literary hero, Virgil, the Roman poet—a virtuous Pagan who dwells in the land of Limbo—who promptly leads him on a magical mystery tour of the nine levels of hell and the seven terraces of purgatory. Along the way, Dante encounters old political enemies, corrupt popes, distinguished forebears, liars and swindlers of every sort. His arduous journey takes him through scenes of unimaginable sorrow and punishment until he arrives at the very gates of Paradise itself, where, to briefly summarize, he is purified by remorse and contrition and "rises to meet the stars," and finally sees his beloved and elusive Beatrice floating in the clouds.

"Whoa," Jack said, glancing at a shop window where a thin young man was attempting to put a lacy brassiere on a shapely window mannequin. "That *doesn't* sound very funny." He glanced over at me, to see if I'd noticed the interesting encounter going on in the shop window. The mannequin appeared to be winning the wrestling match.

I smiled at him and wiggled my eyebrows provocatively. He smiled at me and blushed to his earlobes.

"No," I had to admit. "I guess it's not. But it somehow hooked me. I'd frankly like to try mashing grapes with my bare feet."

"So would I," he agreed.

"What are you two grinning about?" Wendy demanded to know as she held open the door to San Spirito for us after we finally caught up to her and Benedetta a few minutes later and slipped into the church's cool, fragrant, shadowy interior.

"Life. Death. The whole vast human comedy," I explained allegorically to her, wondering if she had any idea the mannequins in Florence were so beautiful and lifelike you almost wanted to give them a hug. Approaching midlife myself, I could personally appreciate Dante's acutely human dilemma, his eternal struggle against the ways of the flesh. No wonder he wound up exiled and wasting away in Ravenna. I'd dearly miss these shop windows, too.

Over the next three hours, Professor Fantugini walked us artfully through a dozen blocks of Firenze and a thousand years of the city's incomparable history and artistic heritage—from Etruscan art to Medici politics, and everything in between. We learned about the ancient art of making frescoes from Arno sand and saw a spot near the Piazza Santa Trinita where legend says Saint Francis brought a child who'd fallen off a nearby roof back to life. We toured a Franciscan monastery and learned about the early wool trade, Florentine architecture, developing craftsmen guilds, and the Arno's violent unpredictability. At the church of Ognissanti, we visited the burial spot of Botticelli and then meandered along the atmospherically narrow Borgo Apostoli, one of Firenze's oldest streets, to a tiny chapel on the Piazza del Limbo—built upon a cemetery for unbaptized children. Into the bright sunlight of the Piazza Signoria we ambled, to see copies of Donatello's Marzocco—an age-darkened lion with his huge paw plopped on the world, the heraldic symbol of the city—and a sublime knockoff of Michelangelo's *David*, which slouched in the square where the original (now kept inside at the Galleria del' Accademia—our afternoon destination) had stood for almost 350 years. A little while later, we stood like a trio of awestruck Iowans beneath Fillippo Brunelleschi's soaring Duomo and admired the exquisite detail work on Ghiberti's incredible Baptistry doors—the "gates to Paradise itself," as Michelangelo supposedly called them.

Far too soon to suit my tastes, the walk came to an end.

The heat of the day was upon us and so were the thrusting tourist crowds, lining up to cram into the Uffizi Gallery and besiege the Museo Nazionale del Bargello where Michelangelo's drunken Bacchus and other treasures of the city would have to been seen another day, preferably in the dead of winter as suggested by our lovely host. After lunch, Benedetta's partner Daphne Mazzaniti was scheduled to lead us on an additional walking tour of Palazzo Pitti, the Galleria Palatina, and (of greatest interest to the budding yardman in me) the famous Boboli Gardens.

And so, with great reluctance, we walked Professor Fantugini to her cute motor scooter which was, she admitted, illegally parked amid a crush of almost identical Vespas and Hondas just off the Ponte Vecchio. I casually asked her if the jewelry shops there were a good place to hunt for a wedding ring.

"Oh certainly, assuming you are *extremely* wealthy," she replied, strapping on her cute little safely helmet. Brad Pitt and Jennifer Aniston had recently purchased their custom wedding rings on the Ponte Vecchio, I'd read somewhere, but were now in the process of suing the jeweler there because he promptly knocked off the rings he sold them and made a small killing. The world never ceased to amaze—and never changed, apparently.

I told this tale of modern intrigue to Professor Fantugini and she laughed, switching on her tiny motorbike.

"Nothing has really changed all that much in a thousand years," she agreed, tightening her chin strap. "I can tell you a funny story, too."

A dear friend of her mother, she explained, recently purchased a beautiful ancient villa in the countryside outside Florence only to discover a crude "sketch" etched into the tiles above the kitchen sink. Believing the sketch might have some appealing historical significance, she summoned a local art expert who soon invited a deputation of government officials into her kitchen.

"The sketch was sort of like, how do you say, um . . . ," she paused to try and find the precise word in English, bundling her long hair expertly beneath her silk scarf, ". . . an innocent doodle?" She laughed again. "The experts decided it was done by none other than Michelangelo himself. It was promptly declared a state treasure, officially sealed and protected, and now at least one day a week—sometimes on weekends, too, I believe—the public is not only permitted by law but even *encouraged* to come straight into my mother's friend's kitchen and admire the doodle. Her beloved kitchen is no longer her own!"

She revved up her little bike and left us with a toss of her head and a musical laugh at the passionate irony of modern Italian life.

"*Ciao,*" she said to us, waving delicately and zooming away in dizzying traffic.

"*Ciao,*" the three of us replied fondly in unison, then traipsed off to find lunch and a cold Coke before meeting Daphne Mazzaniti for the Boboli Gardens.

The famous Medici Gardens were parched and woefully neglected—kind of like my new landscaping scheme back home in Maine due to the drought, according to Wendy.

"I've been waiting for the right moment to tell you that it hasn't rained a drop since you guys left home. Most of what you planted last spring, I'm afraid, has dried up and blown away." We were passing a bone-dry fountain where weeds were growing depressingly from the cracks when she let this news out.

Needlessly to say, I truly wasn't pleased to hear this report from the home front—in part because I've spent years and more folding money than I care to think about trying to create my own little Medici Garden in the big woods, in part because my legs were so danged weary from hiking all over Florence in the sweltering August heat all I could think about was how nice it would be to plunge into somebody's swimming pool and maybe take a nice Florentine nap under a fig tree.

I dug through my pockets to see if I could find the map my friend Robert had sketched to his villa in Siena, but was disappointed to learn I'd somehow lost it.

One reason Jack and I were both whipped puppies was that neither of us had slept very well the night before at Villa Agape. To begin with, the temperature was probably close to a hundred degrees in the room, and according to Jack, who restlessly tossed and turned all night on his noisy bunk, the giant wooden crucifix on the wall above his bed kept doing the Macarena.

"Dad, I think the Jesus is moving up there," his small voice came across to me at one point in the sauna-like darkness.

"Really? I think you're just too hot and imagining that, Boss. Try to relax."

"No, I'm not. It really moved, Dad." There was a pause. "Can I come over and sleep with you?"

"No," I replied. "But I have an idea."

We got up and got dressed and crept downstairs to a cooler sitting room next to the convent's kitchen. Jack promptly went back to sleep in an armchair and I seriously considered trying to raid the kitchen refrigerator to see if the holy sisters kept a cold six-pack stashed there. Instead, I sat there in the silent darkness wondering if Jesus doing the Macarena meant it was time to find a new hotel.

Back out front of the Palazzo Pitti, standing in the blast furnace heat of midday, we thanked Daphne Mazzaniti for her quick but insightful perambulation of the Boboli Gardens and apologized for our wilting enthusiasm for seeing the rest of Florence that afternoon. The walk was supposed to last until five-thirty, but it was scarcely three o'clock and we were thoroughly tuckered out. She commiserated with us, agreeing it was probably best to conclude the tour before somebody suffered heat stroke and we toured another emergency room. "The heat and smog have become a major problem in Florence between May and November. My husband and I never bring our daughter into the city between May and November, if at all possible."

Shading my eyes, I asked if she knew any nice hotels south of town where we might relax a bit and cool our heels—or, better yet, dampen them. She thought for only a moment before suggesting we investigate a country hotel on the road to Siena. It was a lovely old farmhouse among the olive trees called Casa Frassi, she said, and though she didn't know the phone number she felt certain anybody in that area could direct us there.

"I believe they may even have a swimming pool," she added, not unimportantly—basically guaranteeing there wouldn't be a second night with Sister Patrice.

We kissed both her cheeks, Italian style, and offered a damp but grateful good-bye.

*   *   *

We rolled up a dusty lane to Casa Frassi just as waiters were setting out tables for supper beneath the plane trees, a sight to gladden the weariest heart and emptiest stomach. After checking in, Wendy and Jack jumped into bathing attire and went straight off to the swimming pool while I gunned the Audi around a stone barn to the hotel car park, almost knocking over an old man and his mare in the process.

The horse reared and kicked up a cloud of dust and I hopped out to apologize for driving under the giddy influence of not having to spend another night at Villa Agape.

The man clutching the reins was a weathered and handsome old guy, wearing a festively banded straw hat that made him almost a dead ringer for the late golf legend Sam Snead.

"Gosh, I'm sorry," I said to the man clutching the excited horse's reins. He had a deeply lined and handsome face and his hat was not unlike my own dearly beloved headgear. "Didn't mean to upset your horse."

He flashed a set of immaculate teeth at me, stroked the troubled mare's forelock, and murmured something soothing in Italian—probably more to the horse than me. Whoever he was talking to, the horse quickly calmed down.

"Beautiful horse," I said to him, hoping he knew more English than I did Italian.

"*Grazie*," he replied, continuing to stroke the mare's neck. To my surprise, he began speaking to me in a stream of the most pleasant, conversational Italian you've ever heard. Obviously, I had no clue what he was saying, but every now and then he would stop and stare impishly at me beneath his jaunty Sam Snead hat, at which point I smiled, nodded my head, and said things like, "Wonderful," "Oh, I *quite* agree," and "I frankly don't think the relief pitching can hold up till September. But you never know about these things."

Unlike Sister Patrice, the Italian Sam Snead didn't appear the slightest bit bothered by my general functioning stupidity, and in fact, I think he may have even told me some kind of affectionate tale involving himself and the mare. The horse looked old and I got the impression they'd been down many interesting *vias* together over the years, and as he continued on pleasantly speaking about whatever he was speaking about for several unhurried minutes, I moved forward and stroked the animal's head, too.

"What's her name?"

"Juliette," he replied, with another flash of chompers.

"Do you speak English?" I wondered.

"*Non.*" Another pause and dapper smile. "A *leetle* bit onlee."

But that didn't stop him from revving up again, rhetorically speaking. He talked on smoothly for a while in his unrushed provincial way, and I stood there listening and enjoying every unknown word of his horseman's tale. Finally I had to go. I needed a swim. I patted sweet Juliette and lifted a hand to her best friend on earth.

"See you guys."

"*Buona sera,*" said the Italian Sam Snead, actually tipping his straw hat the way my southern grandfather used to do.

"*Buona sera.*"

I went to our room and put on my swim trunks, then came downstairs and followed the sound of splashing and laughter across the lawn to an arbor gate and the swimming pool area. The view beyond the lawn looked like a Titian landscape of dusty vineyards and ageless hills, and I paused at the gate to admire it and a moment later found Wendy lounging in a sun-faded teak chair pretending to look at an Italian fashion magazine but really watching Jack cavort with another kid in the pool.

She shaded her eyes from the low sun and wondered what had taken me so long to come back; after all, I'd been the one so anxious to take a swim. I sat down beside her, peeling off my old boat shoes; tomorrow I was switching to sandals, too. We were in a sandaled landscape now.

"Been talking to a man about a horse."

I guess she thought I was joking—or maybe I'd just been using the john. She nodded discreetly at Nibs.

"Seems he made a new friend." She added quietly, "Cute girl."

I shaded my eyes, not quite so discreetly. By golly it *was* a cute girl. *Eat your heart out, Bethany Bellnap,* I thought, a bit uncharitably. But after a few minutes of shamelessly eavesdropping on the two of them, and not understanding a word she said, I asked my wife what language the little girl was speaking.

Dame Wendy bunched her nose a bit. "French, maybe? Belgian? I honestly can't make it out. But whatever she's saying, he seems to understand it."

A waiter came over and I ordered the cold beer I'd been having unnatural thoughts about since somewhere in the middle of last night at Villa Agape.

And with that, we both tilted our faces to the warm sun of Chianti to nap a bit beneath the trees before dinner. A moment or two later, though, Wendy drowsily asked, "Did you really meet a man with a horse or are you just making that up?"

"Sure did. He looked just like Sam Snead. The man, I mean. The horse looked like Sister Patrice."

I heard the girl laugh at something Jack must have said—so at least one of us was scoring with the ladies. Later that evening we would learn from her parents that the girl's name was Alicia; she was Belgian but speaking in Flemish. She and Jack would exchange addresses and emails, commencing a correspondence that lasts to this day.

But I couldn't have known all of that then. All I knew then was that going from here to there as Dante Alighieri had done, finding a good road and following it, had made me almost inexpressibly happy in the past few days and weeks. Who cared if my garden burned up and we couldn't go to Africa. But, of course, as the sages of this ancient landscape warned, when you're truly happy is when the mischievous gods of Olympus send a bolt to zap you—to keep you awake and on your toes for trouble, if nothing else. Being happy, as Rupert Rivers and Sister Patrice and maybe even those bicycle jerks back in Amsterdam might have pointed out, sometimes makes you an irresistible target for the jealous gods.

For the moment, I didn't care what the idle gods were up to. Instead, I reached over and took my wife's left hand, the hand that still needed to find a ring. I had an idea about that, too . . .

"Sleeping?" I asked, taking another swig of my delicious Italian beer.

"Yes," she replied pleasantly, and a little distantly, like a girl on the very edge of Paradiso itself. "Please don't wake me up."

FOURTEEN

Death in the Afternoon

I pulled over to let Wendy and Jack off on the sidewalk in Vico Equense, a busy clifftop village not far from Sorrento, so they could check out a promising little hotel that clung tenaciously to the rocks high above the blue Mediterranean. This was two days after our restful interlude in Casa Frassi. Purely on the advice of friends who once lived in Italy, we decided to skip the haze and tourist congestion of Rome and make a beeline for Pompeii and the cooler breezes of the Sorrentine Peninsula. As much as I would have enjoyed seeing the Coliseum and Flavian Ampitheatre and hoofing through the Vatican and Sistine Chapel and asking the Holy See if Jack and I could borrow his neat popemobile for a short spin along the Tiber, I halfway suspected Sister Patrice had already been on the horn to John Paul warning him we were in the neighborhood. Besides, if the city was *really* eternal, it would keep until we came back.

Tiny Vico Equense, on the other hand, with its sensational view of the Bay of Naples and mighty Mount Vesuvius, possessed a fragile beauty that seemed to suggest it could slip from the rocks and vanish in the sea at the drop of a Bill Holden hat, a charming little coastal market town that remained lost in time and immune to the tensions of modern urban life.

So much for sweet first impressions, I guess. I'd scarcely gotten my wife and son out the Audi doors onto the bricks of the village, promising I'd be straight back after safely parking the car, before a volley of horns impatiently sounded and angry shouts of a highly personal nature were heard coming from behind.

I waved an apologetic hand and proceeded ahead to a trickling municipal fountain and auto rotary which turned out to actually be the Circus Maximus of Vico Equense whereupon cars and motorbikes were suddenly violently converging on all sides, most if not all drivers laying on their horns at the sight of a dumb flatlander who clearly didn't know the local driving customs. Golly, it took me *three* more complete circumnavigations of the fountain just to make up my mind which congested side street to turn down.

As I braked to turn, finally, a young stud tailgating me on a whiny motor scooter with a voluptuous teenage girl clinging to his twenty-two-inch bare waist rudely thumped the trunk of the Audi with the palm of his hand and then gunned his bike around the driver's side and savagely kicked my door handle with his designer sandal, offering a famous Italian gesture they affectionately call the hook 'em horns sign down in Texas.

I waved back—or, in more precise technical language, gave him the finger. I'm not proud of this act of impromptu flagrant incivility, mind you. But you don't mess with Texas, as they like to say down in G. W. Bush country, and there comes a time in the affairs of men when you don't mess with me, either. I was weary, hot, a little confused, and vaguely worried I might be on a one-way road headed out of town. Besides, this scrawny fascist twerp really had it coming for abusing my rental car.

One of the fun things about driving in Italy, a chap quickly discovers behind the wheel, is that even the smallest chance encounter has the potential to develop into an unforgetable drama. My timeless traffic salutation, for example, really seemed to unhinge the poor kid on the motor scooter. He sat there for a moment murderously staring at me with his dark and brooding bedroom eyes, while his clingy candy-faced girlfriend peeked vacantly over his bare shoulder, then began wildly revving his little motor scooter in some kind of ancient Neopolitan display of precoital machismo.

At this point, for laughs, I yawned and scratched my ear. Or maybe I picked my nose. I forget which I did, to be honest. But it sure revved *him* up.

There was another violent thump on the door handle from the stud's designer sandal and then he gunned his bike and nearly did a wheelie as he went tearing off, whipping violently in front of me and shouting something with a disgusted flip of the hand . . . nanoseconds before he plowed straight into an old man walking a pair of goats across the narrow street.

The goats let out an awful racket. The old man tumbled to the pavement. A fat lady shrieked and dropped a bundle of clothes. Traffic halted. People immediately gathered from everywhere and started yelling at each other. The gorgeous girlfriend got off the stud's motorbike and placed her hands sulkily on her hips. I climbed out to see if the old guy was bleeding from the head. The stud glanced at me and started shouting. He looked about sixteen going on twelve.

For a fascinating anthropological moment, it was tough to determine precisely who was yelling at whom. A blue-shirted policeman eventually sidled up munching a candy bar and attempted to sort things out. He talked to ten people simultaneously. While he did this, I helped the old man to his feet and scratched one of his agitated goats gently behind the ear. The old man shook his head to get the cobwebs out and pointed an accusatory finger at the young stud and said something to the policeman. The stud responded by waving a wild hand at me and one of the old man's goats began to rub itself affectionately against my leg. The gorgeous girlfriend said something to her boyfriend, who said something back rather snippily. I got the impression he immediately regretted this because she suddenly rolled her pretty eyes and flounced off up the sidewalk. This made the young stud noticeably crazier. The bored cop took another bite of his candy bar and waved people back to the sidewalk and shops. The drama, he was saying, was *finito*. People began to shrug, even laugh a bit, and wander away. The fat lady who dropped her clothes bundle picked it up and grinned toothlessly at me, possibly admiring my Bill Holden hat. The young stud fired up his bike, cast me a final evil look, and sped off through traffic chasing his former girlfriend. Traffic resumed its lavalike advance up the narrow street and life in lovely Vico Equense quickly settled back down to its normal level of cliffside civic chaos.

This rich pageant of Italian street life took, I suppose, maybe two minutes to unfold, the upshot being that everybody appeared perfectly fine and maybe even a little grateful for the unexpected entertainment. One of the goats even attempted to get into the Audi with me.

Roughly half an hour after I dropped them off—because I had to drive twelve more kilometers over the mountainside to Positano before I managed to find a place I could turn around without causing another automotive incident—I picked up Jack and Wendy in front of the Hotel Vesuvius.

"Where on earth did you *go?*" Wendy wondered, not unreasonably.

"Just around the block," I answered pleasantly. "Nice town."

The hotel was booked solid, but we found a place on the road back toward Pompeii, a somewhat down-at-the-heels resort, carved into the side of the cliffs, which had a nifty saltwater pool but, mysteriously, few paying guests in its rooms.

Italy is such a divine conundrum. We wondered if the place might be going broke or possibly have been condemned. The floor of our otherwise reasonably attractive room seemed to tilt ever so slightly toward the Bay of Naples. But there were a number of carefree locals sprawled around the salt pool and the English-speaking maître d' assured us that the restaurant did the finest sea bass dinner in the region. For the moment, we were home. We dropped bags, stripped off, and dove into the blue Mediterranean.

In the morning, I woke to the sound of an awful rumble that (for once) turned out not to be my stomach. I padded outside to investigate and heard the rumbling intensify. To make matters worse, the rock terrace where I stood actually gave off the faintest seismic tremor. I padded worriedly back inside and told my sleeping mates, as calmly as I could under the circumstances, "Guys, I think you'd better get up. We may have to pack up *pronto.*"

Jack lifted his groggy head from the pillow, looking like a guy who'd been out drinking milkshakes till the wee hours. For her part, Wendy was still out for the count.

"Why, Dad?"

"I think either Mount Vesuvius might be going off or this place is being bulldozed."

I switched on the TV and was startled to see, in fact, footage of a volcano violently erupting. Wendy and Jack sat bolt upright in their beds.

"Is that . . . *here?*" She sleepily posed the relevant disturbing question.

We watched in silence until the CNN announcer, in Italian followed by English, said something about Mount Etna on Sicily dramatically erupting for the first time in over two decades. I'll admit feeling deeply relieved by this news. I hated to think we might have to execute a classic cliff dive from our balcony and begin swimming for our lives to Capri.

The frightening rumbles and tremors beneath us turned out to be something far more commonplace than a dormant volcano coming to life—another sign of modern values meeting the ancient landscape—as we discovered on the winding coastal road down to Pompeii a couple of hours later. Emerging from a short tunnel through the rock cliffs about a mile and a half below the hotel, we came across a construction crew dynamiting the rocky coastline for a new luxury hotel.

We had paid our admission fee to the ruins at Pompeii and were filtering up the dusty hill toward the Marina Gate, following a colorful group of late-morning sightseers—a joyfully smiling and visibly proud Italian grandpapa and his tittering clan of visiting American relatives, a delightfully noisy group of adults and children that included several young girls about Jack's age, a family reunion on a day trip to the world's most famous city of the dead—when a well-dressed man with a bright orange umbrella approached us, bowed elegantly, and politely inquired in English if we wished to engage his services as a personal tour guide.

Perdition take all guides—that's how Twain dismissed local tour guides when he wandered through these same ruins over a century ago. But we'd had excellent luck thus far with guides, and this chap—late middle age, rawly barbered gray hair, rimless spectacles beneath his straw hat (not unlike my own!), and a no-nonsense academic mien that the Queen Mum would have liked—was not only registered with the regional Bureau of Antiquities but turned out to be an associate professor of Art History at the University of Napoli and, as we later learned from the gallery brochures he gave us, an accomplished land-scape painter in his own right.

Professor Geraldo "Please call me Jerry" Vespucci was a bit on the pricey side but turned out to be worth every lire as we had only an hour or two at most to spend before attempting to drive to Bari for an evening ferry to Greece. He hauled beautiful illustrations and helpful diagrams of the ancient city from his canvas kit bag as he popped open his orange umbrella, aimed us up the hill past the Temple of Venus toward the ruins of the Forum, and slipped into a dramatic monologue worthy of a PBS pledge program about how the great city appeared prior to that fateful noontime eruption in A.D. 79.

Among other things, we learned that the city, located at the mouth of the River Sarno, was a thriving center of sea trade and land com-merce and multicultural life heavily influenced by the art and gover-nance of early Greeks long before the Imperial Romans took possession about the fourth century and began an extensive program of innovative road construction and ambitious temple building. Ro-mans, of course, as any eighth grader who can give you the classical finger knows, were the master builders of the ancient age—leaving an extraordinary design legacy of roads, bridges, aqueducts, baths, public forums, arches, theaters, athletic coliseums, palaces, and monuments strewn across Europe that exist, and in some cases are still used, to this day. Roman public architecture remains the basis of much of the West-ern world's civic and religious building.

"At Pompeii," said Professor Jerry, sounding a little like an Italian James Earl Jones, "this gift for creating beautiful and efficient public spaces came to an early flowering. Tell me, Jake," he asked Jack, "do you have any idea *why* these stones are raised in the middle of the road and what they would have been used for?"

Jack, who didn't seem the slightest bit bothered to be called Jake, studied the peculiar, spaced square stones that rose perhaps half a meter from the ground and crossed the throroughfare at in-tervals by the Forum as well as along most of the city's neat grid of stone roads.

"Were they, like, put there to prevent guys from, I don't know, rac-ing chariots or something through the streets?" He'd just seen the film

Gladiator and I nodded, thinking that would have been *exactly* my guess as well—ancient speedbumps for hellions on two wheels.

"An excellent guess," Professor Pompeii rewarded him, smiling. "But, in fact, the stones were low enough to permit wagons and chariots to pass directly over them. No. These were purely pedestrian conveniences, cleverly raised stones which enabled citizens to cross the street without getting their feet wet during poor weather or having to step in anything unfortunate the horse left behind. Very novel planning, don't you agree? Far ahead of its time, young friend."

We moseyed deeper into the ruins, with the silence and heat rising around us. Professor Jerry motioned us up a narrow alley among two private villas and stooped to show us the remains of what appeared to be ancient plumbing, crumbling terra-cotta pipe emerging from a wall which fed in turn to a master pipe that led, according to the professor, to a state-of-the-art central sewage collection system.

"Most of the city, in the days just prior to the eruption of the volcano, particularly in the districts where the finer villas were built, was fully irrigated and enjoyed the benefits of flowing water through an elaborate system of piping. They had flushing toilets and even showers, as you shall see just ahead."

He led us into the town's primary public bathhouse, the Forum Baths—an impressive collection of separate men's and women's bathing rooms decorated with extraordinary frescoes and murals, hot- and cold-running pools, showers, saunas, and even a rudimentary steaming system. A few doors away, we stepped into a "typical" ruling class residence, the famous House of the Tragic Poet, so named for an illustrious painting of a tragic play rehearsal that once hung on its wall. The owner, a wealthy merchant, left a fascinating mosaic message on the entrance floor that even deeply impressed Twain when he wandered through the dwelling. *Cave Canem*, it reads. Beware of Dog.

This was apt because a scruffy female dog lounged in the empty garden pool while a trio of larger male dogs snarled and circled each other and took occasional passes at her. The bitch, I gathered, was in heat. She looked utterly flayed and disinterested in their attentions. One of the preening, annoying male dogs, I noticed, was a dead ringer for the macho teen on the motorbike back in Vico Equense.

"Ah, the dogs of Pompeii." Professor Jerry sighed with distaste, steering us deftly around the action, into the main living quarters. "This is such a problem we have here, and the civil authorities are apparently in no rush to repair the situation. They claim there is not enough money to complete the excavations, which are only something like half-finished—much less take care of the dog problem."

"Where do they come from?" Wendy wondered.

"People bring them here."

"They just *leave* them?"

"Yes. They are old or stray. Some are ill. People decide it is a good way to dispose of an old pet. They simply abandon them here. Their numbers are rapidly multiplying, I regret to say. It seems terribly brutal, eh? The staff here is overwhelmed by them, to be honest, though I suppose there is a certain level of care." He shook his gray head in dismay, keeping his umbrella at the ready in case one of the dogs lunged our way, ushering us back to the intensely hot sun-washed *via* where we turned up the Via Della Fortuna Augusta and eventually wound up at the House of the Vettii, one of the city's more intact dwellings, unearthed about the time Brother Twain came calling, a year after the American Civil War ended.

Owned by a pair of wealthy and ostentatious merchants who weren't shy about showing off their wealth or anything else, the main vestibule of the house was decorated with a bold fresco depicting the god Priapus, his three-foot penis thoughtfully held aloft by a grain scale. Both Wendy and Jack blushed and did double takes when they saw it, and Professor Jerry quickly moved to explain that the painting was not intended to be pornographic but principally designed to "ward off evil spirits" and deter anyone who coveted the wealth housed within. He showed and explained other beautiful frescoes on the grounds, including one depicting the myth of Cyparissus (the young hunter who slew the stag so dear to Apollo). In the center of the villa lay a handsome courtyard surrounded by an arched peristyle where lavender beds were growing nicely in the parched soil.

"Isn't that great looking?" I observed to Wendy as we shuffled past. "Wish *my* lavender would grow like that."

"Your lavender *is* growing like that, Love," she pointed out. "Thanks to the drought, Maine looks like Pompeii this summer."

"I'm glad we're here then," I said, taking my bride's hand. "Even if we have to outrun a waking volcano."

She smiled but looked a little vexed, as if the combination of the heat and dust kicked up by the desperate dogs and the poignant sight of the human figures we'd happened upon from time to time, caught unaware two thousand years ago by the shower of volcanic ash that buried the city and "froze" them in place for eternity—some writhing in agony as they were asphyxiated, others solemnly bowing their heads as if to quietly accept their fates—were suddenly, collectively, all a bit overwhelming.

Professor Jerry had just finished telling us the sad story about Pliny the Elder, who watched the holocaust from a ship just offshore and lost his life attempting to rescue a close friend who resided in the doomed city (a tale vividly recounted in the subsequent letters written by Pliny the Younger, his admiring nephew) when the wretched female dog suddenly bolted past us pursued by a pack of suitors.

A savage melee involving several of the larger male dogs erupted just ahead of us in the courtyard of the House of the Fawn, kicking up a cloud of dust and slinging ropes of blood and saliva onto the ancient stones underfoot. Professor Jerry immediately seized Wendy's arm, hurrying her past a pair of brutes fighting to the death, and I grabbed Jack by the hand and rapidly towed him past the violence.

Just beyond this scene of mayhem, though, a large crowd was gathering solemnly at an intersection of the Forum, where we heard, as we approached, the unmistakable sound of children weeping. *Oh, great.* I thought. *Dead dog.* But as we approached, I realized a human figure had collapsed in the heat. It turned out to be the smiling patriarch of the happy collection of people we'd followed into the ruins a couple hours ago, the big proud Italian grandpapa. An Italian policeman had just abandoned his attempts to revive the old guy and was solemnly placing his straw hat over the man's serene Roman face, shielding it from the brutal glare of the sun until the authorities could come and remove his body.

Death always comes too early or too late, someone said. Whatever else is true, it changes worlds. Without fully realizing it, I momentarily paused to survey the scene of the tragedy—subconsciously searching, I think, for the sobbing American granddaughters—only to realize Jack was taking it all in, too, with eyes like Pompeiian saucers.

I came to my senses and whispered respectfully, "Guys, let's go," herding them into a temple courtyard that appeared to reconnect on the other side of a crumbled wall with the *via* to the Marina Gate. Unfortunately, though, it led us directly to a vestibule where the grandmother had taken the dead man's grandchildren for refuge from the sun and the stares of horrified tourists.

Professor Jerry, who'd paused to speak to one of the policemen, came hurrying after us but failed to catch us before we bumbled straight into the three American girls, all clinging to their Italian grandmother and sobbing their eyes out. She, on the other hand, had the calmest brown eyes I'd ever seen and was murmuring consoling words to her heartbroken daughter's daughters. Queen Dido with her brave Carthaginian heart as callow Aeneas sails for the underworld.

As Professor Jerry reached us, I realized Jack was staring even more intensely than I was at the weeping granddaughters, a couple of whom were very close to his own age. I touched his arm again and nodded to Wendy, backing up and saying, "Let's give them some privacy. Follow me." Perdition take all guides, indeed. Especially when they assume command and lead the innocent from bad to worse.

We said good-bye to Professor Jerry by the Temple of Isis, accepted one of his brochures, and wandered off to get some air and, hopefully, some much needed perspective. Jack had never witnessed a human death—only the death of his beloved golden retriever Bailey, who sat with her gray muzzle serenely resting on his lap until the narcotic painkiller did its intended job. He'd cried and I'd cried and that was that.

But this was different. This was a child's worst nightmare that had come calling in the middle of a sunny day, grief unbidden, death on Roman holiday. A little while later, the two of us wound up sitting high up on the hot stone seats of Pompeii's incredible ampitheater, where there was a bit of a breeze off the Bay of Naples.

Wendy waited for us in the shade of a plane tree downstairs, purportedly studying the map for the best route across southern Italy to the evening ferry at Bari.

"That was tough, Boss. I'm sorry we had to see that," I began and then fell silent, not entirely certain how I should proceed from here. All sorts of consolations, famous quotes on death, and bits of this and that ancient wisdom entered my head. But in light of the circumstances they all seemed not a little trite. Life's very impermanence makes it precious beyond belief, but that's a revelation that only comes with living. *Life happens, Nibs, and so does death. You never know when your number is up. Look on the bright side—he was with the people he loved most on earth when he crossed the River Styx. Enjoy each moment, that's the message here. Cave Canem AND Carpe Diem, son.*

So, in the absence of anything profound, I simply said nothing, merely allowed my hand to rest on Jack's left shoulder, letting him know I was there with him, feeling probably exactly what he felt, if not fearing what he feared. If things held true to form, Jack would require a few days to mentally process what we'd just witnessed. But then, probably when I least expected, out would come the questions, one upon the other, and I would try my best to answer them honestly and helpfully.

It's as natural to die, said Marcus Aurelius, as to be born—and one can't happen without the other. But try telling that to a boy who really hasn't begun to live yet and you can understand why I chose to sit in that ancient place of stones and ash and let death eloquently speak for itself—at least for the moment.

Down below on the ampitheater floor, a couple of teenagers, a boy and girl, were tossing a Frisbee around on the hard-packed ochre earth.

"You okay?" I finally asked Nibs after we'd sat there in silence for many minutes, just listening to the sea wind and watching the Frisbee fly.

He nodded, still staring at the two happy teenagers down in the arena. The guy would fling the Frisbee high into the air and the girl would lope after it letting out squeals of frustration. Jack watched them while I studied the impressive stonework along the opposite side of the amphitheater wall, idly wondering if the stone fences I was building back home in Maine had any chance at all of making it a couple thousand years. Probably not.

Finally he spoke.

"Dad," he said, "is this where the Romans used to put the Christians in with the lions?" By this point the plastic discus throwers had given up their game and gone to find an icy lemonade by a stand near the front gates of Pompeii. We would join them there in a little while.

"I think that was Imperial Rome, Nibs. We'll see that next trip. Pompeii was more of a minor league town. Kind of like the Portland Seadogs to the Boston Red Sox. I think they only put agnostics in with abandoned dogs here. Like the Queen Mum in a former life."

It was one of my better jokes, I thought. But once again he didn't seem to hear me.

We had a hell of a time making the ferry to Greece—or, for that matter, getting onto it when we did. After a three-hour race across the boot of Italy to Bari, the old Moorish seaport mentioned as one of the places Aeneas and his Trojan band made land en route to civilizing Hesperia, as the wild uncharted West Country of Italy was called in classical times, I hurried into the ferry ticket office where the clerk appeared to still be having his lunch at five in the afternoon. There was a clutter of empty wine bottles and dirty plates piled up. The clerk rubbed his unshaven double chin and belched. Our conversation went more or less as follows:

Me: Is this the ferry to Corfu?

Clerk: To Corfu? *Si.*

Me: Great. I'd like three tickets and an overnight cabin for tonight, if possible. Two adults, one child.

Clerk: So you have *bambini*?

Me: Yes. A boy of eleven.

Clerk: He wishes to go as well?

Me (laughing a little): Yes. That's the general idea of traveling together.

Clerk (yawning): You wish to go tonight?

Me: Yes. If possible. Assuming there is availability.

Clerk (tapping the world's oldest computer keyboard): For *bambini*? Yes. Is possible.

Me: How about for *bambini's* parents?

Clerk (genuinely surprised): You wish to go to Corfu as well?

Me: It would help. *Bambini* gets lonely traveling alone.

At this point, the clerk swiveled around in his chair and conferred with a pair of older women seated at desks behind him in the ticket office. They appeared to be relaxing and filing their nails, resting up from a big lunch. After a few words were exchanged, a terrible row erupted among the three of them, highlighted by lots of (by now familiar) expressive Italian hand waving. Several minutes later, the clerk swiveled back and shrugged, scratching the hairs on his double chin.

Clerk: Is not possible, I'm afraid.

Me: *What's* not possible?

Clerk: Going to Corfu tonight on ferry. There is room for *bambini* but not for you.

He said the first availability for us *all* would be in five or six days. I asked if there wasn't another ferry service to Greece down in Brindisi, 120 kilometers down the coast of Hesperia. Wendy, who'd boned up on the boat schedules, assured me there was a boat to Igoumenítsa or someplace I'd never heard of that left around nine that night.

"Perhaps," the clerk said with another shrug. He yawned. It was nearly time for his post-lunch *siesta*. "I do not work in Brindisi."

I thanked him for his valuable time and then he swiveled around and said something more to the women. As I left, they were shouting at each other again and preparing to hurl bottles.

We reached the old pirate town of Brindisi at six-thirty, establishing a new benchmark land speed record for vacationing Mainers along the southern coast of Italy. As it turned out there were three or four *different* ferry lines with ships headed to Greece that evening, and for a change I did something right. I picked a ship of Greek registry aptly called the *Aeolus* and got in the line where the fewest violent arguments with the clerk appeared to be in progress. Within minutes, triumphantly, I held three one-way tickets to Igoumenítsa and a main-deck outer cabin that was safely booked in our names.

"Where exactly is Igoumenítsa?" I casually asked the female clerk, who also had a two-day stubble of beard.

"Near the Albanian border."

Moments later, out on the vast and mostly empty town docks where the *Aeolus* had just tied up and was being thoughtfully Hoovered prior to boarding for the evening passage, I invited Wendy and Jack to get comfortable with our bags while I went to find the Hertz dealer and dispose of our trusty Audi. Both my companions opened books and Wendy opened a warm bottle of Italian beer.

By the time I managed to return, though—maybe an hour, tops— the dock area resembled a movie scene from the Book of Exodus. The dock was jammed with thousands of waiting passengers, most of whom appeared to be Greek or Turkish refugees carrying most of what they owned on their backs.

For a few tense moments I couldn't spot my wife and *bambini* any- where and then I saw a hand waving frantically at me from the middle of the vast surging crowd. I pushed politely through sweating bodies, excusing myself and collecting dirty looks, and found the home team huddling with a couple of bronzed American college kids from Virginia who were sharing scholarly thoughts with Jack about *The Lord of the Rings*. Dame Wendy looked hot under the collar and about to clock someone with her empty beer bottle.

"These people," she declared, "have never *heard* of a line."

Just then, the *Aeolus* gave a mighty blast of her horn and dropped her gangway and all hell broke loose as a couple thousand sweaty, anx- ious passengers simultaneously attempted to sprint up the narrow four- foot-wide metal boarding ramp to the ferry. Before I realized it, we were nearly being pushed over the dock's edge and individually sepa- rated by the mad crush of pressing bodies. Suddenly I lost Jack's hand.

"Jack! Where *are* you?" I barked, Notre Dame–style, whipping my head around directly into the blank faces of a couple bearded guys smoking cigarettes who'd shoved him out of the way and moved up closer to my hind portion than any two non-consenting men had a right to be.

"Dad! Here!" I heard a welcome voice—but no sight of the lad himself.

"I've got him," Wendy called back. She was now four or five feet off to my right and slightly behind me, at which point I heard her declare indignantly, "Do you *mind?*" and swear in a manner that probably wouldn't have pleased Sister Patrice one bit. The next thing I knew, Dame Wendy was burrowing through the crowd with Jack clinging to her belt.

"This is unbelievable, isn't it?" I attempted to make pleasant conversation with her; unfortunately, as both straps of the large duffel bags I was carrying were constricting my windpipe, everything I said came out as a wheezy croak. "What are you *doing?*"

She had that look in her eyes that said she was not a woman to be trifled with. Puccini's kind of gal, a regular Golden Girl of the West.

"You've obviously never been to Filene's Basement when they put wedding dresses on sale," she declared. "Follow me, boys, and hold on tight."

And with that, we formed a human wedge with Dame Wendy on point, pushing our path up the gangway. Others fell into the conga line directly behind us, and at one point I heard an Englishman remark over my shoulder, as he shoved his mousy wife ahead of him, "Guess it's a question of picking your poison, dear. I mean, one is either beaten to a pulp on the dock or perishes like a vagabond on the sea."

Foolishly, I looked back and asked him what he meant—forgetting that Jack the Worrier was directly in front of me, clutching his ball glove and Professor Tolkien and soaking it all in despite the violently jostling crowd.

"Well," said the Englishman, turning to glare balefully at a small woman in a grubby head scarf who was nudging him from the rear, "isn't this the selfsame ferry that sunk last year during an evening crossing simply because some idiot Greek cabin boy neglected to properly shut the ferry door down below? Eight or nine hundred casualties. Very nasty business, as I recall."

"Oh." *Wonderful.* Far more than I needed to know at this point, Horatio.

"Believe it is, dear boy. Believe it is."

After tossing our bags into our minuscule stateroom, we followed the crowds to an open upper deck, where it became clear why there was such a rush to board the *Aeolus*. Those passengers who held the cheapest tickets would be overnighting on hard benches or sleeping "rough" on the floor of the ship's exposed top deck for the ten or twelve hours it took to cross the Ionian Sea.

Jack looked startled by the sight of elderly travelers and entire families spreading everything they owned out on the hard metallic floor, old men stretching out gingerly to take possession of hard plastic seats, children making beds beneath the ship's lifeboats. I was a bit startled by the sight, too—having seen a great deal in this world but nothing quite like this.

"Can't they come down where we are?" Nibs wondered as we went down a set of steps to the recreation deck of the ship, where the swimming pool had been roped off and tables were spread around a small dance floor. I wondered if people might be sleeping in the net over the swimming pool before the trip was over.

As we got Cokes and snagged a small table, I explained that there are two kinds of tickets in life—first class and traveling with children. He didn't get the joke, so I elaborated that this was probably the best those folks could afford, but at least they were together and it was supposed to be a balmy night with a decent moon.

A family of five—man in his late foties, wife in a beautiful blue head shawl, granny in a bright red scarf, two small kids—was seated at the table beside us. We were having drinks and they were not; they looked as if they meant to occupy the table all night long, which they probably did.

"You are English?" the man said to me; he looked either Turkish or Greek, and his accent was so thick I could scarcely understand him at first.

"No," I said, hesitating a moment. Someone early on our trip had advised me that if we dipped into either Greece or Turkey, given present turmoils, to simply say we were *Canadians* and let it go at that. "We're from Maine."

He nodded and inhaled his cigarette. I asked if they were Greek.

He shook his head and explained that he and his family came from a village outside Istanbul. They were headed to Igoumenítsa to catch another ferry to an island in the Aegean where they would connect with a third ferry to a port in Turkey. There was no direct ferry service to Turkey, due to age-old religious hostilities, and it would take another fifteen to twenty hours for the family to reach their home.

I asked if Igoumenítsa was an interesting place. It was about as far north in Greece as one could physically go without being in Albania. The man shrugged.

"Not so much of a nice town, perhaps because it was once destroyed by the Germans. Everything there is for the ships. Most of these people"—he suddenly waved his smoke at the huddled masses up top, many of whom already appeared to be sacked out and sleeping—"are only going there to collect relatives from the civil war. The ferries from Albania have been shut down temporarily."

I nodded solemnly, remembering that a civil war was raging not far away, exactly the kind of war that made the Queen Mum think so little of organized religion. One faith was duking it out with another in the name of God or divine national sovereignty. The family's small children were unusually still, I noticed—perhaps frightened by all this hullabaloo of boarding and getting settled. I asked the man if he had an opinion on the civil war.

He studied me for a moment. "I believe the Christian minority is trying to drive the Muslims into the sea—or at least into Macedonia. It is an old story here."

At least he offered a sad smile as he said this, lighting a fresh smoke off the embers of his finished cigarette. The wife smiled at Wendy. Wendy smiled back and said, "That's a lovely shawl. Is it Turkish?"

"I'm afraid my wife doesn't speak any English," the man explained, but the wife replied to Wendy in Turkish as if she knew exactly what she'd asked her.

"She says there is a village not far from Igoumenítsa you may wish to see. Many English people like it. It is down the coast a little way. It is called Parga. Very lovely. Sometimes too many tourists. But we had a nice time there once. Many nice boats. Some excellent restaurants."

"We'll check it out," I promised, glancing at Wendy.

"Sounds nice," Wendy agreed, the evening sea air fluttering her auburn hair.

The dark-eyed woman simply nodded a little and smiled beneath her beautiful head shawl.

*   *   *

I woke abruptly and looked at my illuminated watch, feeling the ship's engines surge and throb beneath us. It was quarter to five in the morning, my usual waking time back home in Maine. We had been on the sea almost eight hours, in bed for six. I climbed out of my bunk and quietly dressed in the darkened cabin, careful not to wake my snoozing companions. Then I rooted around in my bag for a somewhat dog-eared paperback of Robert Fagles's translation of *The Odyssey*. I also found my Bill Holden hat and plopped it on my head.

According to my crude navigational calculations we would soon be passing the island of Ithaca, Odysseus' mythical home, the much beloved place he spent twenty years trying to get back to, according to the blind poet Homer. It was kind of corny, but I had this overwhelming desire to stand at the rail and read some of my favorite passages of the epic poem as we glided past Ithaca into the Grecian dawn, hoping nobody I knew spotted me doing such a sappy English major thing.

As I straightened up to go, though, I realized I was being watched by a pair of unsleeping eyes.

"Hey," I whispered to Jack. "Why are you awake, Boss?"

"I don't know."

"Have you slept at all?"

"A little. Not really."

I knew exactly what was chewing at him—that asinine remark the Englishman had made about the ship going down with nine hundred hands. After the *Aeolus* was fully loaded, I'd expressly taken Jack down to the car deck so we could both watch the ship's crew safely shut and seal the boat's great hydraulic doors. That had eased my tensions over the matter somewhat, though clearly not his.

"I'm going up on deck to watch the sunrise. We're almost to Greece. Want to go?"

"Sure," he said, slipping off his upper bunk fully dressed, as if he'd been merely waiting for such an invitation—or to sprint to the lifeboats. He picked up something but I couldn't quite see what it was.

Up on deck, the stars were still faintly shining and the sea winds were lively but warm. Only a few people were up, moseying about the rails. The sky to the east was showing the first smudges of pink and, passing the sleeping shapes on the upper deck floor, we found a good spot at the ship's forward rail, just below the pilot's house.

"You brought your chess set," I remarked to Jack, realizing what he'd carried up top with him.

"Yes, sir. I thought maybe we could have a game or something. What did you bring?"

I showed him my book.

"Oh," he said, "if you want to read we don't have to play chess."

"I'd rather play chess with you," I lied, which I guess really wasn't a lie after all. One can read Homer any old day. Besides, the point of *our* odyssey was for me to be with Jack, not a blind poet from Asia Minor.

We went to the starboard side of the deck, found a spot out of the wind, and set up the board on a locked box of life jackets. Several people were sleeping on the floor all around us. Jack invited me to take the first move, so I did. After several minutes of play, I'd taken four or five of his pawns and a bishop but he'd only taken two of my pawns.

"You're not letting me win, are you?"

"No, sir."

I moved my bishop a bit daringly—and took his rook.

"Dad," he said, almost conversationally, "are you afraid of dying?"

I wasn't surprised at this question—merely how much quicker it had come than I'd predicted. On the other hand, maybe Jack had been lying there awake all night simply processing what he'd seen happen at Pompeii and not worrying about the ferry sinking with all hands on board, after all.

"No, actually."

I explained to him why not. I said that the older I got the more I accepted the fact that most of my life was behind me now, and I told him some of the thoughts I'd had while sitting with him at the top of the Amphitheater in Pompeii and added I sometimes worried about *how* I might depart this blessed realm for the next one, but even that didn't bother me nearly as much as it once had.

"Do you think that man who died at Pompeii is, like, still alive somewhere and sad?"

"I think he's very much alive . . . somewhere," I replied. "I think his only sadness comes from the grief of abruptly leaving his granddaughters and frightening them." I made another move, lifting his second bishop off the board.

"Grief, like beauty, fades away, Nibs. But you might keep that man in your prayers when you speak to the ferry pilot upstairs. Better yet, think of his grandchildren, his children, and his wife. They could probably use a little divine intervention about now. But in time, trust me, they'll only remember what a cool guy their Italian grandpapa was."

Trying to strike a lighter note on life's heaviest subject, I added that his own Native American ancestors believed there was such a thing as a "good" day to pass away and that I genuinely wouldn't mind going to meet my maker in a manner similar to that gentleman at Pompeii, quickly and without too much bother, surrounded by the people he loved most in this world. In my case, perhaps, I'd politely keel over after making a twenty-foot putt for eagle on a famous par-five hole or finish up the mulching and mowing and sit down to drink a glass of freshly made iced tea with the people I love most, including *his* thoughtful children and Maggie's rambunctious brood, all of whom would be gushing embarrassingly about their granddad's Monet-like garden wizardry, at which point I would simply smile, listen to their happy conversations about this and that, shut my eyes for a little snooze in the late summer sunshine, and drift away.

I'm not sure Nibs the Lost Boy found these images nearly as reassuring or entertaining as I did, nor perhaps could he fully fathom why such an end was to be more than hoped for in this violent day and age. But at least he smiled, albeit thinly, as if willing to countenance the possibilities.

After studying the rolling surface of the Ionian Sea for a moment or two, he nodded and concentrated a little more closely on the game, and we played on for several minutes with only the rumble of the ship and the soft hiss of the waves below and the sigh of the sea wind to be heard, each of us pausing from time to time to stare at the water between moves. Suddenly the gray shape of an island loomed, much nearer than I at first realized. Within a minute or two I could make out small lights, jagged mountaintops, even white fishing boats with boom nets in the distance.

"I think that's Ithaca," I said, probably more to myself than to Jack, who dutifully glanced up, remarked a bit absently, "Really? Cool . . ." and promptly got back to trying to figure out his next move, obviously a champ in catch-up mode. A few minutes later, my queen put his Crusader king in checkmate for my first chess victory ever. The Moors had beaten the Christians *on* the sea if not driven them into it.

The win, to be honest, was a little anticlimactic. But maybe I was just tired from the previous long day and the strains of the overnight passage. We closed up the set and wandered to the bow of the ship to stand and watch the sunrise come in earnest now. There was a dramatic rocky coastline visible to the east—*a foretaste of Heaven,* as Mark Twain called mainland Greece upon first seeing it in the distance.

I leaned out over the rail, with one hand on Jack's shoulders and another lightly holding the brim of my Bill Holden hat. A sudden gust of sea air made me sneeze, though, and just like that my beloved hat blew off into the sea.

"Oh well." I tried to be philosophical about the loss as we watched it bob in the waves and then disappear. "I know a woman who is going to be extremely happy when she wakes up this morning.

"By the way," I said. "You didn't just *let* me win, did you?"

"No, sir. You really won. Honest."

"Good." I placed my arm back around Jack and wiped my leaky nose in the wind, hoping I wasn't catching one of those awful summer head colds. "I just had to make sure because I'd hate to have to toss your lying butt into the sea and make you swim after that hat. Wendy would be really mad at us *both*."

Jack laughed a bit of his old laugh and that, under the circumstances, was a little Greek night music to my ears. If I taught him nothing else on this road to somewhere, I hoped he would learn the value of finding humor amid life's sudden and constant sorrows—for that's sacred and healing ground, too. If nothing else, I wanted him to learn the value of taking the world seriously enough to take himself lightly, to have faith, to keep laughing, and to find a way to keep on going no matter what.

Around us, families began to stir on their hard plastic seats and the rolling ferry deck. The light brightened and children and their parents sleepily joined us at that high ship's rail, rubbing their eyes, a new day and even older world approaching.

FIFTEEN

The Navel of the World

"I think, under the circumstances, we should name the car," Wendy proposed. "If ever a car deserved a nickname, this funny little thing is *it*."

A few colorful possibilities came immediately to mind, but I remembered there was an impressionable lad stuffed somewhere in the back so I simply nodded and, having obviously read too many chivalric romances, suggested, "What about Rocinante?"

"Who's that?" someone wondered.

I explained for the benefit of my traveling companions who hadn't read *Don Quixote* that Rocinante was an aged but loyal horse, famous for charging windmills and other futile giants. Even without my beloved Bill Holden hat, the addled hopes of our original quest to wander the world's byways were beginning to make me feel a little bit like Miguel de Cervantes' confused country gentleman of La Mancha. Technically speaking, that cast Wendy in the role of Sancho Panza and made Jack just some dusty urchin we'd picked up along the road and stuffed into the boot of the world's smallest car.

In order to find our Rocinante, I'd been forced to wake up half of slumbering Igoumenítsa on a tranquil Saturday morning, but find it I had, hiring it straight out from under the only car rental agent in town who knew of a functioning vehicle anywhere in northern Greece. When he pulled up in it, I wasn't sure he hadn't simply swiped a bumper car from a traveling carnival or pinched a toy from one of his sleeping children. Whatever it was, the little car was electric green and glowing radioactively.

"How about the Maaaaph Grrrree Peeeeffff?" A somewhat muffled voice proposed from the general direction of the luggage.

"What's that?" I called back over my shoulder and the roar of the morning wind as we sped out of town on a craggy and somewhat desolate high coastal road, heading south along what is called the Epirot Coast toward tiny Parga; the windows were fully cranked open because the car didn't come equipped with an air conditioner and the day was already beastly hot. As it was, all of our bags filled up the backseat and Jack was creatively wedged somewhere among them. A small head appeared between bags.

"I *said*," he clarified, "how about the Mad Green Pea?"

The Mad Green Pea. I thought about it and glanced at Wendy, who now had her knees folded pertly beneath her chin and her pretty face tilted to the sun, auburn hair billowing like Aurora in the Greek morning.

"I like it," she voted without even opening her eyes. I liked it, too. We promptly took a membership vote from the floor and Mad Green Pea beat poor Rocinante, I regret to say, three-to-nil. Even my nicknaming was like tilting at windmills.

"Tired?" I asked my wife, affectionately patting her knee, which was inconveniently blocking the stick shift. Of the three of us, she was the only one who'd managed to actually sleep on the overnight passage from Hesperia.

"No. Just terrified. I don't want to look down. Let me know when we get there."

There *was* something vaguely harrowing about the route I'd chosen, a narrow broken asphalt road winding up and over towering beige cliffs where there seemed to be nary a sign of human habitation and little in the way of interesting flora or fauna and only some kind of little roadside shrine to a Greek Orthodox saint every half a mile or so. We briefly pulled over to investigate one of these and were horrified to discover they were actually private *memorials* to motorists who'd gone over the edge into the wild blue yonder. Greece, it turns out, has one of the highest per capita highway mortality rates in the world.

Parga, maybe an hour farther along the road, though, turned out to be a delightful place spread out between fragrant lemon groves and the bluest ocean water I'd ever seen, a small fishing village with faded pastel houses and cobbled alleys where most of the sunburned tourists appeared to be Europeans and apparently nobody had ever heard of Maine. In no time flat we secured a large room on the top floor of the Hotel Paradiso, tossed open the shutters on a sea of tiled rooftop TV aerials, and stretched out for the customary three-hour noon Greek siesta beneath lazily turning ceiling fans. Then we wandered down to the boat-cluttered waterfront, where waiters were already beginning to stir again and set out chairs and tables at a dozen tavernas strung along the water.

The sun was still fiercely hot but not as hot as before. We decided it was not too late to find a beach and take a swim.

A barrel-chested boatman named Balti said he knew the perfect beach for us, waving us into his elderly wooden launch. As we chugged out of the snug harbor in his long passenger boat with maybe half a dozen other late afternoon beachgoers aboard, I realized with a mild start who Balti reminded me of. He was a dead ringer for Wendy's father, Bill, and for a scary moment or two as we bobbed around ancient pitted rocks where the Sirens had attempted to lure Odysseus to his doom, and passed through a number of bottle-green secret grottoes where beautiful Calliope had made love to the wayward mariner, I began to worry that he might actually *be* Bill Buynak, somehow inexplicably turned up here having abandoned Wendy's mom and fled to a carefree life of worthless tourist ferrying and endless nights of grappa drinking. I gently nudged my sleepy-eyed wife, nodded to the smiling boatman who was schmoozing a pair of fleshy young Englishwomen, and whispered, "Hey. Who does Billy the Greek remind you of?"

She studied him thoughtfully for a moment.

"You in another ten or fifteen years? It's only a guess," she admitted.

"Very funny. Look again. Picture him inhaling pork rinds and channel surfing from female weightlifting to extreme skateboarding. Imagine him yelling at you in tennis. Coming to dinner in his dress sweats. Sports Center's man-of-the-year . . ."

She glanced again. Her mouth fell open.

"Oh my gosh," she said. "What's *he* doing here?"

The private beach Billy the Greek transported us to resembled a postcard from Greek Tourism, a perfect tidy crescent of sparkling white sand set between an old hotel and a high stone cliff. There were scores of children splashing happily in the crystalline water and maybe a dozen nice-looking mothers—if you care to notice such things—sunbathing without their tops up on the sand.

"Dad," Jack said to me after he and I leapt into the water, resurfaced, and began splashing around like toddlers in over their heads, "do you think Wendy is going to, like, take *her* top off or something?"

Funny how a boy's mind works, or, come to think of it, his father's. That thought, frankly, hadn't really occurred to me, nor probably to Dame Wendy either, for that matter. But now that he mentioned it, as we watched her disembark from Balti's launch and wade to shore with her straw carryall, she appeared to be about the only woman on the beach who wasn't missing the top of her swimsuit, and I wondered, to be on the safe side, if it would make Jack uncomfortable to see his stepmother discreetly baring her bosom to the gods and a guy who looked scarily like her own father.

"Of course not," he replied, treading in the blue water beside me. He reminded me of all the nude statues we'd seen in the previous weeks, the Classical ideal of human beauty we'd learned about in various museum tours, not to mention all those bare-chested grandmothers and daughters on the beach back in France. "I mean, Dad. Breasts are just breasts, right? Everybody has them."

"True. Some are better than others, though. That's a very mature attitude on your part, son. Try not to make a big deal out of it if she decides to do it, which knowing her she probably won't. Better yet, don't look or the gods will strike you blind."

Wendy was up on the beach now, stretching out between several intensely suntanned, lightly clad couples on a tubular lounge chair Balti had thoughtfully fetched her from the hotel. She was reading a provocative novel about Florence, art restoration, papal intrigue, and sex behind ornate closed doors. So maybe anything was possible on a designated day of seaside rest and Greek hedonism.

Nibs and I swam for a while, diving down for interesting shells and cute little sponge-like aqua plants that were probably on somebody's endangered species list, and then wandered up to show our gathered sea treasures to Wendy and join her in the sun.

"How's the book?" I asked, plopping down on my tubular lounge like a beached whale, dearly wishing I still had my beloved Bill Holden hat. Some grizzled Ithacan fisherman was probably mending his nets this very minute and having village neighbors tell him he looked just like a famous American movie star.

"Wonderful. How's the water?"

"Awful. I hate this place. Let's go home."

With her wide-brimmed straw hat, dark glasses, and sculpted designer one-piece suit, Wendy looked like a mysterious American heiress or gay divorcee—or so I told her as we lay there together. Jack, who was never much for idle suntanning, had already gotten to his feet and wandered down the beach to look for interesting shells or discreetly check out the other mothers.

"How's the worried barefoot boy?" Wendy wondered conversationally, when he was safely out of earshot, not even looking up from her book.

"Great. He asked me if you planned to take off your top, though," I explained with a wry chuckle. "Virtually every woman on this beach, by the way, is missing hers, in case you hadn't noticed. When in Greece and all of that."

"I wouldn't *dare*," she said and laughed a little nervously. "Not with Jack around."

"Breasts are breasts," I carefully pointed out. "Everybody has them. Especially that woman right over there rubbing suntan oil on herself."

Wendy glanced discreetly over the top of her Ray-Bans.

"A regular Venus de Milo. Amazing what you can get from catalogs these days."

"Well, it's the thought that counts. Size, too, I guess. At least for your average guy, that is."

"What *is* it about women's breasts," she wondered philosophically, "that makes serious men such silly little boys? Even my father."

"I don't know," I admitted. "I'll have to ask Jack and Bill the Greek and get back to you later on that."

"Well," she said, a touch primly, diving safely back into her book, "we'll see. Maybe when Jack is safely out of sight. But *only* then. Don't hold your breath, Mr. *Average*."

This remark stung. But I reached over and touched my modest bride's hand in a highly romantic way, stroking the finger that had yet to achieve a decent wedding ring. The wedding gold we'd eyeballed on the Ponte Vecchio and a few other places on the trip was either laughably expensive or looked like something Liberace might have been embarrassed to wear. We needed something simple and cheap and a little worn down by life, just like us.

"I'm really glad you came on this part of the trip," I explained affectionately to the exotic profile of my almost-new wife. "Believe me when I say that it means a lot to me *and* to Jack to have you with us, with or without your top on. We're three for the road! Pods from the same mad green pea! Even if you stubbornly refuse to behave like Calliope on the beach with Odysseus . . ."

She leaned over and kissed me sweetly on the mouth, a full-blooded Melina Mercouri smooch on the lips. Then she punched me sharply in the rib cage with a balled fist.

"That's for you *and* Billy the Greek."

A funny thing happened on the way to supper that evening. I nearly killed an adorable little girl with a soccer ball.

It happened as we strolled along the busy waterfront in Parga checking out posted taverna menus. Up ahead, in a little plaza by the seawall, a group of boys about Jack's age were engaged in an intense soccer match while a group of elderly women in traditional black robes, a deputation of Greek grannies, sat gossiping and keeping watch and enjoying the evening air along the wall. The tiny girl was seated in their midst, playing quietly with a long-haired doll.

As we approached the crowded plaza, I noticed that Jack had gone ahead and already insinuated himself into the heat of the game and was doggedly attempting to outmaneuver a couple skinny-legged Greek kids while his "teammates" frantically hollered and waved their arms at him, urging him to shoot. Nibs dribbled left, feinted right, paused and booted the ball toward the goal we were approaching, but the shot was wide and bounced off a statue and rolled toward us.

"Hey, Dad," he barked out joyfully. "Kick it back, will ya?"

I stopped the ball with my foot.

"Sure. No problem."

I stepped back, advanced on the ball, and gave it a savage kick. The ball flew low and hard straight at the players but suddenly hooked toward the seawall and the unsuspecting grannies and caught the little girl with the doll squarely in the face, flipping her backward off the seawall like a dummy in a carnival shooting gallery. The Greek grannies all let out appalled noises and everyone in the plaza paused in shock to stare.

By the time I reached the seawall, I could only imagine the worst. The sea was churning on the rocks below, and the jagged rocks were ten feet below the wall. The grannies were collectively on their feet peering anxiously over the stone. But as Lady Fortune would have it, I saw a couple tiny feet poking straight up in the air. The tiny girl was safely resting on her back upon a shelf of flat rock, maybe two feet below the wall, still clutching her dolly and staring up at me with startled brown deer eyes.

"Sweetheart, are you *okay*? I'm so sorry that happened . . ."

Immediately, I hopped over the wall and picked her up gingerly, placing her back on the wall. She must have realized I'd been the imbecile who kicked the ball because she pushed away my hands, issued an offended "Hmmmp," and set about consoling her frightened dolly.

The Greek grannies burst out laughing and one of them with a face like Ray Nitschke babbled something to the effect that she no longer planned to curse my offspring's offspring. Jack and his soccer pals found it fall-down funny, too, and Wendy was chortling with relief when I took her arm and hustled her into the closest taverna. For the life of me, I couldn't picture Billy Holden having an embarrassing travel moment like this one.

"That was most exciting," observed the waiter wryly, after he brought us a fine chilled bottle of something expertly wrung from Greek grapes. "It will be the talk of Parga for a week."

"I don't know who I frightened most—that little girl or myself. Good thing we're leaving town tomorrow, I guess."

"She'll be okay. She is a feisty one, my Pia."

"You *know* her?"

"Yes. She is my daughter."

He smiled, presenting us menus. "She is fine. Tough as the boys. Just be glad her mama isn't here or you might have to swim across the harbor." He recommended the baked sea bass and a vegetable boureki and I was happy to make no more trouble in Parga that night.

Jack jogged up several minutes later, hot, sweaty, happy as those summer days back at Summer Fields. Naturally, he wanted to keep playing soccer rather than eat, so I figured what the heck. I told him we'd save him a bread roll and a warm Coke.

"Thanks," he chirped, darted off, and then paused to look back. He grinned. "Hey, Dad. That was the funniest thing I've *ever* seen you do."

"Glad I could amuse you. I live for that alone."

"How does it feel to be the talk of the town?" my nicely tanned and deeply amused wife asked, sipping her fizzy water, when he'd scampered away.

"Slightly Byronic," I said, reaching for the wine.

Messalonghi, on the other hand, was a grave disappointment to the arrested English major in me. You'd think the place where Childe Harold finally met his maker and discovered eternal rest whilst dressed ridiculously like Alexander the Great, squandering whatever was left of his impressive literary fortune by paying off corrupt Greek tribesmen, drilling a bored and drunken militia for weeks on end and rowing himself around in a dismal mosquito-infested bog to kill time while he waited to do battle with a Turkish army that inconsiderately failed to show up, eventually contracting a fever and, heavily dosed on quinine, babbling affectionately about his woefully neglected former wife and child and sister, alternately ordering Napolean brandy and strong coffee, ranting about his London critics, finally apologizing to God for being such a bother and quietly expiring with the gentle injunction "I must sleep now," author and victim of his own legend in just his thirty-seventh year—well, you'd think after all of *that* the locals would do something slightly more fitting than raise a simple alabaster statue of Lord Byron sitting in a postage stamp park next to an empty sweet shop where there was nary a soul visible save an elderly dog with cloudy eyes and a muzzle as gray as Argus, idly scratching his fleas as we rolled up in the Mad Green Pea around noon the very next day.

True, as I pointed out to my thirsty companions, able to use a bit of my English Lit degree at long last, almost every town in Greece supposedly has a street named *Vyronos* in tribute to the crazy poet and the government did eventually declare England's greatest Romantic bard a Greek national hero for his part in helping whip up sentiment against the Ottomans. More to the point, Byron's much-publicized death back home helped galvanize popular support across Europe for England and France sending a joint naval expedition force to chase out the Turks. But after effectively tracing his route from the dungeon at Chillon to the salons of Florence and thence across the Ionian Sea, I thought for sure we would find more revealing traces of the tortured poet in the place he chose to finish his flamboyant passage through life, though I can't say exactly what I expected—a museum containing his outrageous Alexandrian armor, or maybe a couple folio pages of "Childe Harold" (which he completed en route here) under glass, or at least a decent British pub serving real ale and Byronic 'neeps and tatties.

All we found in sleepy Messalonghi besides the itchy dog was a chubby guy taking a siesta on the counter in his sweet shop. The Cokes he sold us were only slightly cooler than the day outside. We got back in the MGP and sped away as unobtrusively as we'd come, determined to remember Lord Vyronos the way he wanted to be remembered, as a brilliant nutcase who made his mark in the world by faithfully following his muse to the very end.

Besides, our muse was telling us to get on to the Oracle of Delphi ASAP—the Navel of the World, as the ancients called Greece's most sacred spiritual place, high up on the sides of Mount Parnassus overlooking the mighty Gulf of Corinth. Everybody we met, including the guy who owned the dog in Messalonghi, informed us it was complete madness to proceed up to Delphi, owing to the time of August and the annual tourist occupation in that popular area. There wouldn't be any rooms anywhere to be had for the night, they warned us. We would be sleeping under the stars with the scorpions, they predicted.

Curiously, though, the famous soothsaying town was empty, darn

near a ghost town, when we rolled in after a long trek up the mountainside that same afternoon. The clerk in the lovely open-air hotel
lobby where we dropped our bags and checked in had a couple theo-
ries why Delphi was so unexpectedly empty at peak travel season.
"Could be all of this talk of terrorists," he said with a Delphic shrug,
swiping my Amex card. "We've had almost no Americans here this
summer. Or possibly it's the earthquake."

"Which earthquake would that be?" I tried to be as nonchalant as
possible in seeking this useful information.

He smiled, calmly presenting me back my card and a key to a room
with a fifty-mile view. "Some prominent Athens geologist, I believe,
predicted there may be a large earthquake any day now around Delphi.
But there have always been earthquakes around Delphi. Trust me,
friend, you are as safe from earthquakes as from terrorists in Delphi.
You can ask anybody." He smiled puckishly. "Including the Oracle."

Pocketing our key and picking up a street map that would lead us
through the town and over to the sacred ruins, I promised I would try
and remember to do just that, if a November 17 terrorist or a scheduled earthquake didn't get us first.

The overriding point, I guess, having come this far and climbed this
high, was that each of us felt more than a slight romantic obligation as
a thoughtful tourist to ask *something* of the famous mystical Oracle—
even if the whole exercise fell into the category of hokey make-believe
or silly pagan fantasy. If one thought about it, on the other hand, was
the exercise really any different from people of good faith seeking
moral guidance and divine intervention from sacred holy relics, praying for deliverance from the Parisian flood with antique carpenter
nails? Wendy hit the nail directly on the head, so to speak, when she
observed (during our glorious morning stroll through the churches of
Florence with Benedetta) that European churches have evolved from
houses of worship into "museums of faith" where former experiences of
the divine were put on display and sold like Impressionist prints at
Musée d'Orsay.

Under laws as old as the hills, in any case, pilgrims who made the
arduous and dangerous climb up Mount Parnassus were entitled, upon
making some sort of material sacrifice, to submit one (at most two)

questions inscribed on lead tablets to the Pythian priestesses who in turn presented the inquiries to the Oracle at the Temple of Apollo and then interpreted the answer from vapors allegedly rising from the navel of the world. To my mind the whole thing sounded suspiciously like Dorothy going to Oz, but on the Mad Green Pea's slow ascent up the sacred mountain Wendy read to Jack and me about the complicated and violent history of the Oracle and the creation of the town and the vast treasuries of wealth that foreign kings and would-be potentates dispatched to Delphi (and later ungraciously pillaged), prompting me to admit that there was, in fact, one question weighing rather heavily on my mind. I told them what it was.

"When the *hell* is it going to rain again in Maine?"

"I don't know if you're actually supposed to *tell* people your big question before you ask the Oracle," Wendy cautioned, searching the guidebook for better information on ancient oracular protocol. "You might want to pick another question or two to be on the safe side."

"So it's like . . . ," Jack wondered idly, "a birthday wish or something?"

At least, I decided, I wouldn't be like King Croesus who showed up at the height of the Oracle's power in the fourth century B.C. and wondered if he should undertake a war against neighboring Persia. According to the legends, the Oracle advised him that he would destroy a great kingdom, which he subsequently did—his own. So, clearly, if you believed in such pagan nonsense, you had to be careful what you asked, or at least pretty savvy about what you heard.

Interestingly, I'd recently read in *National Geographic* or maybe a supermarket tabloid that a scientific team of researchers from Wesleyan University had just discovered a pair of previously hidden fault lines crossing directly beneath the first temple of Apollo, a place specifically mentioned by Plutarch in his extensive writings on Delphi, the spot where mysteriously rising fumes were believed to inspire visions about the future and provide critical answers to age-old questions regarding war, love, business, bear market portfolio investing, and single-parent dating.

Gazing into a sacred bronze bowl and clutching a laurel leaf or possibly a paperback edition of Edgar Cayce's greatest prophecies, the Pythian priestesses apparently inhaled, according to the geology geeks from Wesleyan, a powerful petrochemical stimulant called ethylene, a vapor known to induce bouts of euphoria and promote a general sense of well-being.

Anyway, that's why we'd come—to sniff around, as it were, Plutarch-style, and pose a few innocent questions about the future of civilized life as we knew it and see what there was to see in the ruins of Delphi.

Before that, though, we wandered out along the town's empty main drag to see what was cooking and wound up sitting with steaming plates of moussaka and asparagus soup and other delicious local delicacies wrapped in leaf vine, on a beautiful flower-strewn balcony overlooking the hazy Gulf of Corinth.

At the table next to us sat a most interesting French couple who'd just finished hiking up Mount Olympus with their teenage sons. The sons—matching college-aged boys—were presently off on their own checking out Delphi's dubious nightlife, but their weary adventuresome parents were pleased to hear that Jack and his *père* had just partied in the streets of Paris on Bastille Day. Falling into deeper conversation with them in the empty restaurant, we learned they hoped to spend American Independence Day during the summer of 2003 seeing the back roads of America the way we were aimlessly knocking about Europe.

"Perhaps you have some useful advice for us?" asked the mother, an elegant, fine-featured lady with pulled-back graying hair.

I suggested they skip, as de Tocqueville had, the golden arches, avoid taking the Interstate if at all possible, and stay clear of all shopping malls. Every shopping mall in America was basically the same, a commercial blanding out of the landscape that rendered small towns featureless and made it nigh impossible for even the locals to get their proper bearings at any given moment in America. As I said this, I realized what a pleasure it was that *we* hadn't eaten a Big Mac, traveled a congested super highway, or wandered mindlessly around in a mall all summer long. I said they might want to come visit us in Maine, where we'd happily stuff them full of Cundy's Harbor lobster and send them on their way to delightful rural folk we knew in upstate New York.

"I suspect that may be the last trip for us as a family," the father allowed, a touch wistfully, tasting his somewhat goaty house red. (We were having the same stuff from a glass pitcher.) "It seems only five minutes ago that I took zee boys up zee Eiffel Tower for the very first time. Now they want to find zee discothèque in Delphi."

I tasted my wine and said I knew exactly what he meant, though I really didn't. For the moment at least I still had a fractional piece of Jack's childhood to cling to, a good boy's heart to try and preserve and protect. On the other hand, time really did fly and I knew I would soon have to release him the way Daedalus had released Icarus, hoping he would choose the Middle Way. A moment ago I'd been my son's age, wondering what the Labyrinth at Knossos was really like. Now I was the same age as Plutarch when he died, Twain when he passed this way a hundred and some years ago, and time, as Nick the Greenwish tour guide said, really was a rascally old bald deceiver. "At least you *got* up the Eiffel Tower," I said attempting to cheer him up, explaining about our failed assent of the famous landmark on Bastille Day. He found this news amusing and generously offered that if we ever returned to Paris and were interested, he would personally escort us to the top of France's greatest monument.

"Great," I said, topping up his glass with our pitcher. "But by then my knees will be shot and Jack will probably be more interested in checking out the discothèques of Paris."

We all laughed in the way about-to-be-left-behind parents must do in order to retain any shred of their sanity.

"Where do you suppose everybody *is?*" Wendy asked the woman, lowering her voice so some little brassy type from the Delphi Chamber of Commerce didn't leap out and begin haranguing us that there was no more danger from sudden earthquakes than terrorists up here in these violent old sacred hills. Not only was the restaurant nearly completely empty but good old Lord Byron could have fired one of his Greek cannons down Delphi's picturesque Main Street and not hit a clubfooted housefly.

"I don't know," the woman observed pleasantly, pulling on her silk shawl as we paid our bills and the six of us, counting Jack and Harold the Defender (who was in his knapsack), filtered slowly toward the front of the restaurant and the deserted street, "but Maurice and I plan to take advantage of this moment and the boys' absence. My feet are killing me from that climb up Olympus, so I'm going back to our hotel and run a bath and open the shutters to that beautiful moon." She smiled meaningfully at her husband, then glanced at the moon and finally us. "We'll see what happens next."

I glanced up and there was indeed a nice runcible moon hanging over the Gulf of Corinth. In two or three nights' time, I guessed, or more or less about the time we were supposed to turn for home, it would be full.

"Cover your ears, Jack," I commanded Nibs. "Lest French age corrupt American youth."

We bid our fellow wanderers a pleasant good night and walked back up the empty street to our empty hotel, pausing to admire a gorgeous chess set in a lighted shop window which featured classical Greek figures made from bronze and pig iron. We brazenly decided to come back and purchase that chess set and have it shipped home, whatever the cost—something to remember for years to come this day, this night, this road trip that turned out pretty nicely after all.

"Dad," Jack wondered, a little sleepily, as we moved on. "Why is it that when you fall asleep it only feels like a few minutes have passed when you wake up?"

"You know," I was forced to admit to him, "I don't know. Might ask the Oracle that." Our trip, come to think of it, felt a little like a quick, pleasant sleep, too. It had felt like it took forever to actually begin; and now it had unfolded and passed away in the blink of an Oracle's eye.

But even sleepers are builders of what goes on in the universe—that's what I explained to my walking companions, poorly paraphrasing Heraclitus, the same guy who pointed out that character is *fatum*. The death of each day's life, sore labor's bath, the chief nourisher of life's feast—these were a few other descriptions for welcome sleep I was able to pull from my mental attic of useless familiar quotations. Finally there was Mark Twain, who observed there simply ain't no way for a snorer to properly know when he's snoring. Jack dutifully laughed at my mangling of famous quotes.

"I could tell you when you snore, dear," my plucky bride spoke up right on cue, taking my arm. "But that would wake you up."

"Very funny. First my hat, now my snoring. It's a wonder you could convince yourself to marry me."

"I needed to keep my feet warm."

Back at the hotel, we changed and had a nice long swim in the pool before turning in. The last thing Jack did before hitting the pillow was place Harold the Defender securely by his bed to make sure no terrorists came unchallenged through our open windows. The last thing I did before turning in was fling the shutters open to the runcible moon and ask whatever thoughtful ancient deity was keeping watch out there not to let that big earthquake come tonight. And then I turned around to discover that both my weary road pals were in their respective beds soundly asleep, already nourishing their feasts.

That same splendid isolation was waiting for us the next morning at the entrance to Delphi's archaeological museum and ruins. Nobody was in the place save a couple museum maintenance men wrestling with large and tippy pedestal fans—trying to cool down the air in the museum even though it wasn't yet ten in the morning.

A little decadently, we had the run of the place to ourselves. Wendy wandered off to study in scholarly detail the famous Silver Bull of Delphi and spectacular friezes recovered from the ruins of places like the Siphnian Treasury, while Jack moseyed back to hunt for the Naxian Sphinx and the world famous Charioteer of Delphi. After about half an hour of standing directly in front of the largest fan in the museum entrance, hogging the breeze from the few other paying customers who straggled in, I went in search of them both and found my wife intricately examining a beautiful third-century B.C. statue of a naked man.

"Look at that incredible detail," she whispered in awe.

"Which detail?" I asked, for a laugh, idly resting my hand on the head of a nearby two-thousand-year-old Nubian woman. I wondered if she—my wife, that is—had any idea how to identify the best man at a nudist wedding. She suddenly went a little pale around her suntanned ears.

"Did that head you're touching just *move?*"

"Not much."

"You're not supposed to *touch* these statues," she whispered. "Can't you read the signs? Please take your hand off that woman's head. Ve-ry carefully."

"Okay," I said with a shrug, pointing out to her that the signs were written in a foreign language and thus mostly Greek to me. "But if I do, don't blame me if it falls off. They must not have had very good glue back in the old days."

I removed my hand and the Nubian's head stayed in place.

We collected Jack from the Charioteer and headed straight outside to climb the Sacred Way up to the Sanctuary of Apollo and the stadium where in ancient times the Pythian Games were conducted by naked athletes with all their incredible details showing. I think the unsettling crash we heard behind us as we exited was simply one of the electric fans falling over on the marble floor. Hope so, at any rate.

As it turned out, the Oracle wasn't *up* the Sacred Way at the "new" Sanctuary of Apollo, which dated from the sixth century B.C. but *down* the slopes across the road, at the shabbier Temple of Athena—or so an English tour guide lecturing to a group of geriatric Ohioans tersely explained to us from beneath his broad-brimmed hat, a straw headpiece that made the one I'd lost in the Ionian Sea look positively elegant by comparison.

As a result of this information, we foolishly marched all the way up the Sacred Way in the monstrous heat to have a look at the spectacular stadium and classical amphitheater, then wandered back down the steep stone path past the Temple of Apollo and the elderly Ohioans with our own tongues beginning to flop out, dying for a drink of water. At that point we crossed the highway and meandered down a winding path through scrubby pines until we came to a lower "gymnasium" and, finally, a couple more terraces farther down the hill, the remains of what we *thought* belonged to the Temple of Athena, a bunch of broken columns sticking up in the dust. Nothing in our guidebook indicated this fact, though.

"Is this *it?*" Wendy wondered, perplexed, glancing around at perhaps the most neglected corner of the famous ruins.

"This isn't right," she decided. "I think that Englishman intentionally misled us so we couldn't eavesdrop on his lecture."

"I think you're probably right," I agreed, plopping down next to Jack on a broken pillar. The touring Ohioans now appeared to be ants clustered on the Sacred Way. Heat waves were shimmering off the mountainside and I wasn't thrilled about the idea of trekking all the way back up the path, oracle or no oracle. "If I had the strength," I added, "I'd march straight back up that mountain and ridicule his hat. Or at least pinch his water bottle."

"Why don't I at least go get us all some water," Wendy volunteered with a sigh, starting toward the path that led to a small snack shop up by the road. "We can figure out what to do next. You guys wait here and take a break."

"I'll go with you," Nibs proposed, hopping up.

"I'll wait here and take a break," I suggested helpfully.

Left alone with my thoughts and roughly two thousand years of Greek history, give or take a rare Nubian head, I glanced around at the ruins of Athena's palace and thought how ironic it was we'd come this far and gone all the way up and down a sacred mountain only to *miss* the opportunity of a lifetime to pose a question for the ages to the Navel of the World. That seemed to be the story of our mall-free vagabond summer. Next time, Slick, the moral of the tale seemed to be, sign up for the guided tour.

Athena, on the other hand, if I recalled correctly, was a pretty cool customer in Greek mythology. The powerful Olympian deity sprung from Zeus's forehead, consort of Pan, goddess of war and peace, patron of the world's arts and crafts, the armored virgin for whom the Parthenon was built and dedicated by good King Pericles in the Golden Age of Greece. Even though her temple at Delphi was admittedly a little down at the heels, Athena was clearly no poor relation in the family hierarchy, and it suddenly occurred to me, perhaps due to the early stages of heat stroke, that maybe *she* could somehow hear my question and convey it to the Oracle, wherever the blazes it was located.

"Okay, Athena," I said aloud just for the heck of it, "here's my big question . . ."

I was just preparing to ask if Nibs the Lost Boy would ever stop worrying so much, and to inquire about how he might get along in his life, when a guy who was even larger and more out of shape than me came stumping down the dusty path, sweating profusely beneath a grimy Mets baseball cap. He plopped his broad butt down on one of the sacred Athenian stones not four feet away.

He glanced over at me, wiping his broad face, and grunted, "Hotter'n hell here, ain't it?"

I smiled and nodded as best I could, sorely tempted to tell him he was invading my sacred holy space and to buzz off before I picked up one of Athena's sacred rocks and flattened his skull with it. On the other hand, he was a fellow countryman clearly as confused as I was about these ancient mysteries. Perhaps if I'd evolved a little more as a human being I might have just smiled and said something truly neighborly to him. Instead, I just sat there marinating in body sweat and wishing he'd go rejoin whatever tour bus brought him. The truth is, I genuinely loathe the Mets—who robbed the Red Sox of a World Series they clearly deserved to win in 1986, you may recall, not to raise a sore subject or anything, and may Bill Buckner enjoy the rest of his days on this earth before he fittingly roasts in Hades.

"The tour I'm on went up the hill to see the stadium," he explained, squinting up at the hazy Sacred Way. "So I come on down here to look around. Good thing I brought my own water. Hey," he added, as if the thought had just occurred to him, "is this the place where that ole oracle used to be? I can't tell a dang thing from the map . . ."

"No," I provided. "I think it's back up the hill at the Temple of Apollo."

"Shit. Now I gotta walk all the way up *there*."

And with that, he ripped the cap off a huge bottle of mineral water and drank most of it down in four or five baboon-sized gulps.

I stared at this sweaty ape's Mets cap and vaguely wondered if his sudden appearance was some kind of *sign* from Athena, goddess of war and baseball.

As I say, I had every good intention of asking the Navel of the World about my only beloved son's fate—his chances of someday at least making the Red Sox farm team, let's say, or maybe what kind of wholesome corn-fed Iowa girl or belle of Flanders he would eventually bring home from Oxford or Cambridge, the world chess championships or the Formula One circuit, to meet the extended Maine family, and so forth.

But some things in this life, I suppose, as the sages advised, truly are better left unrevealed until they just, well, *happen*. Whatever Jack will be will be, to paraphrase goddess Doris Day, and I decided on the spot that whatever Nibs turned out to be in his life—based on what a fine young man he already was here and now—that would be just fine with his old man.

Before I realized it, though, another timeless question flew straight from overheated brain to parched lips on the wings of Mercury.

"Listen, Oracle," I heard myself mumble aloud, "will the damn Red Sox *ever* beat the Curse of the Bambino?"

The guy in the Mets cap turned his blocky head and stared at me as if I must be having a heat stroke or speaking in Naxian tongues.

There followed a moment of eerie silence, save for the faint soughing of the winds as they swirled up the dry mountain terrain into the scraggily Delphic pines. I might even say it was reverentially quiet, as if all Nature herself had paused to consider my question.

But then the Mets guy got to his Nikes with a grunt and waddled a few yards, pausing to turn up the last of his water bottle. Wiping his mouth, he regarded the sweeping view from Greece's most sacred spiritual summit, gently belched, and then—and I *swear* on Athena's pretty warlike head I'm not making this up—kicked a sacred stone and passed gas loudly as he wandered back up the dusty path to locate his missing tour group, tossing his empty bottle to the ground.

Was this my answer? Unfortunately I had no euphoric Pythian priestess to properly interpret this unexpected release of vapors. So I abandoned the silly cause, picked up the Mets guy's discarded bottle, and went to find Wendy and Jack, realizing that the older I got the more I disliked people who littered in public places.

Jack discovered his own form of Paradise—and I discovered why nobody was up country at Delphi—two afternoons later on Crete where, arriving late in the day, we encountered everybody but the Mets guy and the elderly Ohioans jammed around the main swimming pool and ninety-foot waterslide at the poetically named Cretan Village Hotel.

Perhaps I should explain how we wound up in such a depressing spot—the Old World replica of a Disneyworld resort. Once again, the fault was not in our stars but in my erring travel judgment. After roaming around in the boggling traffic and dense smog of Athens for several hours, before finally locating the city's swank new airport that's been hastily thrown up to accommodate the 2003 summer Olympics, we dumped the Mad Green Pea and impulsively got in line at a Greek airline to purchase tickets to Crete—figuring that, if Herodotus could be believed, Greek culture itself evolved from the famous Minoan island, and Western Civilization pretty much began there, as well.

Besides, it was basically as far as we could go in the world that had made us, and had one of the oldest human histories on earth, including the Palace of Knossos, a place I'd been keen to see since I was knee high to a Nubian statue. Some friends of ours spent an entire winter on the island several years ago, recovering from the death of their teenage daughter, getting away from their hectic American lives, living simply among the locals, learning the customs, exploring Crusader caves and so forth. They described Crete as a healing paradise, an ancient Mediterranean spa, exotic and unhurried and entirely wonderful.

"If I may ask, why do you wish to go to Crete?" asked the pretty young airline clerk, however, scrunching up her nose as she checked on flights to the island.

"Because we have only three days left before we have to go home to Maine," I explained. "Besides, Crete is the backyard of Western Civilization."

She gave a pained little smile. "Perhaps so. But this time of year it is also very crowded with Germans and English people."

"Where would you go?" Wendy put it to her.

"Santorini is very beautiful. I would go there."

As she said this with great conviction, the stubborn kid in me realized I simply *hated* to let Crete go. The aging Daedalus in me was dying to see the labyrinth at Knossos, hoping the Icarus in Jack would get the point of that timeless cautionary tale. Also, our friends made Crete sound so lovely and far away, a place of small miracles influenced by the ocean currents of both East and West. An idea percolated in my head.

"Maybe we could fly to Crete and see the Palace of Knossos and then take a ferry back to Santorini," I proposed, showing my companions a nifty description of a coastal hotel not far from the ruin at Knossos which sounded ideal for our purposes. *An oasis of rustic simplicity and charm set down between mountain and sea. A true reflection of ancient Minoan culture in Crete.* In my mind's eye I pictured Cretan Village Hotel as a cross between a seaside cave where the Apostle Paul napped in the afternoon and a wattle hut with only rudimentary services and ancient graffiti etched into the stone floor revealing that *Erasmus slept here.* The hotel came with five stars, the guide's highest recommendation, which meant it must be good. Time to splurge a little.

"What do you think?" I asked the young clerk, who seemed to really know her way around the Greek islands. "We're kind of making this up as we go along."

"I would skip Crete and go straight to Santorini. Go see Crete when the Germans are gone. The winter is nice there."

Wendy and Jack stared blankly at me, the man who'd gotten us into this fine predicament, dumping the whole thing into *my* lap. Somebody had to make an executive decision fast because the clerk's fingers were hovering above her keyboard, Jack was thumping his ball mitt, and the crowd in line behind us was growing visibly churlish.

"Crete it is. Tomorrow or the next day we'll take a boat to Santorini. That'll leave us a whole final day to see the Acropolis before we fly home."

So, in a nutshell, arriving too late to make other accommodations, that's how we wound up at Cretan Village, basking in the late afternoon sun with a bunch of greased-up topless German people. In retrospect, it should have been a tip-off that the hotel was the *only* hotel on that part of the island that actually had rooms available for the night. But, honestly now, who could possibly have guessed from the inspiring bit of guidebook prose that Cretan Village would turn out to be simply the Minoan version of a beached Carnival Cruise ship as Wendy accurately summed it up, a ridiculous American-style hotel teeming with families wedged around a concrete lagoon that was unnaturally warm due to baby pee.

"Think of this as a nice way to prepare for going home." Wendy gamely attempted to put an upbeat face on yet another unexpected situation as we settled into lounge chairs amid blaring rock music, seminude strangers, and the attentions of a relentlessly circulating bottle-blond social director who kept threatening us with her clipboard and wondering if we'd signed up yet for the conga lessons or the weekly foosball tournament.

"Besides," Wendy added with a chuckle, preparing to safely escape into her Florentine art mystery, "Jack thinks this place is next to heaven. It is pretty amusing, if you think about it."

I wasn't exactly laughing at yet another gross travel miscalculation on my part, but Jack admittedly was having a high old time. At that very moment, in fact, the happy boy in question made a dramatic appearance, whooping to beat the conga band as his slippery frame came rocketing around the final curve of the waterslide and splashed ecstatically into the baby pee.

"Dad," he called to me from a scrum of Eurokids in the pool. "Come try this slide. It's really *awesome!*"

I waved, thanked him, and politely declined, noting that I was well over the age and weight limit for that sort of crude public display. But after a moment or two of further reflection, I realized there was plenty of time left in life to be an old fart. So what if Crete turned out to be Myrtle Beach with a heavy Greek accent? I got to my hind legs and followed my boy up the waterslide and down that twisting hunk of plastic, I must tell you, with all the athletic grace a sack of grain falling from a moving train. Though several incontinent infants nearly drowned in the resulting tidal wave, Jack clearly loved it, and when I finally climbed out of the pool, the blond social director was waiting there to pounce on me with her relentless smile and clipboard.

"Are we having a good time, sir?" she demanded to know with the vigor of a Nazi interrogator.

I looked at her and smiled. This wasn't even remotely how I'd imagined spending our final hours at the edge of Western Civilization, but I guess the gods were determined once again make the point that it's human folly to have great expectations about what you'll discover down the road. Better to climb the waterslide and go down with a war whoop and make the biggest splash you can make.

"It's fine," I replied, dripping on her a bit, figuring it was pointless to try and explain any of this hard-earned road wisdom.

"Excellent," she said, duly noting my response on her clipboard. In parting, she wished to know if I and my "girlfriend" would be joining the hotel staff for the special "Karaoke Carribbean Buffet" that evening in the hotel's main dining hall.

"Maybe," I said. "I'll have to ask my wife first."

We fled Cretan Village before dawn the next day, skipping the cruise-ship breakfast buffet, hoping to find someplace, well, a little *less* American for our final full day in the Minoan empire. After spending the early morning searching for Crusader caves on the island's south side, we ventured off to check out Sir Arthur Evans's unearthed Palace of Knossos, only to encounter ranks of gassy tour buses and vast queues of tourists waiting to enter the ruins. We dutifully got in line, paid our admission, and eventually found ourselves walking through a landscape of lamely "restored" palace columns and stone arches that looked, on the whole, like something you might see at Epcot—except that Epcot is, sadly, more authentic looking.

Barely a hundred years ago Knossos existed only in mythology, but then Englishman Sir Arthur Evans got permission from the local Ottoman tribal bosses to excavate the site in the stony hills south of Iráklion and not only dug up the remains of an empire that was believed to have reached its cultural peak three thousand years ago but liberally "restored" the royal apartments and royal halls of the palace according to his own fine conjecture. The resulting re-creation set off a furious debate among archaeologists and historians that rages to this day. Among the more garish touch-ups, several apartment walls were painted blood red and featured hokey "frescoes" and artfully faded paintings of the sacred bull and double axes, symbols of power and fertility to the ancient Minoans.

"Where exactly *is* the labyrinth Daedalus made for the Minotaur?" Jack wondered after we'd shuffled along a wood ramp behind a boisterous group of Italians for maybe half an hour. The Italians appeared to find the place almost as laughably phony as most serious archeologists seem to.

"Down there," I replied, leaning over the rail and pointing toward the ground.

Jack peered confusedly over the edge for several moments, then glanced at me and smiled as if he understood what coming to Knossos had meant to the arrested eighth grader in me, and he probably guessed how disappointed I was to find it just another roadside tourist attraction. Some things are better left unearthed and only imagined. The legendary Minotaur was still in the ground, hidden from view, locked in the stones of mythology, where I couldn't help wishing Sir Arthur had left Knossos.

Afterward, we drove into the heart of Iráklion for a late lunch in the busy marketplace overlooking the ancient Venetian fort. None of us, I think, wanted to come out and say what a disappointment the palace had been, and our spirits were admittedly pretty low. The narrow streets were full of dust and vendors, and that lively district of the old city, on the other hand, would have been an excellent backdrop for an Indiana Jones film. As the three of us sat at a table waiting for our lamb gyros and Cokes to arrive, watching a man nearby entertain a crowd with a brightly hued snake that was crawling in and out of his nose, a shabby little girl suddenly appeared at our table.

She was as tiny as the imp at Parga, brown-haired, barefoot, dressed in a dirty green gingham dress, perhaps five years old. She stared briefly at me and then shifted her attention to Jack, silently lifting a cupped right palm like a supplicant at communion. Nibs scarcely hesitated before he reached into his safari shorts and withdrew several wadded drachmas, which he pressed into her palm.

Just then, the waiter brought our lunches.

"Go away now," he said, swatting an irritated hand at the tiny girl, and like that she melted away into the crowds.

"Dad," Jack said a few moments later, his gyro untouched, still looking after her, "is the drachma the oldest currency in the world?"

I said I thought it was—and because it was about to be replaced by the Euro, he might wish to take a few home to show good old Andy Tufts.

He nodded, taking a bite of his sandwich, looking past the guy with the snake in his nose.

"Do you think she, like, has a home?"

"Probably." I had no clue, of course. The waif looked like she lived in the streets of Indy's Iráklion, to be honest.

"She didn't have any shoes."

"I know. You were nice to give her some of your money."

"I feel bad for her."

"That just shows what a good heart you have."

We continued eating in silence. But moments later, of all things, the little girl was back, holding up a huge sandwich wrapped in foil that was brimming with fresh cut veggies and fragrant meat of some kind. Behind the sandwich was one of the most radiant smiles I'd ever seen. Her large brown eyes were shining and I suddenly remembered Muhammad's line about God wanting to see laughter in our eyes. She turned and skipped away into the teeming bazaar.

Some pictures, I guess, really are worth a thousand words, and Dame Wendy maybe said it best for all of us when any of us could manage to speak again. She cleared her throat and wiped an eye, looking off at the snake charmer and his fascinated audience.

"That smile alone was worth coming here for, eh, boys?"

Later that afternoon, we found a delightful old hotel down the coast west of Iráklion in Ayia Palaya, a remote seaside town which had a lovely rock-and-sand beach and a string of waterside tavernas rivaling Parga.

There, predictably, Jack quickly made friends with a lonely English boy named Oliver, and soon the two of them were engaged in a fierce chess match by the pool, while Wendy and I went down a set of crumbling stone steps for a romantic honeymoon swim in the Aegean— that famous sea, remember, named for a grieving papa who thought he'd lost his son.

"I'm so glad you agreed to come with us after all," I said to her as we splashed around like a couple giddy newlyweds. "It just wouldn't have been a honeymoon without you. With or without your top on."

"It's been more married fun than I've ever had," she confirmed. "But I do wish we could have found a couple wedding rings so Sister Patrice would believe we really are husband and wife. And I'm sorry you boys didn't get to Africa and Egypt and China."

I shrugged, which is nearly impossible to do in water over your head I discovered, managing to swallow a couple quarts of the very seawater where Homer's grandkids peed, give or take three thousand years, before us.

"There's always tomorrow." I tried to strike a philosophical pose, coughing up saltwater. "I guess that's the point."

She kissed me and swam off on her lonesome for a while, scissoring through the waves like a young Queen Dido before angling into shore and going up to lie in the Cretan sun to finish up her art mystery.

I swam around for a while on my own until a friendly otter head suddenly bobbed up beside me in the gorgeous green water. It was none other than good old Jack!

"Hey, Nibsy." I greeted him the way King Aegeus would have greeted his son if he'd only known the whole story. "Who won the chess match?"

"Oliver."

"You didn't let him win, did you?"

"Well, kind of. I mean, see, he's with his father and his new stepmother and his older brothers. I guess they're all kind of mean to him or something—his brothers, I mean. And his father drinks a lot, he said. I sort of felt sorry for him. He lives with his mom somewhere near Oxford."

He wondered if we might be able to take Oliver to supper with us, a request I should have seen coming from half a mile at sea.

I said that was okay with me. This was our last night on Crete and we were hoping to have a nice meal before turning in to rest for tomorrow afternoon's ferry ride to Santorini.

"Thanks," Jack said and then glanced at the crowded shore. He casually added, "Hey, Dad. Look. She did it."

"Did what?" I glanced blankly at the shore, but all I could make out was a blurry impression of human bodies that seemed very far away indeed. On the other hand, we were probably a quarter of a mile at sea and I wasn't wearing my glasses.

Jack smiled. "Wendy finally took her top off. Just like all the other ladies."

"Oh, right," I said. "Try not to look," I advised him. "She'd have to murder you if she knew you saw her. Even worse, she'd murder me."

"Dad," he said, "it's *no* big deal."

"I know. You've grown up a lot on this trip. And that's a little worrying because it means pretty soon only *one* of us will be childish."

He smiled at me as if I were merely joking around again.

And for a change, I guess I wasn't.

Truth be told, I was still reflecting on these matters two evenings later as the three of us raced pell-mell through the incomprehensible traffic of downtown Athens to try to reach the Acropolis and scale its heights before sunset. I realized it truly *was* about time for me to leave my inner eighth grader behind and get back in touch with my repressed responsible adult side.

By then, to summarize a final time, we'd taken the late night ferry from Crete to Santorini and found it every bit as peaceful and spectacular as the airline clerk had said. Early in the morning on our last day in Greece, we hoofed around the Great Caldera of Thira, which Plato asserts may have been all that was left of the mythical city of Atlantis, and then found, in a crowded bazaar, out of the blue, in a box of cheap antique jewelry, a pair of silver wedding rings made by unknown Minoans. They were old and slightly dented—just like us, Wendy cheerfully pointed out—but beautiful slender silver braids of fine workmanship, priced to sell, and perfectly lovely Gordian knots of second-chance optimism. We knew the moment we saw them they were meant for us. Dame Wendy's fit perfectly and mine was only a little too large, which meant I still had room for personal growth.

The stones of the Parthenon, that Periclean hymn to human democracy, were glowing pinkly in the expiring light when we finally reached the base of the Acropolis. The taxi let us off and we bolted along an ascending path to the entrance gates—only to have them shut rudely in our faces and be informed that the Western World's most famous tourist site was closing shop two hours earlier than normal due to a special concert in the ancient amphitheater below the Parthenon.

Phillipe Entremont, the world famous violinist, was giving a special concert, Joseph Haydn's Clock Symphony and a couple sonatas beneath the full moon.

This seemed to be a fitting coda to our pilgrimage and an apt conclusion to our Crosby and Hope road trip—a day late, a drachma short, maybe just a summer or two off the perfect trip around the world.

What else could we do? We purchased tickets to the concert and strolled across the street to an empty café where we had a fabulous Greek dinner with the kind of timeless view you just can't get back home in Maine. Jack phoned his buddy Andrew from the dinner table, promising he'd be home by his birthday in three days.

Afterward, seated high up in the amphitheater where there were fewest people, Wendy nudged me and pointed to Jack. He'd gotten up and drifted over to a high wall overlooking the famous temple ruins and the glittering city beyond. As Entremont sweetly sawed out Haydn's tribute to the old bald deceiver beneath a moon that looked as if it had been sketched by Edward Lear, Jack seemed to be deeply in thought and having a final look at the ancient world.

I sat there watching him, I confess, for the longest time, tuning out Haydn and Entremont and wondering what sort of things were running through his agile mind and what he might eventually choose to remember from the summer we attempted to go around the world but only managed to get halfway there.

On the down side we'd missed all of East Africa, the Great Pyramids, and a walk along the Great Wall. But on the plus side we'd met a real live Cathar and an old man who'd walked home from a world war. Jack had survived Shakespeare with machine guns and I'd survived punting down the Cam as well as his daring Formula One driving skills. We'd both become certified fools and I'd learned chess from a true master. Speaking purely for myself, I'd never forget the way Florence looked at dawn or the way the Italian Sam Snead had cherished his mare, or the dazzling smile that turned everything around on Crete. Looking back on it all from the benefit of a final hilltop, that seemed like an awful lot for one summer vacation.

I decided to join him at the wall for a last long look at the world we hadn't quite reached. In truth, I was more than a little homesick for

Maine and suspected he was, too. The gods only knew how my new hydrangea bushes were managing without me.

"Dad," he said quietly, when he realized the figure approaching in the moonlight was just me. "Can I tell you something?"

"Sure thing, Boss," I said, wondering what small but interesting nugget Nibs the not-quite-so Lost Boy was about to come out with next—although, for a second or two, I had a sudden fear that he was having flight jitters all over again. Our tickets required us to fly back to London early tomorrow and make a direct flight back to Boston in the afternoon.

I leaned against the wall beside him, hoping I didn't show my worry about this, gazing out at the fine night and the porch lights of old Athens.

"We haven't thrown the baseball in almost two weeks," he revealed.

I smiled with relief. The lights of Athens suddenly looked like a million distant campfires or the glittering stars of a mythical heaven painted on some old-fashioned theater ceiling. It's funny how a young boy's mind works. Or for that matter, his father's. Why did this news temporarily banish my own worries and fill me with both incredible homesick *and* happiness?

"We'll do something about that the minute we get home," I promised Jack, placing my arm around his shoulders. He admired the view for a moment more and then put his arm around *me* and wondered, "Do you think you'll *really* coach my baseball team next spring?"

"You bet. I need to trash another Volvo."

Any lingering doubts about Jack's fitness to fly were cleared up that next afternoon, shortly after our American Airlines flight lifted into the sky from Heathrow.

Across the aisle from where we sat—Wendy plugged into British *Vogue*, Jack staring blankly out at Windsor Palace, me pretending to read my unfinished bio of Dante but really thinking about that great meal in Chianti and clandestinely watching Nibs for telltale signs of trouble—a small dark-skinned boy sitting next to a mother holding a newborn began to raise quite a ruckus.

"I believe he is just frightened," the toddler's mother explained to the flight attendant when she finally came forward at ten thousand feet to see what was up. "Our flight from Cairo, you see, was terribly bumpy. He has never flown before."

"Maybe an electronic game would help," the flight attendant said and hurried to fetch a couple hand controls. A moment later she was back, plugging them in and attempting to explain some electronic gizmo to the worried little boy. This seemed to divert him briefly, but the moment the attendant left he started shouting even louder in a foreign language I couldn't quite make out. They looked Middle Eastern.

"Dad," Jack said suddenly, nudging my elbow, "can I show him how to play it?"

I glanced over at the mother, who looked harassed beyond belief and was now trying to calm the infant in her arms as well. She looked maybe twenty-five, tops.

"That would be great, Jack," I said, getting up so he could slip past me into the aisle.

A moment later, Nibs was kneeling by the frightened boy. He politely took command of the hand controls and was soon showing the little fella how to move the figures of the electronic game around. The tears dried up as if a spigot had been turned, and a faint smile came to the lad's round swollen face.

"Would you like to sit here?" the mother asked Jack, offering him her seat, visibly relieved. This prompted me to offer to move to the center seat next to my wife and give her my seat on the aisle so she could remain beside her son. We played musical airplane seats, and soon the grateful mother and newborn were seated beside me and Dante Alighieri as the boys disappeared into the thrall of the electronic game.

"Have you ever played chess before? By the way, you don't have to worry about flying in airplanes . . . ," I heard Nibs reassure the little boy as he settled in beside him for the long ride above the clouds to America.

The mother said to me, "My son doesn't speak much English yet. But your son certainly seems to know what to say."

"He's a champ," I agreed, letting it go at that.

She turned out to be an Egyptian graduate student on her way to meet her husband, a visiting professor of Mathematics at M.I.T. We talked for a while about this and that as she coaxed the infant back to sleep. Her husband was about to accept a full-time position at a large university in Iowa and the family was moving there.

"I'm not even certain I know where Iowa *is*," she admitted with a shy smile, lightly bouncing her baby in his blankets.

I told her it was somewhere out west of Boston. They grew excellent corn and football teams there. Lots of winter, too.

"I suppose I'll have to get a good winter coat," she said, as if the complexity of going to a vast New World had suddenly struck her.

Wendy leaned over and told her about Filene's Basement. The two of them chatted pleasantly for a while and I attempted to get back to Dante Alighieri's plight. The lonely Guelph was about to be banished to Ravenna and never see Beatrice or those splendid shapely mannequins in the shop windows of Firenze again.

"Have you all been on holiday in Europe?" the woman asked me a little while later, glancing over to check on her charge, who was now so totally absorbed in Jack's computer wizardry he was actually leaning on Nibsy's shoulder.

"Yes," I said, deciding to spare her the details.

"It's good to see other places," she observed, almost as if trying to reassure herself that it was true, touching her sleeping baby's cheek and adjusting the blanket.

I agreed with her on this, and then, following her baby's lead, I closed my book and took a much-needed nap, too.

ABOUT THE AUTHOR

James Dodson is the author of *Final Rounds*, a bestseller in 1996 that has been translated into six languages; *The Dewsweepers*; *Faithful Travelers*; and the *New York Times* bestseller *A Golfer's Life*, coauthored with Arnold Palmer. Dodson has written for numerous national magazines and is the recipient of the T.H. White Award for Public Affairs Journalism, is a four-time winner of the prestigious Golf Writers of America Award, and received the 1998 "Golf Reporter of the Year" award. He lives with his wife and four children on the coast of Maine.